The Complete Gluten-Free Whole Grains Cookbook

The Complete Gluten-Free Whole Grains Cookbook

125 Delicious Recipes from Amaranth to Quinoa to Wild Rice

Judith Finlayson

Robert
ROSE

For complete cataloguing information, see page 212.

Disclaimers

The recipes in this book have been carefully tested by our kitchen and our tasters. To the best of
our knowledge, they are safe and nutritious for ordinary use and users. For those people with food
or other allergies, or who have special food requirements or health issues, please read the suggested
contents of each recipe carefully and determine whether or not they may create a problem for you.
All recipes are used at the risk of the consumer.

We cannot be responsible for any hazards, loss or damage that may occur as a result of any
recipe use.

For those with special needs, allergies, requirements or health problems, in the event of any
doubt, please contact your medical adviser prior to the use of any recipe.

Editor: Carol Sherman
Recipe Editor: Jennifer MacKenzie
Copy Editors: Sheila Wawanash and Karen Campbell-Sheviak
Design and Production: Kevin Cockburn/PageWave Graphics Inc.
Photography: Colin Erricson
Food Styling: Kate Bush and Kathryn Robertson
Prop Styling: Charlene Erricson

Cover photo: Peppery Chicken Quinoa (page 104)
Page 7: Southwestern Turkey Stew with Cornmeal Dumplings (page 115)
Page 8: Pork Pozole (page 146)

Additional photo credits:
©istockphoto.com/IndigoBetta (page 2), ©istockphoto.com/Roel Smart (page 34),
©istockphoto.com/Sasha Radosavljevic (page 48), ©istockphoto.com/clemarca (page 64),
©istockphoto.com/Stepan Popov (page 82), ©istockphoto.com/Viktor Lugovskoy (page 98),
©istockphoto.com/Viktor Lugovskoy (page 118), ©istockphoto.com/schantalao (page 130),
©istockphoto.com/1MoreCreative (page 154), ©istockphoto.com/Alejandro Rivera (page 170),
©istockphoto.com/Lehner (page 190).

We acknowledge the financial support of the Government of Canada through the Book Publishing
Industry Development Program (BPIDP) for our publishing activities.

Published by Robert Rose Inc.
120 Eglinton Avenue East, Suite 800, Toronto, Ontario, Canada M4P 1E2
Tel: (416) 322-6552 Fax: (416) 322-6936
www.robertrose.ca

Printed in Canada

1 2 3 4 5 6 7 8 9 TCP 21 20 19 18 17 16 15 14 13

FSC
www.fsc.org
MIX
Paper from
responsible sources
FSC® C011825

Contents

Introduction

I'm a foodie, plain and simple: someone who strongly believes that eating is one of life's great pleasures. But I'm also committed to eating food that is nutritious. I expect my diet to keep me healthy and provide me with the energy and enthusiasm I need to enjoy my life and accomplish my objectives on a daily basis. That's why I avoid processed foods. I like to know what I'm eating, choosing instead fresh fruit and vegetables, naturally raised meats and sustainable seafood. For many years, I also enjoyed a diet rich in whole grains and in 2008 even published a book on the subject (*The Complete Whole Grains Cookbook: 150 Recipes for Healthy Living*). Although I love the many different kinds of whole grains, since I reside in the developed world, it's not surprising that wheat constituted a significant component of my whole-grain consumption.

I won't bore you with the details, but over a period of time, I began to realize that I wasn't my optimal self much of the time. I often felt lethargic and bloated and my stomach was easily upset. My favorite pair of jeans was banished to the back of my closet because I knew wearing them would make me uncomfortable. Through a process of trial, error and self-education, I came to the conclusion that I (like a surprising number of people I know) had a problem digesting wheat. I won't say it was easy to wean myself from this ubiquitous grain but within four months of eliminating wheat from my diet, I had lost five pounds and felt more energetic. My stomach became increasingly resilient to upset and, once again, my beloved jeans became part of my life.

In addition to wheat, gluten is found in barley and rye. Triticale is a hybrid of wheat and rye and obviously contains gluten, as do "ancient" forms of wheat such as Kamut, emmer (also known as farro), spelt and products made from wheat such as bulgur and couscous. Some people with wheat sensitivity are unable to digest "conventional" wheat, but can comfortably consume other grains that contain gluten, including older forms of wheat, such as emmer and spelt. Others, such as those with celiac disease, cannot tolerate gluten at all.

Fortunately, my health issues fall into the realm of gluten sensitivity rather than celiac disease, which is a far more serious problem. I have a great deal of sympathy for people with celiac disease because in today's world, avoiding gluten is a major challenge. Hidden gluten appears in a startling number of food products, from breakfast cereals to deli meats. Manufacturers often add ingredients that contain gluten (such as dextrimaltose, modified food starch and artificial flavors) to prepared foods and it is very difficult to avoid hidden gluten at fast food chains, although some now advertise gluten-free options. Even dining at high-end restaurants can be challenging. Although I've found that most will accommodate my problem, avoiding gluten does seriously limit my mealtime choices.

In the process of exploring the ins-and-outs of eating gluten-free, I made another interesting discovery: many foods and recipes that meet the needs of people who have problems digesting gluten did not meet my definition of healthy. A steady diet of white rice and refined starches, such as cornstarch, which often substitute for wheat flour, is not nutritious. I quickly came to the conclusion that in the process of avoiding gluten many people were making very poor food choices.

There is absolutely no reason why people should be denied the benefits of eating whole grains just because they can't tolerate gluten. There are many delicious gluten-free whole grains, from amaranth to wild rice, and all contain a wide range of health-promoting nutrients. Moreover, they are delicious. Their flavors vary from earthy and slightly grassy to nutty and sweet. All are appetizing on their own, marry well with a wide variety of seasonings and add taste and texture to any dish.

A quick look at my existing whole-grains cookbook confirmed that a significant number of recipes already qualified as gluten-free because they were built around ingredients such as brown (or black or red) rice, quinoa, buckwheat (which despite its name has no relationship to wheat) and millet. Moreover, since that book was published, gluten-free has

expanded as a category and appropriate options (for instance, whole-grain Job's tears, a yummy grain that can be used in place of barley in just about any recipe) have become more widely available. I decided that it was time to update my book, making it gluten-free.

Once you begin to enjoy eating gluten-free whole grains on a regular basis, I'm convinced you will become a convert to this nutritious way of eating. If your palate has been seduced by processed foods, you may need to be eased into the stronger taste and more robust texture of whole grains. If that's the case, experiment to find a few you like — quinoa and millet are particularly mild with a very pleasing, almost sprightly texture — and build upon expanding your repertoire over time.

I decided to write this book because I wanted to reinforce the message that you can enjoy a highly nutritious diet that doesn't sacrifice taste and yet is gluten-free. I hope you'll use the recipes in this book to become better nourished and that it will help you enjoy the experience of eating more. Happy healthy cooking.

— *Judith Finlayson*

What is Gluten and Why Does it Matter?

Gluten is a kind of protein found in wheat (and its relatives spelt, farro, emmer, Kamut, barley, rye and triticale). It also appears in a surprising number of prepared foods, ranging from salad dressings to dairy products. More and more people are having difficulty digesting gluten. Those with celiac disease have an autoimmune disorder that perceives gluten as an attacker, initiating a potentially serious allergic reaction.

Wheat and Diabetes

In his best-selling book *Wheat Belly*, Dr. William Davis reported on his clinical success helping his overweight, diabetes-prone patients reduce their blood sugar levels by eliminating wheat from their diets. While he does not provide statistics, he states that by replacing wheat-based foods with healthy low-glycemic foods, these patients lowered their blood sugar levels from diabetic range to normal. Many also reported other positive benefits, including the disappearance of gastrointestinal issues such as acid reflex and irritable bowel syndrome.

Hidden Gluten

People who have problems digesting gluten, particularly those with celiac disease, need to be constantly on the lookout for its presence. Gluten appears in a wide variety of prepared foods, from canned broth to deli meats and spice blends. Because manufacturers are constantly changing their formulae, gluten may suddenly appear in a familiar product that previously was gluten-free. Cross contamination may also be an issue. Although a product may not contain gluten, it may have been processed in a facility where foods containing gluten are prepared. As a result it may come in contact with or attract gluten. It is important to read labels carefully as additives often contain gluten. Ingredients such as hydrogenated vegetable protein, hydrolyzed plant protein, textured vegetable protein, monosodium glutamate, malt and modified food starch may signal the presence of gluten. When in doubt, contact the manufacturer.

A Whole Grains Primer

What are Whole Grains?

Whole grains are the seeds of certain plants. The inedible outermost layer (husk) of the grain is removed, leaving the resulting "berry" or "groat." They differ from grains that are not whole (refined) because they contain all three parts of the grain: bran, germ and endosperm.

Currently, most of the grains typically consumed in North America — for instance, white wheat flour, white rice, pearled barley and steel-ground cornmeal — are highly refined. During the milling process, the bran and the germ, which contain valuable nutrients, are removed, leaving the endosperm. While the endosperm is the largest part of the grain, it also has the fewest vitamins and minerals. Although refined grains are subsequently "enriched" with the addition of some nutrients, such as riboflavin, thiamin and iron, they are far less nutritious than whole grains. Not only do they lack the full range of vitamins, minerals, healthy fats, antioxidants and phytonutrients found in whole grains, refined grains provide far less fiber. They also lack the synergistic benefits of whole foods, which scientists are just beginning to explore. For instance, recent research suggests the phytonutrients found in plant foods fight disease more effectively when they work together, rather than as supplements on their own.

Why Should I Eat More Whole Grains?

Not only do whole grains taste good, they contain a wide range of nutrients. Although the nutrient content of individual grains varies, in general terms, most whole grains will provide at least small amounts of B vitamins (niacin, riboflavin, thiamine and folate), vitamin E, manganese, magnesium, potassium, iron, copper and selenium. They also contain fiber, beneficial fatty acids, antioxidants and phytonutrients. All these substances work together to fight disease and keep you healthy.

As we understand more about the relationship between diet and health, it's becoming increasingly clear that eating nutritious food can help to reduce the risk of illness and disease. Today our nutritional focus is shifting, from limiting how much we eat toward understanding that eating certain foods can actually be beneficial to our health.

Research has linked eating whole grains with a wide range of health benefits. Studies show that regular consumption of whole grains:

- reduces the possibility you will develop Type-2 diabetes
- makes it less likely you will have a heart attack
- helps to keep your blood pressure under control
- reduces your risk of having a stroke
- lowers your risk for certain types of cancer
- assists with keeping your weight under control and helps to ensure that you have a healthier waist-to-hip ratio
- helps to keep your cholesterol levels low
- fights gum disease
- promotes regularity

And, if that isn't enough, scientists are actively engaged in studying substances contained in whole grains, such as lignans and oligosaccharides, which function as prebiotics. Prebiotics are ingredients that stimulate the growth of healthy bacteria, such as lactobacilli and bifidobacteria (which are known as probiotics). By promoting the growth of beneficial intestinal flora, prebiotics help to keep your gut in tiptop health. In addition, prebiotics appear to have a wide range of other health benefits, from preventing hair loss to reducing menopausal symptoms.

Why Gluten-Free Whole Grains?

In the past, baked goods suitable for people with gluten intolerance or sensitivity were often made with significant amounts of highly refined ingredients such as white rice flour, tapioca flour and cornstarch. These ingredients were energy dense (high in calories) but low in nutrients. Flours made from whole grains such as sorghum, brown rice and buckwheat are far more nutritious because they contain all parts of the grain. I speak from experience when I say that baked goods made with a combination of whole-grain flours, with the addition of a small amount of refined starch, which lightens the result and aids in browning, can be as delicious as those made from wheat.

What about Fiber?

When scientists started noticing that the consumption of whole grains was linked with certain health benefits, they initially attributed these positive results to their high fiber content. We now know that fiber is just one of many healthful substances found in whole grains. By keeping you regular, a fiber supplement may help to keep you well, but it won't help your body to ward off disease.

There are two kinds of fiber — insoluble and soluble. The substance we traditionally associate with fiber is insoluble fiber, which doesn't dissolve in water. (It's what my mother called "roughage.") Insoluble fiber absorbs water in your digestive track and moves waste through your system, preventing constipation. The other kind of fiber, soluble fiber, does dissolve in water, forming a gel-like substance. It helps to lower blood cholesterol levels and to control blood sugar levels.

Despite its many benefits, most people in North America do not consume enough fiber. Adult women should consume 21 to 25 grams a day, while men should eat 30 to 38 grams a day. Some health professionals recommend that children should consume, on a daily basis, an amount equal to or greater than their age plus 5 grams. A diet high in whole grains will help you to meet these goals.

The fiber in whole grains is concentrated in the bran, which explains why whole grains (which also include the endosperm and the germ) may contain less fiber per comparable weight than some refined cereals, such as bran. However, the whole grain does contain the entire package of nutrients, which may create synergy in the health-promoting effects.

Fiber Fights Fat

Did you know that fiber helps to keep your weight under control? Because foods that are high in fiber take longer to chew, your body has time to recognize its appetite has been satisfied, reducing the possibility you'll overeat.

Whole Grains and Antioxidants

In 2004, Dr. Rui Hai Liu and his colleagues at Cornell University discovered a previously unknown benefit to eating whole grains: They contain potent antioxidants. Although scientists have been aware of the antioxidant power of fruits and vegetables for many years, the ones in whole grains were overlooked because they appeared in a different form and there was no known way of identifying their presence. These qualities help to explain why diets high in whole grains appear to be protective against diseases, such as diabetes and heart disease, as well as colon, breast and prostate cancers. Over 80% of these protective substances are found in the bran and the germ, which are removed when the grain is refined.

Whole Grains and Cancer

Whole grains contain a number of substances that appear to have cancer-fighting properties. These include antioxidants and phytochemicals, such as lignans, saponins and phytoestrogens. They also contain fiber, the consumption of which has been linked with reduced cancer risk. When the American Institute for Cancer Research combined data from 40 studies, they concluded that people who consumed large amounts of whole grains reduced their cancer risk by 34% when compared with those who ate small quantities.

Whole Grains and Heart Health

A study published in *Nutrition, Metabolism and Cardiovascular Disease* concluded that eating whole grains benefits cardiovascular health. People who consumed on average 2.5 daily servings of whole grains reduced their risk of heart disease and stroke by 21%, compared with those who consumed only 0.2 servings.

How Much Should I Eat?

When the U.S. Dietary Guidelines were updated in 2010, they recommended that adults consume three to five servings of whole grains every day. Canada's Food Guide recommends three to four servings of whole grains daily. The USDA defines a serving of whole grains as any food containing 16 grams of whole grain or an "ounce equivalent" (28 grams) of bread or cereal. Sixteen grams is just a little more than half an ounce — so three servings (48 grams) of whole grains are just under two ounces.

Recognizing Whole Grains

Increasing your intake of whole grains may be challenging because it's not always clear from labels whether grains are whole or refined. You can, however, look for the whole-grain health claim on food product labels. It reads: "Diets rich in whole grain foods and other plant foods and low in total fat, saturated fat and cholesterol, may help reduce the risk of heart disease and certain cancers."

A food bearing this label must contain 51% or more whole grains by weight. Canadians will see these labels on imported whole-grain products.

The Whole Grains Council, an industry association in the United States, has developed an eye-catching stamp, a sheaf of grain on a golden-yellow background, with a black border. It has two variations: 100% whole grain or whole grain. You'll know you've eaten three servings of whole grains when you eat three foods with the 100% stamp or six foods with the whole-grain stamp. If there is no stamp on the product, the labeling should say "100% WHOLE Grain or Excellent Source."

Gluten-Free Oats

While oats do not appear to contain gluten, until recently it was thought they were unsuitable for people with celiac disease. Recent research indicates that the problem is not with oats per se but rather because the grain is contaminated with gluten from neighboring crops or during processing. Now, organizations, including the American Dietetic Association, agree that most people with celiac disease may consume small amounts of oats from a source that guarantees it has taken the appropriate steps to eliminate cross-contamination. For further information, consult your physician or a reputable celiac organization.

Gluten-free grains

- Amaranth
- Buckwheat
- Corn
- Millet
- Oats (see page 11)
- Quinoa
- Rice
- Sorghum
- Teff
- Wild Rice

Many Whole Grains Cook Quickly

Many people overlook whole grains because they believe they take too long to cook. While this is true of some, many whole grains are actually quick cooking. The following gluten-free whole grains cook in 25 minutes or less: amaranth, buckwheat, millet, quinoa and teff; and Bhutanese red and brown Kalijira rice.

Liquid and Timing are Approximate

When cooking whole grains, be aware that the amount of liquid specified as well as the cooking times I've provided are approximate. As natural foods, whole grains are affected by many variables. These include how much of the bran has been lost in hulling, the size of the grain (it can vary quite a bit), and how long it's been stored, among other things. The best test is taste — when cooked it will be tender to the bite and somewhat chewy, depending upon the grain. How you want it cooked also depends upon how you'll be using the grain — firmer for salads and quite soft if you're serving it for breakfast.

What's a Serving?

- ½ cup (125 mL) cooked brown rice or other cooked grain
- ½ cup (125 mL) cooked hot cereal, such as oatmeal
- 1 ounce (30 g) uncooked whole-grain gluten-free pasta, brown rice or other grain
- 3 cups (750 mL) popped popcorn

Cooking Methods

Whole grains cook nicely on the stovetop in a heavy pot with a tight-fitting lid, and unless your stove has a true simmer, most benefit from having a heat diffuser placed under the pot. However, some do just as well cooked by more convenient methods, such as in a microwave oven, rice cooker or slow cooker. I've provided stovetop instructions for all the grains and, where appropriate, alternative cooking methods. In general terms, I've found that longer-cooking grains (Job's tears and hominy) do not do well in a microwave, but respond favorably to pressure cookers and slow cookers. My rice cooker, which uses fuzzy logic technology to sense grain and liquid ratios and adjust its cycle accordingly, does a fabulous job of cooking most whole grains, but because it incorporates soaking and steaming time, it takes longer to complete its cycle than do conventional rice cookers. I don't recommend using a rice cooker for very tiny grains, such as amaranth and teff, as they will plug the steam vent.

Cooked Grains Soak Up Liquid

When left to sit or refrigerated, cooked whole grains soak up liquid like a sponge. When reheating most dishes, be prepared to add liquid — either additional water or some of the stock in which the dish was cooked.

To Soak or Not to Soak

There are differences of opinion on the subject of soaking grains prior to cooking. Many people feel it cuts down on the cooking time and others think it helps the grains to cook more evenly. I have usually not found that soaking affects either the cooking time or the results. However, in some of the recipes in this book (Brown Rice Risotto, page 173 and Roasted Red Pepper Risotto, page 174) I specifically recommend soaking the rice and soaking cornmeal, grits and oatmeal before cooking as it does produce a creamier result.

There is a second and perhaps more important reason for giving your grains a good soak before cooking: some people have difficulty digesting grains, even those that do not contain gluten. Grains contain substances such as tannins, lectins and phytic acid (phytate), which, in general terms, are not easily digested and in some cases interfere with your body's ability to absorb nutrients. Take phytic acid, a so-called anti-nutrient, for instance. While ruminant animals such as cows produce an enzyme called phytase, which breaks down phytic acid, humans are not so lucky. In our stomachs phytate impairs the absorption of important minerals, such as phosphorus, calcium, magnesium, iron and zinc. (On the other hand, it should be noted that while these substances may be hard to digest, they may also have potential health benefits, which scientists are currently exploring.)

In any case, if you have the time, it is a good idea to give your digestive system a boost by soaking grains before you cook them. Studies show that soaking grains in a generous amount of filtered water, covered and at room temperature, for at least 2 hours (and up to 6 hours) will improve digestibility. (Results vary among the grains.) You can improve mineral bioavailability by "souring" your grains. Simply add about 1 tbsp (15 mL) of whey, sauerkraut juice, lemon juice or vinegar to the soaking water and set aside at room temperature for 12 hours. Studies show that when grains have been soaked in an acid then cooked, their phytic acid content is significantly reduced. After soaking, rinse and drain the grains.

Sprouted Grains

While it is still in the initial stages, there is a growing body of research confirming the health benefits of sprouted whole grains. Grains sprout after they have been soaked long enough to germinate. At that point, a small sprout will emerge from the kernel.

In general terms, sprouting, like soaking, makes grains more digestible, breaking down the anti-nutrients and making certain nutrients more bioavailable. In fact, a group of grain scientists found that sprouting grains produced changes that are similar to those that occur during fermentation. (For more information on sprouted grains, visit wholegrainscouncil.org.) Although you can easily sprout grains yourself, more and more producers are providing sprouted grains and flour made from sprouted grains. Look for them at well-stocked natural food stores or Whole Foods.

Non-Grain Ingredients used in Gluten-Free Baking

Almond Flour (sometimes called almond meal) is ground almonds. It is very nutritious and is often used in baked goods to add moistness and density. Because almonds contain unsaturated fats, almond flour can become rancid quickly and should be stored in the refrigerator or freezer.

Coconut Flour is made from the residue left over in the process of making coconut milk. It has a very appetizing nutty aroma and is high in both fiber and protein. Used along with other flours, it is excellent for baking.

Guar Gum is a thickener made from the seed of a plant. It is very high in fiber and because it may create digestive issues for some people I have not used it in this book.

Potato Flour is made from dried ground potatoes and as a result, it has a pronounced potato flavor. It can be used to make baked goods chewier and as a thickener for sauces and gravies. It plays an important role in food for the Jewish feast of Passover when leavened grains cannot be consumed for religious reasons.

Potato Starch, which should not be confused with potato flour, is a neutral-tasting starch made from potatoes. It adds lightness to baked goods and promotes crispiness in fried foods. In general terms it can be substituted for cornstarch and vice versa.

Tapioca Flour (also known as tapioca starch) is a starch derived from cassava root. It is a thickening agent, and adds lightness to baked goods and aids in browning. In general terms it can be substituted for cornstarch and vice versa.

Xanthan Gum is a fermented product that works as a binder, replacing the glue-like function of gluten in gluten-free baking. It should be used sparingly, as too much produces a gummy texture. Conventional wisdom suggests that it contains corn and as a result should not be used by people with a corn allergy. However, Bob's Red Mill, which makes xanthan gum, says theirs does not contain any corn. However, if you prefer, you can substitute a slightly larger quantity of guar gum for the xanthan gum in these recipes. A good rule of thumb comes from Bob's Red Mill, which makes both products. They recommend using 1/4 tsp (1 mL) xanthan gum per cup (250 mL) of flour or 1/4 to 1/2 tsp (1 to 2 mL) of guar gum per cup (250 mL) of flour.

Just the Grains

Amaranth

The name "amaranth" comes from the Greek word meaning "unfading." Amaranth is a bushy plant related to spinach and the leaves, which taste like spinach, are used in various cuisines around the world. For instance, in Asia they are steamed or added to stir-fries and in the Caribbean they add depth to the regional stew, callaloo. The seeds are used as a grain.

Amaranth played an important role in Aztec culture. The emperor Montezuma collected the grain as a tax and it figured prominently in religious rituals. The Aztecs made amaranth cakes, which symbolized the flesh and blood of their gods and were shared like Christian communion, a practice that so horrified the Spanish they banned cultivation of the plant. As a result, it almost disappeared, surviving in only a few remote areas of Mexico and the Andes.

Like quinoa, amaranth grows in adverse conditions and is heat and drought resistant. In India and Mexico, the seeds are popped and made into a candy, and in Peru, they are used to make beer. Amaranth has been grown in the U.S. since the mid-1970s, mainly in Colorado, Wyoming, Nebraska and California.

WHOLE GRAIN FORMS OF AMARANTH

AMARANTH SEEDS, a tiny beige seed resembling a small mustard seed.

AMARANTH FLOUR, which is ground from the seeds.

AMARANTH FLAKES, an ingredient in some commercially prepared breakfast cereals.

amaranth seeds

Culinary Profile

Amaranth is a bit of an acquired taste because it has a strong earthy flavor and almost gummy texture. In my opinion, it usually works best in dishes with an abundance of zest to provide balance. You can mellow its effect somewhat by toasting the seeds before cooking.

I enjoy amaranth as a breakfast cereal, combined with millet (see Hot Millet Amaranth Cereal, page 44), but it can also be served as a side dish. In that case, I'd cook it like polenta and flavor it with assertive ingredients, such as chiles and tomatoes, which share its native habitat. Just be aware that once it is cooked, amaranth should be served promptly because it releases a starch and becomes glutinous on standing. Although it doesn't fluff up when

Nutritional Profile

Amaranth is a highly digestible gluten-free grain. It is a source of complete and high-quality vegetable protein and provides valuable nutrients, such as magnesium, iron, copper and zinc.

Nutrients per ½ cup (125 mL) cooked amaranth

Calories	73
Protein	2.8 g
Carbohydrates	12.9 g
Fat (Total)	1.3 g
Saturated Fat	0.3 g
Monounsaturated Fat	0.3 g
Polyunsaturated Fat	0.6 g
Dietary Fiber	3 g
Sodium	6 mg
Cholesterol	0 mg

- **Good source of** magnesium and manganese
- **Source of** phosphorus, iron, zinc and copper
- **Contains** a moderate amount of dietary fiber

How much whole grain am I eating? Based on the USDA definition of a serving of whole grains, ½ cup (125 mL) cooked amaranth provides 1.2 servings of whole grains.

cooked, it becomes soft while retaining a slight pleasant crunch.

Amaranth flour can be used to make flatbreads and pastas.

Worth Knowing
Amaranth contains a relatively high proportion of the amino acid lysine, which makes it one of the best sources of vegetable protein.

Buying and Storing
Compared to some other whole grains, amaranth is relatively high in polyunsaturated fats, so unless you're using it immediately, store both the seeds and the flour in the refrigerator or freezer to prevent rancidity. It will keep in the refrigerator for up to 6 months or in the freezer for up to 1 year.

Cooking
Many people prefer the taste of amaranth if it is toasted before being cooked. To toast amaranth, cook in a dry nonstick skillet over medium heat, stirring often, until fragrant, about 4 minutes.

GENERAL COOKING INSTRUCTIONS (APPROX.)			
Grain Quantity	Liquid Quantity	Cooking Time	Yield (approx.)
1 cup (250 mL)	2½ cups (625 mL)	20 minutes	2½ cups (625 mL)

Stovetop
Bring water to a boil and add the grain in a steady stream, stirring well. Return to a boil. Reduce heat to low. Cover and simmer, stirring occasionally, until tender and thickened, about 20 minutes.

Storing Cooked Amaranth
Cover tightly and refrigerate for up to 2 days. Amaranth does not freeze well.

Buckwheat

While buckwheat is technically not a grain — it is the seed of a plant related to rhubarb that is native to northern Europe and Asia — it is classified as a grain because it has many of the characteristics of wheat. Buckwheat, too, grows better in cooler climates, such as Canada, Russia and northern Japan. In that country, the seeds are ground into flour where they form the basis of soba noodles, which, depending upon the quantity of buckwheat they contain, may be the world's most nutritious noodles (see Asian-Spiced Beef with Soba Noodles, page 142, Soba Noodles with Broccoli Sauce, page 158, and Cold Soba Noodles, page 88). Buckwheat flour is also the essential ingredient in blini (see Buckwheat Blini, page 54), the tiny pancakes traditionally served with the world's best caviar. In Italy, buckwheat flour is used to make pizzoccheri, a pasta that is the basis for a rich comfort food dish of cheese and potatoes called Pizzoccheri Valtellina.

Buckwheat groats play a significant role in Jewish cooking in dishes such as Varnishkes (see Mushroom Varnishkes, page 162) and knishes. They are commonly served as porridge or in pilaf-like dishes and can be used in salads (Kasha and Beet Salad with Celery and Feta, page 92) and added to soups.

In North America, many consumers are familiar with buckwheat through its association with honey. The flowers of the buckwheat plant are particularly attractive to bees and buckwheat honey is a robustly flavored variety produced in regions where the grain is cultivated. Buckwheat is also malted to produce gluten-free beer.

WHOLE GRAIN FORMS OF BUCKWHEAT
BUCKWHEAT GROATS (or kasha) is whole-grain buckwheat. Groats are the kernel from which the inedible outer hull has been removed. You can buy buckwheat groats either unroasted or roasted, in which case they will be called kasha. For the mildest taste, buy the unroasted version and toast them yourself (see Cooking, page 16).

BUCKWHEAT FLOUR is ground groats. It is used to make noodles, pancakes and baked goods, such as quick breads. You can buy buckwheat flour in natural foods stores or well-stocked supermarkets or you can grind your own, using a flour mill or blender.

Culinary Profile
Buckwheat has a unique intense flavor, which may take a bit of getting used to. However, once you have learned to appreciate it, buckwheat can become something of a delicacy. The grains,

known as groats, are usually toasted before using or can be purchased already toasted under the name "kasha." Buckwheat is a quick-cooking grain, ready in about 15 minutes. It is also very versatile. Use buckwheat in salads and pilafs, as a substitute for some of the ground meat in meat loaves, or, in its flour form, to make quick breads, noodles or that North American classic, buckwheat pancakes (page 38). If you find its taste

buckwheat groats

kasha

overpowering, but still want to add it to your diet, try stirring a portion of cooked buckwheat into cooked rice and enjoy it as a side dish.

Worth Knowing

In a placebo-controlled study, Canadian researchers found that buckwheat may be particularly beneficial in managing diabetes. Buckwheat extracts lowered blood glucose levels of rats from 12 to 19%. They believe the compound d–chiro–inositol, which is found in relatively high amounts in buckwheat but not commonly found in other foods, may be responsible for this positive effect and further research is underway.

Buckwheat contains high levels of phytase, which helps to neutralize its phytic acid content (see page 12). According to one study soaking buckwheat for 12 hours reduces its phytic acid content by 25%. Adding acid to the soaking water will break the phytic acid down even more, increasing the bioavailability of its valuable nutrients.

Buying and Storing

Buy buckwheat from a purveyor with rapid turnover. Store, tightly sealed, in a cool dark place for up to 6 months. If you live in a warm climate, keep it in the refrigerator. Buckwheat flour should be stored in the refrigerator, where it will keep for up to 2 months, or the freezer for up to 6 months.

Cooking

If you're using buckwheat groats rather than kasha, which has already been toasted, toast the groats in a dry skillet over medium-high heat, stirring constantly, until fragrant, about 4 minutes. Then cook as follows.

Nutritional Profile

Buckwheat is a source of high-quality vegetable protein as it contains all the essential amino acids. A half-cup (125 mL) serving of cooked buckwheat provides a range of valuable nutrients, such as magnesium, folate, pantothenic acid, phosphorus, iron, zinc, copper and selenium. Buckwheat is also rich in phytochemicals. For instance, it is the major food source of the bioflavonoid rutin, a powerful antioxidant, which researchers are studying for its medicinal properties.

Nutrients per ½ cup (125 mL) cooked buckwheat groats

Calories	113
Protein	4.2 g
Carbohydrates	24.6 g
Fat (Total)	0.8 g
Saturated Fat	0.2 g
Monounsaturated Fat	0.2 g
Polyunsaturated Fat	0.2 g
Dietary Fiber	3.3 g
Sodium	5 mg
Cholesterol	0 mg

- **Excellent source of** manganese
- **Good source of** magnesium
- **Source of** niacin, folate, pantothenic acid and phosphorus, iron, zinc copper and selenium
- **Contains** a moderate amount of dietary fiber

How much whole grain am I eating? According to the USDA definition of a serving of whole grain, ½ cup (125 mL) cooked buckwheat groats provides 2.1 servings of whole grains.

hominy

Stovetop

Toasted groats or kasha: In a saucepan over medium–high heat, bring 2 cups (500 mL) water to a boil. Add salt to taste, if using. Add 1 cup (250 mL) of the grain in a steady stream, stirring constantly. Reduce heat to low. Cover and simmer until all the liquid is absorbed, about 10 minutes. Remove from heat and let stand, covered, for 5 minutes. Fluff with a fork.

Rice cooker

In rice cooker bowl, combine 1 cup (250 mL) toasted groats or kasha and 2 cups (500 mL) water. Add salt to taste, if using. Stir to combine. Cook on Regular or Brown Rice setting until completed, about 25 minutes on Regular setting. Let rest on Warm cycle for about 15 minutes. Fluff with a fork.

Storing Cooked Buckwheat Groats

Let cool, then cover and refrigerate for up to 2 days. Cooked buckwheat does not freeze well.

Corn

Corn is one of the most popular foods in North America, so not surprisingly it is eaten in a variety of forms. The sweet corn we enjoy fresh from the field in summer has a high sugar content and, in nutritional and culinary terms, is considered a vegetable. Field corn, which is starchier, is different. Although some is eaten fresh, most is allowed to dry on the stalk. During this process, the sugar is converted into starch. A significant amount of field corn is used as animal feed, but some is ground into grits, cornmeal or flour, which may or may not be whole-grain products. Cornstarch is the highly refined starch ground from the kernel's endosperm. It is commonly used as a thickener. In gluten-free cooking it adds lightness to baked goods and aids in browning. Popcorn, which

Nutritional Profile

Most of the cornmeal sold in supermarkets is ground with steel rollers, which removes the bran and the germ and, in the process of refining, strips away most of the B vitamins, fiber, iron and healthful phytochemicals, although iron may subsequently be returned through fortification. Whole-grain yellow cornmeal contains more than twice as much magnesium, phosphorus and zinc and significantly more potassium and selenium than the de-germed variety. Corn also contains many powerful phytonutrients. For instance, whole-grain yellow cornmeal contains the carotenoids, beta-carotene, lutein and zeaxanthin. Carotenoids have been linked with a variety of health benefits.

Nutrients per ½ cup (125 mL) cooked stone ground yellow cornmeal

Calories	63
Protein	1.2 g
Carbohydrates	13.4 g
Fat (Total)	0.7 g
Saturated Fat	0.1 g
Monounsaturated Fat	0.2 g
Polyunsaturated Fat	0.3 g
Dietary Fiber	2.3 g
Sodium	4 mg
Cholesterol	0 mg

- **Source of** magnesium
- **Contains** a moderate amount of dietary fiber

How much whole grain am I eating? According to the USDA definition of a serving of whole grains, ½ cup (125 mL) cooked stone-ground yellow cornmeal provides 1.1 servings of whole grain.

WHOLE GRAIN FORMS OF CORN

HOMINY (also known as pozole): Whole dried kernels of corn cooked in a solution of lye or slaked lime to loosen the hull, which is discarded. In the course of being washed, the remaining kernels swell and are subsequently dried. This process, which has an alkalizing effect on the grain, making it particularly digestible, is known as nixtamalization. When hominy is partially ground, the result is hominy grits. Hominy flour is used to make masa harina, the basis for Mexican tortillas. Hominy is widely available already cooked and canned and can be found in its dried form in Latin American food stores.

You can buy dried hominy that has already been nixtamalized or you can nixtamalize it yourself. To nixtamalize hominy, bring a large pot of water to a boil. Add 2 tbsp (30 mL) calcium hydroxide (this should be available in small packages where your purchase the hominy) and stir to dissolve. Add 5 cups (1.25 L; about 2 lbs/1kg) of dried "uncleaned" pozole and return to a boil. Reduce heat and simmer until the skins begin to come away from the kernels (about 15 minutes). The corn will turn a shade of orange. Set aside until cool. (You can leave this overnight.) Drain and rinse well. To prepare the corn for "flowering" after it has been rinsed, remove the pointed germ from each kernel. Rub the corn between your hands to remove the skin. Discard skins. The hominy (nixtamal) is now ready to be cooked. If you are very ambitious, you can dry it thoroughly and grind it into flour.

To cook soaked dried hominy: Combine 1 part hominy with 4 parts water. Cover, bring to a boil, reduce heat and simmer until hominy puffs and is tender, 2 to 3 hours.

HOMINY GRITS: Broken grains of hominy.

MASA HARINA: Flour made from hominy. Used for making tortillas.

STONE-GROUND CORNMEAL: Dried ground corn, which is crushed between millstones and ground the old-fashioned way with the power of water. It has a coarse texture and, because it is very perishable, should be freshly ground. Italian versions of cornmeal are often known as polenta. Although most polenta sold in North America is made from refined dried corn that has been hulled and degermed, some artisanal producers, both in North America and Italy, are producing whole-grain polenta. Check the label to ensure the product is whole grain. Cornmeal comes in white, yellow and blue varieties, depending upon the corn. All are equally nutritious so long as the product is stone-ground. Stone-ground cornmeal is available in well-stocked supermarkets and natural foods stores.

STONE-GROUND GRITS: The coarsest grind of whole corn. For the best flavor and nutrition, look for coarse texture and dark flecks of germ and bran scattered throughout. The best grits are available online or by mail order from artisanal producers in the U.S., such as Anson Mills or Hoppin' John's, who make their product from heirloom varieties of corn.

Soaking cornmeal or grits in a solution of warm filtered water with the addition of whey, buttermilk, lemon juice or apple cider vinegar for a minimum of 8 hours makes them easier to digest and improves the bioavailability of their nutrients. After soaking cornmeal or grits, drain, rinse and cook as usual. The result will be particularly creamy.

CORN FLOUR: Finely ground cornmeal. Check the label to make sure it is whole grain.

POPCORN: A variety of corn that pops when heated. It is a whole grain and, so long as it isn't slathered with butter, a nutritious, low-cal snack.

was first cultivated by the Incas for snacking, is a whole-grain food. Corn is traditionally used to make "moonshine" and is the basis for bourbon, a whiskey originating in Kentucky, which is aged in charred oak casks.

Culinary Profile

Whole-grain corn is dried kernels of corn sold whole (hominy) or ground (cornmeal or grits). Hominy has undergone a process called nixtamalization (see above), which makes its nutrients much more easily absorbed. Stone-ground cornmeal is processed the old-fashioned way, with water-powered millstones, and as a result, it has more texture and flavor than refined versions. Hominy is a great addition to soups, salads and stews. Because it takes a long time to cook, I recommend cooking big batches and freezing portions. Grits make a sumptuous soft porridge that is a staple of Southern cooking. Cornmeal is the basis for polenta (see pages 58 and 182), which can be topped with a wide variety of sauces. It is also delicious made into cornbread (see Old-Fashioned Cornbread, page 40, and Cheesy Jalapeño Cornbread, page 42) and muffins or as pie-like crusts for chilies and stews or as a coating for fried foods. When cornmeal is finely ground, it becomes corn flour, which, depending upon the type of cornmeal used, may or may not be a whole-grain product. Corn flour shouldn't be confused with cornstarch, which is a highly refined product used for thickening sauces or, in small quantities, adding lightness to gluten-free flour blends.

stone-ground cornmeal

white corn grits

Worth Knowing

A recent study shows that corn is particularly high in antioxidants.

Corn doesn't contain much phytase but it is high in phytic acid, which means it benefits from being "soured" (see page 13).

Buying and Storing

Because the germ is loaded with healthful unsaturated oils, whole-grain corn is very perishable. Buy it from a source with high turnover. Store it in an airtight container, in the refrigerator, for up to 2 months. You can also store it airtight in the freezer for up to 6 months.

Cooking
(See also Basic Polenta and Grits, page 182)

GENERAL COOKING INSTRUCTIONS (APPROX.)			
Grain Quantity	Liquid Quantity	Cooking Time	Yield (approx.)
1 cup (250 mL)	4½ cups (1.125 mL)	20 minutes to 2 hours	3½ cups (825 mL)

Stovetop

Bring 4½ cups (1.125 L) water or stock to a rapid boil. Season to taste with salt and freshly ground black pepper. Add 1 cup (250 mL) stone-ground cornmeal or grits in a steady stream, stirring constantly and ensuring the water maintains a rapid boil. Reduce heat to low. Cook, stirring frequently, until thickened, about 20 minutes for finely ground cornmeal and up to 2 hours for coarse-ground grits. Stir in butter to taste, if desired.

Microwave

In an 8-cup (2 L) baking dish, combine 1 cup (250 mL) stone-ground cornmeal or grits with 4 cups (1 L) water or stock. Season to taste with salt and freshly ground black pepper. Cook, uncovered, on High for 10 minutes. Stir well. Return to oven and cook for 8 minutes. Stir in butter to taste, if desired. Serve warm or cool and cut into squares.

Rice Cooker

Using 4 cups (1 L) water produces polenta with a creamy consistency. If you prefer a slightly firmer consistency, reduce the quantity of water to 3¾ cups (925 mL). In rice cooker bowl, combine 1 cup (250 mL) stone-ground cornmeal or grits and 4 cups (1 L) water. Add salt to taste. Stir to combine. (If you don't have a fuzzy logic rice cooker and have the time, allow to soak for 1 hour.) Cook on Regular or Brown Rice setting until completed, about 30 minutes. Let rest on Warm cycle for at least 15 minutes.

Storing Cooked Cornmeal or Grits

Cooling cooked cornmeal causes it to solidify. Spread any excess in a lightly greased baking dish in a 1-inch (2.5 cm) thin layer. Smooth, cover with plastic wrap and chill until firm, about 2 hours or for up to 3 days. To use, turn out, cut into squares and top with your favorite sauce. Or, if you prefer, heat a small amount of oil in a heavy skillet and sauté the squares until golden, about 1 minute per side.

Job's Tears (hato mugi)

A tropical plant, native to Asia, Job's tears is becoming increasingly available in North America. The grain is used widely in China, Japan, Vietnam and Korea. Traditionally, its presence in the West has been associated with macrobiotic diets. The grain looks like a cross between white oatmeal and pearled barley with a brown stripe down the center. It can be found in natural foods stores and well-stocked Asian markets and can be ordered online. In China and Korea, hato mugi is often made into a tea-like beverage or distilled into liquor. The name "Job's tears" comes from its hard seed casings, which resemble tear-shaped beads. As a result, the "tears" are often used to make prayer beads and jewelry.

Culinary Profile

Job's tears is chewy and has a distinctive nutty taste. It can easily be substituted in most dishes calling for barley. In fact, it is often referred to as "Chinese barley" (see Southwestern Bean and Chinese "Barley" Salad with Roasted Peppers, page 85, or Fragrant Beef and Chinese

---

WHOLE GRAIN FORMS OF JOB'S TEARS

Whole-grain Job's tears is ivory colored and looks like barley with a brown line running down the center. When cooked, it looks a bit like pumped-up barley. Its taste also resembles that of barley. It can be purchased in well-stocked Asian markets, natural foods stores and online.

"Barley" Soup with Shiitake Mushrooms, page 66) even though, unlike barley, it does not contain gluten. It can be combined with brown rice (1 part Job's tears to 3 parts rice) to make a wonderful side dish. Add it to soups or stews along with other long-cooking whole grains such as hominy or rice (see Southwestern Turkey Chowder, page 75).

Worth Knowing

Job's tears is commonly used as a medicinal food in Asia, where it is used to treat joint conditions such as arthritis and is considered to have anti-inflammatory properties.

Buying and Storing

Store Job's tears in an airtight container in the refrigerator for up to 3 months or in the freezer for up to 6 months.

Cooking

Nutritional Profile

In traditional Chinese medicine, Job's tears is used as a digestive aid and an anti-inflammatory and in the treatment of acne.

Nutrients per ½ cup (125 mL) Job's Tears

Calories	140
Protein	5.7 g
Carbohydrates	24 g
Fat (Total)	2.3 g
Dietary Fiber	0.3 g
Sodium	2 mg
Cholesterol	0 mg

- **Good source of** phosphorus
- **Source of** thiamine, niacin

How much whole grain am I eating? According to the USDA definition of a serving of whole grains, ½ cup (125 mL) cooked Job's Tears provides 2.3 servings of whole grain.

GENERAL COOKING INSTRUCTIONS (APPROX.)

Grain Quantity	Liquid Quantity	Cooking Time	Yield (approx.)
1 cup (250 mL)	2 cups (500 mL)	60 minutes	2½ cups (625 mL)

Stove Top

Some suggest toasting the grains before cooking, although I haven't found this to be necessary. To toast Job's tears, place in a dry skillet over medium heat and cook, stirring, until fragrant, about 5 minutes. Meanwhile, bring 2 cups (500 mL) water or stock to a boil. Add 1 cup (250 mL) Job's tears. Return to a boil. Reduce heat to low and simmer until grains swell and become tender, about 1 hour. Remove from heat and let stand, covered, for 10 minutes.

Rice Cooker

In rice cooker bowl, combine 1 cup (250 mL)

Job's tears

Job's tears and 2½ cups (625 mL) water. Stir to combine. (If you don't have a fuzzy logic rice cooker and you have time, allow to soak for 1 hour before starting the machine.) Cook on Regular or Brown Rice setting until completed, about 45 minutes. Let rest on Warm cycle for at least 15 minutes.

Storing Cooked Job's Tears

Because Job's tears is a long-cooking grain, it's a good idea to make more than you need. You can refrigerate the extra, tightly covered, for up to 3 days. It can also be frozen for up to 3 months. Before freezing, cool thoroughly and, for convenience, add to resealable plastic bag(s) in 1-cup (250 mL) increments. Defrost overnight in the refrigerator, or remove from the plastic bag and microwave. You can also defrost frozen Job's tears on the stovetop in a heavy pot. Add 1 tbsp (15 mL) or so of liquid, cover and steam over low heat.

Millet

An ancient grain that is still a major form of sustenance in much of the world, including northern China, Africa and India, millet is possibly the world's oldest crop, predating wheat and rice as a cultivated grain. Herodotus

VARIETIES OF WHOLE-GRAIN MILLET

MILLET GRAINS, a small round grain, usually yellow, with a mild flavor.

MILLET FLOUR can be used as part of a blend in baked goods.

TEFF GRAINS, a very tiny grain, darker in color with a more intense flavor than millet.

TEFF FLOUR can be used as part of a blend in baked goods.

described it growing in the hanging gardens of Babylon and it covered the base of the Colossus in Rhodes. Before corn was grown in Italy, it was the original ingredient used to make polenta. Teff, which is prominent in Ethiopian cuisine and is now grown in the United States, is a variety of millet. It is notable for its very tiny seeds and perhaps best known as the major ingredient in injera, the Ethiopian flatbread, upon which various cooked dishes are served.

Culinary Profile

Light gold in color, millet resembles mustard seeds in appearance. It cooks quickly, has a mild nutty flavor and is easy to digest. A quick toasting prior to cooking brings out its

Nutritional Profile

As a grain, millet has two big advantages: not only is it gluten-free, it is also particularly easy to digest. A half-cup (125 mL) serving of millet is a good source of magnesium, which helps to keep bones strong and supports the nervous system. It also contains a moderate amount of dietary fiber. Millet also provides manganese and small amounts of the minerals phosphorous, zinc and copper, as well as an assortment of beneficial phytochemicals.

Nutrients per ½ cup (125 mL) cooked millet

Calories	108
Protein	3.2 g
Carbohydrates	21.4 g
Fat (Total)	0.9 g
Saturated Fat	0.2 g
Monounsaturated Fat	0.2 g
Polyunsaturated Fat	0.5 g
Dietary Fiber	2.7 g
Sodium	2 mg
Cholesterol	0 mg

- **Good source of** magnesium
- **Source of** thiamine, niacin, folate, phosphorus, manganese, zinc and copper
- **Contains** a moderate amount of dietary fiber

How much whole grain am I eating? Based on the USDA definition of a serving of whole grains, ½ cup (125 mL) cooked millet provides 1.8 servings of whole grains.

millet grain

teff grain

full flavor. Millet can be eaten as a breakfast cereal Almond-Flavored Millet with Cherries (page 46), in salads (Cranberry Pecan Millet Salad (page 95) or as a substitute for other grains, such as rice or quinoa. It makes a tasty pilaf (Saffron-Scented Millet Pilaf with Toasted Almonds, page 189). Millet flour can be used in some baked goods, such as flatbreads, and to thicken soups and stews.

Teff is usually brown in color with a sweet molasses-like flavor. It has a more intense flavor than millet and is used as a breakfast cereal or in polenta-style dishes. To cook teff, follow the instructions for cooking millet. However, do not use a rice cooker. It, too, benefits from being toasted.

Worth Knowing

A report in the *Archives of Internal Medicine* found a link between the intake of dietary fiber and magnesium and a reduced rate of diabetes. People who consumed the most cereal fiber and magnesium had a much lower risk of developing diabetes than those who consumed the least amount of those nutrients.

Buying and Storing

Compared to some other whole grains, millet is relatively high in polyunsaturated fats and, therefore, is more perishable. As a result, it is particularly important to buy it from a source with high turnover. Millet will keep in a cool dry place for up to 2 months, in the refrigerator for up to 4 months, or tightly wrapped in the freezer for up to 6 months.

Cooking

For best results, before cooking toast millet in a dry skillet over medium heat, stirring constantly, until fragrant, about 5 minutes.

GENERAL COOKING INSTRUCTIONS (APPROX.)

Grain Quantity	Liquid Quantity	Cooking Time	Yield (approx.)
1 cup (250 mL)	2½ cups (625 mL)	25 minutes	3½ cups (875 mL)

Stovetop

In a saucepan, bring 2½ cups (625 mL) water or stock to a rapid boil. Add toasted millet in a steady stream and season with salt and freshly ground black pepper to taste. Return to a rapid boil. Reduce heat to low. Cover tightly and simmer until liquid is absorbed, about 25 minutes. Remove from heat and let stand, covered, for 5 minutes. Fluff with a fork before serving.

Note: if you're eating millet as a cereal, increase the quantity of cooking water (use about 4 cups/1 L per cup/250 mL of millet) and stir occasionally while cooking to produce a porridge consistency. Cooking millet by this method produces a creamy texture. The result could also be used like polenta. You can cook teff the same way.

Rice Cooker

In rice cooker bowl, combine 1 cup (250 mL) toasted millet and 2 cups (500 mL) water or stock. If using water, add salt to taste. Cook on Regular or Brown Rice setting until completed, about 35 minutes. Let rest on Warm cycle for at least 15 minutes. Do not cook teff in a rice cooker. The grains are too small.

Storing Cooked Millet

Cooked millet can be refrigerated for up to 2 days. Millet doesn't freeze well.

Oats

Although oats have earned their place in history — for instance as the only food Alexander the Great would feed to his legendary horse, Bucephalus — they also have the distinction of being the most popular whole grain in North America. To some extent, this is due to the fact that oats are easy to grow in parts of the continent because they thrive in cooler climates, but probably the most significant reason is that most oat products are not refined. Unlike other grains, oats contain a natural chemical that acts as a preservative. This means it isn't necessary to refine the grain to extend its shelf life. Normal processing for oats consists of roasting and hulling, which leaves the bran and germ layers intact.

In North America, most oats are consumed at breakfast in the form of cereal or used in baking. In Scotland, oats are an integral ingredient in the national dish, haggis, a sausage-like mélange of seasoned sheep's heart, liver and lungs, also mixed with suet and onions and boiled in a casing of sheep's stomach. I've tried it and wasn't impressed, but I do know native Scots who find it a great delicacy.

WHOLE GRAIN FORMS OF OATS

OAT GROATS: The whole oat kernel, which has not been cut or flattened in any way. They are good for breakfast or can be used in grain salads, like barley and wheat berries.

STEEL-CUT OATS (also known as Irish or Scottish oatmeal), these are whole oat groats cut into smaller pieces. Flavorful and nicely chewy, they are the ultimate breakfast cereal.

ROLLED OATS: Less toothsome than steel-cut oats, these are groats that have been softened by steaming, then rolled. The form of oats usually used in baking, they also make a great cooked breakfast cereal or an ingredient in muesli or granola.

OAT FLOUR: A flour made from ground whole oats, used in baking. You can easily grind your own in a food processor.

Culinary Profile

Unlike other grains, after being harvested and cleaned, oats are roasted, which gives them their unique flavor. Because they are high in soluble fiber, they easily become smooth and creamy

Nutritional Profile

One half-cup (125 mL) cooked oatmeal is a good source of the antioxidant manganese, which slows down the aging process. They also contain beta-glucan, a type of fiber that is particularly beneficial in controlling cholesterol levels and may reduce the risk of heart disease. A recent University of Ottawa study showed the consumption of oat bran, which is high in beta-glucan, stabilized blood sugar, which may also make it beneficial to people with Type-2 diabetes.

Nutrients per ½ cup (125 mL) cooked rolled oats

Calories	45
Protein	1.8 g
Carbohydrates	7.9 g
Fat (Total)	0.8 g
Saturated Fat	0.2 g
Monounsaturated Fat	0.2 g
Polyunsaturated Fat	0.3 g
Dietary Fiber	1 g
Sodium	4 mg
Cholesterol	0 mg

- **Good source of** manganese
- **Source of** phosphorus and magnesium

How much whole grain am I eating? Based on the USDA definition of a serving of whole grains, ½ cup (125 mL) cooked rolled oats provides 0.7 servings of whole grain.

when cooked with liquid, making them an ideal thickener for soups and puddings. They have a natural sweetness, which makes them appealing for baked goods, such as cookies. They are often used as extenders for dishes, such as meat loaf or stuffing.

rolled oats

steel-cut oats

oat groats

(250 mL) oat groats. Reduce heat to low and simmer, stirring occasionally to prevent sticking, until liquid is absorbed and oats are tender, about 50 minutes.

Steel-Cut Oats: In a saucepan, bring 3 cups (750 mL) water to a boil. Add salt to taste and stir in 1 cup (250 mL) steel-cut oats. Reduce heat to low and simmer, stirring occasionally to prevent sticking, until liquid is absorbed and oats are tender, about 30 minutes.

Rolled Oats: In a saucepan, bring 2 cups (500 mL) water to a boil. Add salt to taste and stir in 1 cup (250 mL) rolled oats. Reduce heat to low and simmer, stirring occasionally to prevent sticking, until liquid is absorbed and oats are tender, about 10 minutes.

Microwave

Steel-Cut Oats: In an 8-cup (2 L) baking dish, combine 1 cup (250 mL) steel-cut oats with 4 cups (1 L) water and a pinch of salt. Cover and cook on High for 8 minutes. Stir well. Return to oven and cook, uncovered, for 8 minutes. Cover and let stand for 5 minutes.

Rolled Oats: In an 8-cup (2 L) baking dish, combine 1 cup (250 mL) rolled oats, $2\frac{1}{3}$ cups (575 mL) water and a pinch of salt. Cook, uncovered, for 4 minutes on High and stir well. Return to oven and cook for 4 minutes. Let stand for 1 minute.

Slow Cooker

Use a small ($3\frac{1}{2}$ quart) slow cooker. If you're using a large (minimum 5 quart) slow cooker, double or triple the quantity.

Oat Groats or Steel-Cut Oats: In lightly greased stoneware, combine 1 cup (250 mL) steel-cut oats and 4 cups (1 L) water. Add salt to taste. Cover and cook on Low for 8 hours. Stir well.

Rolled Oats: In lightly greased stoneware, combine $1\frac{1}{4}$ cups (300 mL) rolled oats, $\frac{1}{2}$ tsp (2 mL) salt and 4 cups (1 L) water. Cover and cook on Low for 8 hours. Stir well.

Worth Knowing

Oats contain avenanthramides, a powerful antioxidant that has been linked with a reduced risk of heart disease. The compound prevents LDL (bad cholesterol) from becoming oxidized. Interestingly, when vitamin C was consumed along with oats, the combination created synergy, significantly extending the positive effect of the phytonutrient. So enjoy a glass of orange juice with your oatmeal every morning, and give your heart a hug. Because they are low in phylate (the substance that neutralizes the anti-nutrient phytase), it is beneficial to soak oat groats with some acid (see page 13) before cooking. Most of the phytase is contained in the bran, some of which has been removed in the process of making rolled oats.

Buying and Storing

Because oats, unlike most whole grains, are not highly perishable, acceptable products are widely available. Oats will keep so long as you use them up within a reasonable amount of time.

Cooking

<table>
<tr><td colspan="4">GENERAL COOKING INSTRUCTIONS (APPROX.)</td></tr>
<tr><td>Grain Quantity</td><td>Liquid Quantity</td><td>Cooking Time</td><td>Yield (approx.)</td></tr>
<tr><td>1 cup (250 mL)</td><td>2 to 4 cups (500 mL to 1 L)</td><td>10 to 50 minutes</td><td>3 to 4 cups (750 mL to 1 L)</td></tr>
</table>

Stovetop

Oat Groats: In a saucepan, brings 4 cups (1 L) water to a boil. Add salt to taste and stir in 1 cup

Storing Cooked Oatmeal
Cover and refrigerate for up to 3 days. Oatmeal does not freeze well.

Quinoa

Although it is considered a grain, quinoa is actually the seed of a leafy plant related to spinach. Originally grown in the Andes, quinoa, which the Incas called "the mother of all grains," was known for keeping their armies strong. It made its way to North America in the 1980s and has been rediscovered as a good-for-you "ancient grain." The plant thrives in circumstances that mimic its origins in the Andes. It loves drought, poor alkaline soil and altitude, conditions under which few grains would even survive.

WHOLE GRAIN FORMS OF QUINOA

QUINOA SEEDS: Quinoa seeds are commonly sold in yellow and red. These varieties are fundamentally the same, although the red version is less common, has a firmer texture and a more striking color.

QUINOA FLOUR: A good flour to use in gluten-free baking, although it has a strong nutty flavor.

Culinary Profile

Quinoa is commonly sold in yellow or red varieties, although black quinoa, which is much less common, is also available. Subtly flavored, quinoa has a mild nutty taste that is very pleasing. It cooks quite quickly (in about 15 minutes) and you can tell when it's cooked because the germ unfolds like a little white tail. When cooked, it fluffs up but maintains an appealing, slightly crunchy texture. It can be substituted for rice, pasta, couscous or potatoes at most meals. Quinoa grains are naturally coated with saponin, a natural detergent found in many plants that has an unpleasant bitter taste. By the time you purchase it, most has been washed off, but a thorough rinsing before use is always a good idea.

Nutritional Profile

Quinoa is known as a "supergrain" not only because it is relatively high in protein, but also because it is one of the few vegetable sources of complete protein, including lysine. A half-cup (125 mL) serving of cooked quinoa is a good source of iron and magnesium, among other nutrients, and, like all whole grains, provides beneficial phytochemicals.

Nutrients per ½ cup (125 mL) cooked quinoa

Calories	106
Protein	3.7 g
Carbohydrates	19.5 g
Fat (Total)	1.6 g
Saturated Fat	0.2 g
Monounsaturated Fat	0.4 g
Polyunsaturated Fat	0.7 g
Dietary Fiber	2 g
Sodium	8 mg
Cholesterol	0 mg

- **Excellent source of** manganese
- **Good source of** iron and magnesium
- **Source of** phosphorus, zinc, copper, riboflavin, niacin and folate
- **Contains** a moderate amount of dietary fiber

How much whole grain am I eating? Based on the USDA definition of a serving of whole grains, ½ cup (125 mL) cooked quinoa provides 1.8 servings of whole grain.

Worth Knowing
Copper is a nutrient that plays important roles in the body, from helping wounds to heal and boosting your energy, to keeping bones strong.

yellow quinoa

red quinoa

In 2006, researchers at the USDA found that copper helped prevent the calcium loss from bones associated with dieting.

You can significantly reduce the phytate levels in quinoa by soaking it for 12 hours (about 65%) or souring it with the addition of an acid for 16 hours (about 80%; see page 13). Sprouted quinoa (see page 13) is available in natural foods stores and well-stocked supermarkets.

Buying and Storing

Compared to other whole grains, quinoa is relatively high in polyunsaturated fats, so buy it from a source that has a high turnover. It should be stored in an airtight container in the refrigerator, where it will keep for up to 6 months. Quinoa flour should be stored in the freezer.

Cooking

Even if you decide not to soak it, it's always a good idea to rinse quinoa before using to remove any bitter saponin residue. Fill a bowl with warm water and swish the kernels around, then transfer to a sieve and rinse thoroughly under cold running water. If desired, toast the rinsed drained quinoa in a dry skillet over medium heat, stirring constantly, until it darkens, about 4 minutes.

GENERAL COOKING INSTRUCTIONS (APPROX.)

Grain Quantity	Liquid Quantity	Cooking Time	Yield (approx.)
1 cup (250 mL)	2 cups (500 mL)	15 minutes	3 cups (750 mL)

Stovetop

In a pot, bring 2 cups (500 mL) water to a boil. Add quinoa in a steady stream, stirring to prevent lumps from forming, and return to a boil. Reduce heat to low. Cover and simmer until tender, about 15 minutes. Look for a white line around the seeds — it's the germ, and when it bursts out, the grain is cooked. If water still remains in the bottom of the pot, remove the lid and stir occasionally until all the liquid evaporates, being careful not to overcook. You want the quinoa to maintain a bit of pleasant pop. Remove from heat and let stand, covered, for 5 minutes. Fluff with a fork before using.

Rice Cooker

In rice cooker bowl, combine 1 cup (250 mL) quinoa and 2 cups (500 mL) water or stock. If using water, add salt to taste. Cook on Regular or Brown Rice setting until completed, about 35 minutes. Let rest on Warm cycle for at least 15 minutes.

Microwave

In a microwaveable bowl, combine 1 cup (250 mL) quinoa and 2 cups (500 mL) water. Add salt to taste, if desired. Microwave on High for 10 minutes. Stir well. Microwave on High for 7 minutes. Remove from oven. Cover and let stand for 5 minutes.

Storing Cooked Quinoa

Refrigerate for up to 3 days in a tightly sealed container. Quinoa doesn't freeze well.

Rice

Rice is the dietary staple for almost half the world's population. In countries such as China, Japan, India and Thailand, it plays a major role in the national diet. First cultivated in China, rice made its way to ancient Greece via Arab traders. It still plays a significant role in Mediterranean cuisine, as evidenced by signature dishes, such as Italian risotto and Spanish paella. The United States has been a significant producer of rice since the late-17th century, when it was first planted in South Carolina. Today, rice is grown in a number of southern states, notably Arkansas, California and Louisiana, as well as in other locations around the world.

Most whole-grain rice is brown, although specialty varieties, such as black and red rice are widely available. Whole-grain rice is husked, but not milled or polished, leaving the outer layers in tact. Milling, which removes the bran and much of the germ, produces white rice, which is no longer a whole grain. Most white rice is polished, which strips away further nutrients from the grain. Interestingly, parboiled (or converted) brown rice that has been steamed under pressure and dried is more nutritious than white rice because technically it is still a whole grain. The rice is left in its hull and boiled, usually under pressure, which forces nutrients

VARIETIES OF WHOLE-GRAIN RICE

LONG-GRAIN BROWN RICE: The grains of long-grain brown rice are long and narrow. When cooked, it is quite fluffy, with individual grains that remain separate.

SHORT-GRAIN BROWN RICE: Short-grain rice has short, stubby grains that tend to stick together when cooked. From a culinary perspective, this means you can easily produce risotto-like dishes with relatively little stirring.

SPECIALTY VARIETIES OF WHOLE-GRAIN RICE: Nowadays, many varieties of specialty rice are quite widely available, either in Asian markets, specialty stores or well-stocked supermarkets, including black, red and brown rice. Other varieties, such as Brown Pecan or popcorn rice from the southern U.S., are available in specialty stores. All these varieties have unique qualities and it's wise to consult the purveyor who sold you the product, or the package it came in for specific instructions.

Black rice includes Chinese black rice, Thai black sticky rice, Italian Black Venere rice, and Black Japonica rice.

Red rice: Several kinds are available, such as Bhutanese red rice, an heirloom variety grown in the Himalayas, Thai red rice, Italian wild red rice, Colusari red rice, red rice from the Camargue region of France, and Wehani rice. Most varieties of red rice can be used interchangeably in recipes, although the cooking times may vary.

Brown Kalijira is a tiny-grained rice, often described as baby basmati, which is destined to become popular because it cooks in less than 30 minutes. It makes an excellent substitute for plain white rice and a side dish or accompaniment for Asian dishes, such as stir-fries or curries.

BROWN RICE FLOUR: In baking, brown rice flour resembles wheat flour but without the ability to bind, so it is usual to add a binder such as xanthan gum. It has a nutty flavor and so long as it has been finely ground, the texture is very smooth. Brown rice flour is available in natural foods stores. Because it contains volatile oils, it is quite perishable. Store brown rice flour in the refrigerator for up to 5 months or in the freezer for up to 1 year.

BROWN RICE PASTA: A wide variety of conventional pasta forms, such as spaghetti, fettuccini, spirals, elbows and lasagna noodles, are made from brown rice. When cooked, brown rice pasta is softer than that made from wheat; it has a mild, very pleasant taste. Varieties of Asian noodles made with brown rice are also becoming increasingly available.

into the endosperm. It cooks more quickly than regular brown rice and produces a fluffier result.

Culinary Profile

Simple steamed rice is the perfect side dish and, in its refined white form, has long been the most common substitute for potatoes in the traditional North American diet. Now, more and more people are finding they actually prefer brown rice and to satisfy consumer demand

---

Nutritional Profile

Although many of the world's population consume white rice, brown rice is far more nutritious. Rich in complex carbohydrates, it contains much more fiber than white rice (½ cup/125 mL of white rice contains 0.3 grams of dietary fiber, while you'll get 1.5 grams from the same quantity of brown). A half-cup (125 mL) serving of brown rice is also an excellent source of manganese, a mineral that helps your body utilize key nutrients and keep your bones healthy. Rice also supplies varying degrees of minerals, such as magnesium, selenium, phosphorus, zinc, copper, thiamine and niacin, as well as valuable phytonutrients. Recent research suggests that brown rice is rich in beneficial antioxidants, particularly phenolic compounds (found in many fruits and vegetables), which have been shown to protect against cardiovascular disease.

Nutrients per ½ cup (125 mL) cooked long-grain brown rice

Calories	114
Protein	2.6 g
Carbohydrates	23.6 g
Fat (Total)	0.9 g
Saturated Fat	0.2 g
Monounsaturated Fat	0.3 g
Polyunsaturated Fat	0.3 g
Dietary Fiber	1.5 g
Sodium	5 mg
Cholesterol	0 mg

- **Excellent source of** manganese
- **Good source of** magnesium and selenium
- **Source of** phosphorus, zinc, copper, thiamine and niacin

How much whole grain am I eating? Based on the USDA definition of a serving of whole grains, ½ cup (125 mL) cooked long-grain brown rice provides 1.9 servings of whole grain.

short-grain brown rice

long-grain brown rice

chefs are adapting by preparing dishes, such as sushi, made with short-grain brown rice or offering a brown rice option with Chinese food. The main types of rice, Indica, Japonica and Javanica, are generally classified according to their length: long, medium or short grain. Rice can also be sticky or glutinous. Whatever kind you use, whole-grain rice is much chewier than its refined counterpart and has a sweet nutty flavor that lends itself to a wide array of dishes, from breakfast to dessert. Most also make a great side, simply cooked. Unless it is a glutinous variety (such as black sticky rice or short-grain brown rice), whole-grain rice generally cooks up to be relatively fluffy. Most varieties take a relatively long time to cook (about 55 minutes), although some, such as brown Kalijira rice from Bangladesh and Bhutanese red rice, both heirloom varieties, cook in less than 30 minutes.

Worth Knowing

The bran layer of rice, which is lost to polishing in the production of white rice, contains the compound gamma oryzanol, which appears to have antioxidant properties. Preliminary studies suggest that this compound may help to keep cholesterol under control.

Brown rice is high in phytates. It benefits from a long soaking (at least 8 hours) preferably with the addition of acid (see page 13). Sprouted brown rice (see page 13) is widely available in natural foods stores and well-stocked supermarkets.

Buying and Storing

Because the germ layer contains healthful oils, brown (and red and black) rice, like most whole grains, turns rancid if not properly stored. As a result, it's important to buy from a source with high turnover. If possible, smell before buying — you'll know immediately if it's past its peak. Before I knew better, I sometimes bought packaged brown rice in the supermarket and was frequently disappointed with the result. Once I opened it at home, one whiff told me I'd made a mistake. Rice should have a fresh nutty aroma with no hint of bitterness. Store whole-grain rice in a cool dry place and use within 1 month of purchase. Or cover tightly and refrigerate for up to 3 months, my favorite method.

GENERAL COOKING INSTRUCTIONS (APPROX.)

Grain Quantity	Liquid Quantity	Cooking Time	Yield (approx.)
1 cup (250 mL)	2½ cups (625 mL)	50 minutes	3 cups (750 mL)

Cooking

These are general instructions that work for all varieties of rice. You may prefer slightly firmer rice, in which case use a bit less water. If you're cooking a type of specialty rice, consult the package instructions. If there are none, follow these general instructions and subsequently adjust the quantity of water or cooking time to suit your preference.

brown Kalijira rice

Italian black rice

Thai black sticky rice

Bhutanese red rice

Camargue red rice

Stovetop

Rinse under cold running water and drain. For 1 cup (250 mL) short- or long-grain brown rice bring approximately 2½ cups (625 mL) water to a boil in a heavy pot with a tight-fitting lid (for specialty varieties of rice, follow package instructions). Stir in rinsed rice and return to a rapid boil over high heat. Reduce heat to low. Cover tightly and simmer until rice is tender and all the water is absorbed, about 50 minutes. Remove from heat and let stand, covered, for 5 minutes. If using long-grain rice, fluff with a fork.

Rice Cooker

Combine 1 cup (250 mL) rice and 2¼ cups (550 mL) water in rice cooker bowl. If you don't have a fuzzy logic rice cooker and have time, allow to soak for 1 hour before starting the machine. Cook on Regular or Brown Rice cycle until done, about 40 minutes. Let rest on Warm cycle for 15 minutes.

Oven

Preheat oven to 350°F (180°C). In a baking dish, combine 2½ cups (625 mL) boiling water and 1 cup (250 mL) long-grain brown rice. Cover and bake in preheated oven until liquid is absorbed, about 45 minutes.

Tip: Rice is cooked when the top looks like a crater.

Pressure Cooker

Before using your pressure cooker, consult the manufacturer's instructions to ensure you are not over- or underfilling the appliance. We used a 7.4-quart (7 L) pressure cooker. Combine 2 cups (500 mL) brown rice, 4 cups (1 L) water and, if desired, salt to taste. Cook under high pressure for 15 minutes. Release pressure and let stand, covered, for 5 minutes. Drain off water.

Storing Cooked Rice

To store cooked rice, place in a shallow container and let cool slightly (the steaming should have subsided) and then refrigerate for no more than 2 days. A toxin often present in rice, called *Bacillus cereus,* can multiply quickly on cooked rice that isn't cooled quickly enough and then stored. Brief reheating (such as stir-frying) isn't enough to destroy the toxin and it can cause food-borne illness.

To freeze, cool rice completely, then transfer to a resealable plastic bag in 2- or 3-cup (500 to 750 mL) quantities. Frozen rice will keep for up to 3 months. Defrost overnight in the refrigerator or remove from plastic bag and defrost in a microwave oven.

Tip: If you're cooking whole-grain rice in a fuzzy logic rice cooker, expect it to take longer to cook than the times I have suggested because the machines allow time for soaking the raw grain and steaming it after it is cooked. This produces more evenly cooked grains, but the cycle takes longer. However, you do not need to allow for a resting period after the cycle is completed, as with conventional rice cookers. I find that brown, red or black rice can take almost 2 hours in my machine, but the results are terrific.

Sorghum

Sorghum, also known as milo, is a tropical plant originating in Northeast Africa. It is a round grain, yellow-beige in color and looks most like millet, although it is lighter in color and significantly larger. (One friend described it as millet on steroids.) It's an ancient grain that can withstand a reasonable amount of drought, making it a particularly valuable food in areas of the world that tend to be arid. Perhaps not surprisingly, it is one of the principal cereal grains grown in Africa and India, where sorghum flour is used to make bhakri, an unleavened bread that is a staple in many parts of the country. In China, it is distilled into beverages, such as maotai, a liquor that achieved international fame when it won a gold medal at the 1915 Panama-Pacific Exposition in San Francisco. In the United States, sorghum has been used to make gluten-free beer. Sorghum syrup, which is made from the juice extracted from the stalks of a non-grain variety known as sugar sorghum, is considered a great delicacy and is used in Southern U.S. cooking.

WHOLE GRAIN FORMS OF SORGHUM

SORGHUM GRAIN: Small beige seeds with a tiny brown dot. It has a chewy texture and earthy taste. It is available by mail order from gluten-free markets.

SORGHUM FLOUR: is a soft, fine flour that has become very popular because it most resembles wheat flour in gluten-free baking. Most is stone-ground, which makes it a whole grain.

Culinary Profile

Most of the sorghum grown in the U.S. is used as animal feed, although it is reasonable to assume that the grain will grow in popularity because it is gluten-free. The actual grain, which is difficult to obtain in North America, is eaten instead of rice in some parts of Asia and ground and made into porridge in Africa. It has a mild, pleasant taste, which is accented by toasting. Sorghum grain makes a tasty pilaf or, cooked simply in stock or water, a good substitute for barley or wheat berries. Add it to soups or stews, along with or instead of other long-cooking grains. Sorghum flour, which tastes more like wheat than any of the other gluten-free flours, is readily available in natural foods stores. It adds a slightly nutty flavor to baked goods.

Worth Knowing

A study reported in the *Journal of Food Science* found that some varieties of sorghum are extremely high in antioxidants and also contain compounds (policosanols) that may be heart-healthy.

sorghum grain

Nutritional Profile

Compared to other whole grains, sorghum is relatively high in polyunsaturated fats, which means it should be stored in the refrigerator or freezer. A half-cup (125 mL) serving also provides phosphorus, iron, thiamine, niacin and dietary fiber, among other nutrients.

Nutrients per ½ cup (125 mL) cooked sorghum grain

Calories	130
Protein	4.3 g
Carbohydrates	28.7 g
Fat (Total)	1.3 g
Saturated Fat	0.2 g
Monounsaturated Fat	0.4 g
Polyunsaturated Fat	0.5 g
Dietary Fiber	2.4 g
Sodium	4 mg
Cholesterol	0 mg

- **Good source of** phosphorus
- **Source of** iron, thiamine, niacin and phosphorus
- **Contains** a moderate amount of dietary fiber

How much whole grain am I eating? Based on the USDA definition of a serving of whole grains, ½ cup (125 mL) cooked sorghum grain provides 2.4 servings of whole grain.

Buying and Storing

Because it contains a relatively high amount of polyunsaturated fat, sorghum should be stored in the refrigerator or freezer. Sorghum will keep, frozen, for up to 6 months.

Cooking

For best results, before cooking, toast sorghum in a dry skillet over medium heat, stirring constantly, until fragrant, about 5 minutes.

GENERAL COOKING INSTRUCTIONS (APPROX.)			
Grain Quantity	Liquid Quantity	Cooking Time	Yield (approx.)
1 cup (250 mL)	2 cups (500 mL)	50 minutes	2½ cups (625 mL)

Stovetop

Bring 2 cups (500 mL) water to a boil. Add sorghum. Reduce heat to low, cover and cook until grains are tender and uniform in color, about 50 minutes.

Storing Cooked Sorghum

Cooked sorghum can be refrigerated in an airtight container for up to 2 days. Cooked sorghum doesn't freeze well.

Wild Rice

Not a rice or technically even a grain, wild rice is actually the seed of an aquatic grass. However, it is categorized as a grain because it is cooked like one and has a similar nutritional profile. Wild rice is native to North American wetlands and has been harvested for centuries by Native people of the northern Midwest

wild rice

(Manitoba, Saskatchewan and Minnesota), where it is known as manomin, "a gift from the Creator." Harvesting has a religious and cultural significance for the Ojibwa people, who gather the crop in canoes, with the use of "knockers," specially designed wooden sticks, which are used to bend the stalks so the grains fall into the canoe. However, today most wild rice is commercially grown, although it can be difficult to ascertain this fact from labeling. Since the best wild rice is foraged, look for the word "organic" and some indication that the product is hand-harvested, although even this is no guarantee that you are purchasing the real thing. Wild rice is traditionally cured after harvesting, which results in a mildly fermented product. It is then dried.

WHOLE GRAIN FORMS OF WILD RICE

All wild rice is whole grain. Wild rice flour is dark in color and has a hearty flavor. It makes a nice addition to pancakes or quick breads but is not suitable for elegant baking. It is relatively expensive but because the grain was cured, the flour is slightly fermented and, as a result, has a long shelf life.

Culinary Profile

Wild rice has a soft chewy texture and a delicious nutty flavor. The naturally grown, hand-harvested varieties are considered to have the most delicate and complex flavors, and although they are the most expensive, connoisseurs believe they are worth the extra cost. In general terms, the longer the grain, the more it costs — premium grains are about 1 inch (2.5 cm) long, while the least expensive are broken grains, which are often added to mixes. In fact, wild rice is most often consumed in a blend with other types of rice or grains because its robust flavor dominates the mix. Its presence can be felt with a ratio of as little as 2 tbsp (30 mL) to 1 cup (250 mL) brown or white rice. It pairs well with foods that are equally assertive, such as smoked turkey, dark mushrooms, dried fruits and nuts, or those that grow in its natural habitat, such as blueberries and cranberries.

Worth Knowing

A 100-gram serving of wild rice contains 26 grams of folate, a B vitamin that helps to keep homocysteine levels under control and

Nutritional Profile

Wild rice is a nutritious gluten-free grain. It is higher in protein and lower in calories than brown rice and provides folate, a valuable nutrient that is not abundant in the North American diet (see Worth Knowing, right). Combining brown (or red) rice with wild rice is a good way to expand the range of nutrients you consume.

Nutrients per ½ cup (125 mL) cooked wild rice

Calories	81
Protein	3.2 g
Carbohydrates	17.2 g
Fat (Total)	0.3 g
Saturated Fat	0 g
Monounsaturated Fat	0 g
Polyunsaturated Fat	0.2 g
Dietary Fiber	1.5 g
Sodium	4 mg
Cholesterol	0 mg

- **Source of** phosphorus, magnesium, manganese, zinc, copper, niacin and folate

How much whole grain am I eating? Based on the USDA definition of a serving of whole grains, ½ cup (125 mL) cooked wild rice provides 1.4 servings of whole grain.

assists in the formation of red blood cells. (A comparable quantity of brown rice has 4 grams of this nutrient.) A vital nutrient for pregnant women, folate prevents neural tube defects, such as spina bifida.

Buying and Storing

Because it has undergone a mild process of fermentation and drying, wild rice (and wild rice flour) has a longer shelf life than most whole grains. It will keep covered in a cool, dark place for up to 1 year.

Cooking

Wild rice should be rinsed thoroughly and drained before cooking. Because the grains can range so wildly in size, it is difficult to be specific about cooking times and the quantity of water required. As a rule of thumb, the longer the grain, the more water it needs. When cooking 1 cup (250 mL) wild rice, count on about 3 cups (750 mL) water for longer grains and as little as 2 cups (500 mL) for the shortest. The safest strategy is to use a bit more water than you think you will need and drain off the excess, although it's wise to be judicious in the quantity of water you add because any that is discarded will carry away nutrients. You will know when the wild rice is done if about half the grains have burst.

GENERAL COOKING INSTRUCTIONS (APPROX.)

Grain Quantity	Liquid Quantity	Cooking Time	Yield (approx.)
1 cup (250 mL)	2 to 3 cups (500 to 625 mL)	45 to 65 minutes	3½ cups (875 mL)

Stovetop

Bring 2 to 3 cups (500 to 750 mL) water or stock to a boil. Add 1 cup (250 mL) rinsed drained wild rice and return to a boil. Reduce heat to low. Cover and simmer until the kernels begin to burst, 45 to 65 minutes. Remove from heat and let stand, covered, for 10 minutes. Fluff with a fork.

Rice Cooker

Combine 1 cup (250 mL) rinsed drained wild rice and 2½ cups (625 mL) water in rice cooker bowl. Stir well. (If you don't have a fuzzy logic rice cooker and have time, allow to soak for 1 hour before starting the machine.) Cook on Regular or Brown Rice cycle until done, about 1 hour. Let rest on Warm cycle for 15 minutes.

Slow Cooker

In a small (3½ quart) slow cooker, combine 1 cup (250 mL) rinsed drained wild rice and 2½ cups (625 mL) water. Stir well. Cover and cook on High for 2½ hours, until water is absorbed and rice is tender. If you're using a large (minimum 5 quart) slow cooker, double or triple the quantity. Cover and cook on Low for 6 to 8 hours or on High for 3 to 4 hours, stirring once or twice, if possible, until desired texture is achieved.

Pressure Cooker

Before using your pressure cooker, consult the manufacturer's instructions to ensure you are not over- or underfilling the appliance. Whole grains generate a great deal of foam, so the cooker shouldn't be more than half full. Combine 1 cup (250 mL) wild rice, 2½ cups (625 mL) water and, if desired, 1 tsp (5 mL) salt. Cook under high pressure for 25 minutes. Drain off water.

Tip: If you're using packaged wild rice, I recommend using the instructions provided by the producer: they know their product. The most effective way to ensure good results is to cook wild rice and most other whole grains in an overabundance of water, then drain off the excess. However, I usually prefer not to do this, as nutrients disappear down the drain.

Storing Cooked Wild Rice

Store cooked wild rice, covered, in the refrigerator for up to 5 days. Freeze for up to 3 months in resealable plastic bags in 1-cup (250 mL) quantities. Defrost in the refrigerator or remove from plastic bag and defrost in a microwave.

Amaranth

Breads and Breakfasts

Cranberry-Orange Pecan Muffins

These muffins are so delicious it's hard to believe they are also nutritious and convenient to boot. You can make the batter ahead of time and refrigerate overnight (see Tips, left). Put them in the oven before you shower, and by the time you're finished, your muffins will be ready to eat.

Makes 12 muffins

Tips

If you're making the batter ahead of time, don't add the cranberries until you're ready to bake. You can chop them, cover and refrigerate overnight. The batter will keep for two nights, so if you're baking half, chop half the cranberries and do the remainder the following night.

Always check the labels of dairy products, such as yogurt, to make sure they are gluten-free.

Use fresh or frozen cranberries. If using frozen, partially thaw them and blot in paper towel before adding to the batter.

Nutrients per serving

Calories	245
Protein	3.6 g
Carbohydrates	32.9 g
Fat (Total)	11.7 g
Saturated Fat	2.1 g
Monounsaturated Fat	6 g
Polyunsaturated Fat	3 g
Dietary Fiber	3.5 g
Sodium	203 mg
Cholesterol	18 mg

EXCELLENT SOURCE OF manganese.
SOURCE OF vitamins C and E (alpha-tocopherol), thiamine, riboflavin, niacin, pantothenic acid, phosphorus, iron, magnesium, zinc and copper.
CONTAINS a moderate amount of dietary fiber.

- Preheat oven to 375°F (190°C)
- 12-cup muffin tin, lightly greased

½ cup	sorghum flour	125 mL
½ cup	brown rice flour	125 mL
½ cup	coconut flour	125 mL
¼ cup	tapioca flour	60 mL
¾ cup	granulated sugar	175 mL
¾ cup	chopped pecans	175 mL
1 tsp	gluten-free baking powder	5 mL
1 tsp	xanthan gum	5 mL
½ tsp	salt	2 mL
½ tsp	baking soda	2 mL
1	egg	1
⅔ cup	plain full-fat yogurt (see Tips, left)	150 mL
2 tsp	finely grated orange zest	10 mL
1 cup	freshly squeezed orange juice	250 mL
¼ cup	vegetable oil	60 mL
1½ cups	cranberries, coarsely chopped (see Tips, left)	375 mL

1. In a large bowl, combine sorghum, brown rice, coconut and tapioca flours, sugar, pecans, baking powder, xanthan gum, salt and baking soda. Mix well and make a well in the center.

2. In a separate bowl, beat egg. Add yogurt, orange zest, orange juice and oil and beat well. Pour into the well and mix with dry ingredients just until blended. Fold in cranberries. Divide batter evenly among prepared muffin cups. Bake in preheated oven until the top springs back when lightly touched, about 25 minutes. Let cool on a wire rack for 5 minutes before removing from pan.

Buttermilk Buckwheat Pancakes

This is one of my favorite Sunday breakfasts. I add a slice or two of bacon for a treat and a good portion of maple syrup. I savor every bite.

2½ cups	buttermilk	625 mL
2 tsp	gluten-free baking powder	10 mL
1 tsp	baking soda	5 mL
½ tsp	salt	2 mL
1 tbsp	light (fancy) molasses	15 mL
1	egg	1
2 cups	buckwheat flour (see Tips, left)	500 mL

Makes 12 to 14 pancakes or 6 servings

Tips

Buckwheat flour is available in natural foods stores. If you don't have it, you can make your own by processing kasha or toasted buckwheat groats in a food processor until finely ground.

You can make this batter ahead and keep, covered, in the refrigerator for up to 2 days. The batter will thicken a bit, so you may need to add a little buttermilk to thin it out. Your pancakes will not be as airy as those made immediately after mixing, but they will still be delicious.

1. In a food processor, combine buttermilk, baking powder, baking soda and salt. Pulse to blend. Add molasses and egg and pulse to blend. Add buckwheat flour and pulse just until combined. Set aside for 5 minutes. Mixture should be of a pourable consistency. If necessary, add more flour or buttermilk and pulse until blended.

2. Heat a lightly greased nonstick skillet over medium heat until water dropped on the surface bounces before evaporating. Add about ¼ cup (60 mL) batter at a time and cook until bubbles appear all over the top surface, then flip and cook until bottom side is browned, about 1 minute per side. Keep warm. Continue with remaining batter.

Nutrients per serving

Calories	92
Protein	4.4 g
Carbohydrates	15.8 g
Fat (Total)	1.8 g
Saturated Fat	0.8 g
Monounsaturated Fat	0.6 g
Polyunsaturated Fat	0.2 g
Dietary Fiber	1.2 g
Sodium	260 mg
Cholesterol	17 mg

GOOD SOURCE OF magnesium and manganese.

SOURCE OF thiamine, riboflavin, niacin, folate, phosphorus, calcium, iron, zinc, copper and selenium.

Blueberry Wild Rice Pancakes

The combination of flavors in these delicious pancakes is quintessentially North American, especially when finished with real maple syrup. They make a great Sunday breakfast any place, any time, but I find them particularly enjoyable at a lakeside cottage. They are a great way to use up leftover wild rice and are not only gluten-free, but also, a friend tells me, diet-friendly at only 1 Weight Watchers® point apiece.

Makes about 12 pancakes or 4 servings

Tip

When measuring flour for this or any other recipe, always use a dry measuring cup so the flour can be leveled off with the back of a knife and be sure not to pack it down.

1 cup	rice milk or milk	250 mL
½ cup	cooked wild rice (see cooking instructions, page 32)	125 mL
1 tbsp	granulated sugar	15 mL
1	egg, separated	1
1 tsp	vanilla extract	5 mL
1 cup	brown rice flour	250 mL
1 tsp	gluten-free baking powder	5 mL
½ tsp	salt	2 mL
1 cup	fresh or frozen blueberries	250 mL
	Maple syrup or blueberry jam	

1. In a saucepan over medium heat, combine milk, wild rice and sugar. Heat, stirring, until sugar dissolves and bubbles appear around the edge. Remove from heat. Stir in egg yolk and vanilla. Set aside.

2. In a bowl, combine rice flour, baking powder and salt. Add to milk mixture, stirring just until blended. Fold in blueberries. Beat egg white until stiff and gently fold into batter.

3. Heat a lightly greased nonstick skillet over medium heat until water dropped on the surface bounces before evaporating. Scoop out ¼ cup (60 mL) of batter per pancake and cook until bubbles appear all over the top surface, then flip and cook until bottom side is lightly browned, about 1 minute per side. Keep warm. Continue with remaining batter. Serve with maple syrup or blueberry jam.

Nutrients per serving

Calories	249
Protein	5.7 g
Carbohydrates	50.1 g
Fat (Total)	3 g
Saturated Fat	0.6 g
Monounsaturated Fat	1.3 g
Polyunsaturated Fat	0.7 g
Dietary Fiber	3.9 g
Sodium	404 mg
Cholesterol	47 mg

EXCELLENT SOURCE OF manganese.

GOOD SOURCE OF niacin, phosphorus and magnesium.

SOURCE OF vitamin C, thiamine, riboflavin, folate, pantothenic acid, calcium, iron, copper and selenium.

CONTAINS a moderate amount of dietary fiber.

Old-Fashioned Cornbread

This traditional favorite is the perfect accompaniment to soups, stews and chilies that have a down-home feel. Use leftovers to make cornbread stuffing, or for a great snack, enjoy with a bit of salsa.

Makes 8 servings

Tips

I have also made this with good results using brown rice milk, which qualifies as a gluten-free whole grain, so if you have a problem with dairy, give it a try.

As with other quick breads, when making cornbread, one key to success is not to overmix the batter.

Nutrients per serving

Calories	195
Protein	5.1 g
Carbohydrates	31.7 g
Fat (Total)	5.8 g
Saturated Fat	2.8 g
Monounsaturated Fat	1.7 g
Polyunsaturated Fat	0.7 g
Dietary Fiber	2.6 g
Sodium	357 mg
Cholesterol	57 mg

EXCELLENT SOURCE OF manganese.

GOOD SOURCE OF phosphorus.

SOURCE OF vitamins A and E (alpha-tocopherol), thiamine, riboflavin, niacin, folate, pantothenic acid, calcium, iron, magnesium, zinc, copper and selenium.

CONTAINS a moderate amount of dietary fiber.

- Preheat oven to 400°F (200°C)
- 8-inch (2 L) square baking pan, lightly greased

1 cup	stone-ground yellow cornmeal	250 mL
½ cup	sorghum flour	125 mL
¼ cup	brown rice flour	60 mL
¼ cup	tapioca flour	60 mL
2 tbsp	granulated sugar	30 mL
4 tsp	gluten-free baking powder	20 mL
1 tsp	xanthan gum	5 mL
½ tsp	salt	2 mL
2	eggs	2
1¼ cups	milk (see Tips, left)	300 mL
2 tbsp	melted butter	30 mL

1. In a bowl, combine cornmeal, sorghum, brown rice and tapioca flours, sugar, baking powder, xanthan gum and salt. Whisk to blend and make a well in the center.

2. In a separate bowl, beat eggs. Add milk and butter and beat well. Pour into well and mix with dry ingredients just until blended. Spread in prepared pan and bake in preheated oven until top is golden and springs back, about 30 minutes. Let cool in pan on wire rack for 5 minutes. Serve warm.

40   BREADS AND BREAKFASTS

Cheesy Jalapeño Cornbread

Slightly spicy, intriguingly savory and deliciously comforting. What more could you want? Serve this cornbread as an accompaniment to dinner or just enjoy it on its own.

Makes 8 servings

Tip

Not only does pulsing blend the dry ingredients, it also aerates them slightly, contributing to a lighter result.

- Preheat oven to 400°F (200°C)
- 8-inch (2 L) square baking pan, lightly greased

1 cup	stone-ground yellow cornmeal	250 mL
½ cup	sorghum flour	125 mL
¼ cup	brown rice flour	60 mL
2 tbsp	tapioca flour	30 mL
1 tbsp	granulated sugar	15 mL
2 tsp	gluten-free baking powder	10 mL
1 tsp	xanthan gum	5 mL
½ tsp	baking soda	2 mL
½ tsp	salt	2 mL
¼ cup	cold butter, cubed	60 mL
1½ cups	buttermilk	375 mL
2	eggs, separated	2
1	jalapeño pepper, seeded and minced	1
1 cup	shredded Cheddar cheese, preferably sharp (old)	250 mL

1. In a food processor, combine cornmeal, sorghum, brown rice and tapioca flours, sugar, baking powder, xanthan gum, baking soda and salt. Pulse to blend. Add butter and pulse until mixture resembles coarse crumbs. In a measuring cup, combine buttermilk, egg yolks and jalapeño pepper and beat well. Pour over cornmeal mixture and pulse just until blended.

2. In a mixer on high speed, beat egg whites until stiff peaks form. Fold in cheese. Fold in cornmeal mixture and spoon into prepared pan. Bake in preheated oven until top begins to brown and sides come away from the pan, about 25 minutes. Let cool in pan on a wire rack for 5 minutes. Serve warm.

Variation

Cheesy Chipotle Cornbread: Substitute 1 minced chipotle pepper in adobo sauce for the jalapeño.

Nutrients per serving

Calories	263
Protein	9 g
Carbohydrates	27.9 g
Fat (Total)	13.4 g
Saturated Fat	7.6 g
Monounsaturated Fat	3.9 g
Polyunsaturated Fat	1 g
Dietary Fiber	2.7 g
Sodium	485 mg
Cholesterol	80 mg

EXCELLENT SOURCE OF manganese.

GOOD SOURCE OF calcium, phosphorus and selenium.

SOURCE OF vitamins A and E (alpha-tocopherol), thiamine, riboflavin, niacin, folate, pantothenic acid, iron, magnesium, zinc and copper.

CONTAINS a moderate amount of dietary fiber.

Multigrain Cereal with Fruit

A steaming bowl of this tasty cereal gets you off to a good start in the morning and will help to keep you energized and productive throughout the day.

Makes 8 servings

Tip

If you're having trouble digesting grains such as oats, amaranth, millet or quinoa, try soaking them overnight in warm non-chlorinated water (about 2 parts water to 1 part grain) with a spoonful or so of cider vinegar. Add some seeds, if desired. Drain, rinse and cook in the morning. A bonus is that your cereal will be creamier than usual.

4 cups	water	1 L
¼ tsp	salt, optional	1 mL
½ cup	long- or short-grain brown rice, rinsed and drained	125 mL
½ cup	wild rice	125 mL
½ cup	Job's tears	125 mL
½ tsp	vanilla extract	2 mL
2	all-purpose apples, peeled, cored and thinly sliced	2
½ cup	chopped pitted soft dates, such as Medjool	125 mL
	Milk or non-dairy alternative	
	Maple syrup	
	Chopped toasted nuts, optional	

1. In a large saucepan over medium heat, bring water and salt, if using, to a boil. Gradually stir in rice, wild rice, Job's tears, vanilla and apples and return to a boil. Reduce heat to low. Cover and simmer, placing a heat diffuser under the pot, if necessary, until Job's tears are tender, about 1 hour. Stir in dates. Serve with milk or non-dairy alternative and maple syrup. Sprinkle with nuts, if using.

Use your slow cooker: Whether you're cooking Multigrain Cereal with Fruit, or a single whole grain, such as rolled oats, your slow cooker makes light work of the job, particularly if you cook your grains overnight. Use a small (maximum 3½ quart) lightly greased slow cooker. Place a clean tea towel, folded in half so you will have two layers) over top of the stoneware to absorb moisture. Cover and cook on Low for up to 8 hours or overnight, or on High for 4 hours. Stir in dried fruits and sprinkle with toasted nuts and seeds, if using.

Nutrients per serving

Calories	168
Protein	4.5 g
Carbohydrates	36.3 g
Fat (Total)	1.2 g
Saturated Fat	0.1 g
Monounsaturated Fat	0.1 g
Polyunsaturated Fat	0.2 g
Dietary Fiber	2.5 g
Sodium	5 mg
Cholesterol	0 mg

EXCELLENT SOURCE OF manganese.

SOURCE OF thiamine, niacin, folate, phosphorus, iron, magnesium, zinc, copper and selenium.

CONTAINS a moderate amount of dietary fiber.

HOT WHOLE-GRAIN CEREALS

I really enjoy having hot whole-grain cereal for breakfast. The recipe above is just one suggestion. Brown rice cooked with rice milk (1:4 ratio) and finished with dried cherries, cranberries or blueberries, and gluten-free steel-cut (also known as Irish) oats, or rolled oats cooked in water (1:4 ratio) are equally delicious. I like to add chopped pitted dates to the oats after they are cooked and finish with maple syrup and milk. A sprinkle of toasted nuts and seeds is always nice, but not essential.

Hot Millet Amaranth Cereal

Here's a great way to start your day and add variety to your diet. Both millet and amaranth are relatively quick and easy to cook — so long as you keep the temperature low, they don't need to be stirred. Use a sweetener of your choice and add dried fruit and nuts as you please.

Makes 6 servings

Tips

For best results, toast the millet and amaranth before cooking. Stir the grains in a dry skillet over medium heat until they crackle and release their aroma, about 5 minutes.

If you're having trouble digesting grains, try soaking them overnight in warm non-chlorinated water (about 2 parts water to 1 part grain) with a spoonful or so of cider vinegar. Drain, rinse and cook in the morning.

2½ cups	water	625 mL
½ cup	millet, toasted (see Tips, left)	125 mL
½ cup	amaranth	125 mL
	Honey, maple syrup or raw cane sugar	
	Milk or non-dairy alternative	
	Dried cranberries, cherries or raisins, optional	
	Toasted chopped nuts, optional	

1. In a saucepan over medium heat, bring water to a boil. Add millet and amaranth in a steady stream, stirring constantly. Return to a boil. Reduce heat to low (see Tip, page 47). Cover and simmer until grains are tender and liquid is absorbed, about 25 minutes. Serve hot, sweetened to taste and with milk or non-dairy alternative. Sprinkle with dried fruit and nuts, if using.

Nutrients per serving

Calories	124
Protein	4.2 g
Carbohydrates	23.3 g
Fat (Total)	1.6 g
Saturated Fat	0.4 g
Monounsaturated Fat	0.3 g
Polyunsaturated Fat	0.7 g
Dietary Fiber	4 g
Sodium	6 mg
Cholesterol	0 mg

EXCELLENT SOURCE OF manganese.

GOOD SOURCE OF magnesium.

SOURCE OF thiamine, niacin, folate, phosphorus, iron, zinc and copper.

CONTAINS a high amount of dietary fiber.

Almond-Flavored Millet with Cherries

Since millet is particularly easy to digest, it's an excellent way to get your day off to a great start. Although it's an extra step, I recommend toasting millet before cooking, as it really brings out its pleasing nutty flavor. Once the pot is on the stove, it simmers away on its own requiring no attention from you.

Makes 6 servings

Tips

Almond milk is available in natural foods stores.

I like to add the dried cherries along with the liquid, as they rehydrate while cooking, becoming almost plump.

If you're having trouble digesting grains, try soaking them overnight in warm non-chlorinated water (about 2 parts water to 1 part grain) with a spoonful or so of cider vinegar. Drain, rinse and cook in the morning.

1 cup	millet	250 mL
4 cups	vanilla-flavored almond milk	1 L
½ cup	dried cherries	125 mL
	Maple syrup or honey	
	Toasted sliced almonds, optional	

1. In a saucepan over medium heat, toast millet, stirring, until it crackles and releases its aroma, about 5 minutes. Transfer to a bowl and set aside. Add almond milk to saucepan and bring to a boil. Gradually stir in millet and cherries and return to a boil. Reduce heat to low (see Tip, page 47). Cover and simmer until liquid is absorbed, about 30 minutes. Remove from heat and let stand, covered, about 5 minutes. Serve with maple syrup and sprinkle with almonds, if using.

Nutrients per serving

Calories	227
Protein	4.9 g
Carbohydrates	45.5 g
Fat (Total)	3 g
Saturated Fat	0.3 g
Monounsaturated Fat	0.3 g
Polyunsaturated Fat	0.6 g
Dietary Fiber	4.6 g
Sodium	105 mg
Cholesterol	0 mg

GOOD SOURCE OF magnesium and manganese.
SOURCE OF thiamine, riboflavin, niacin, folate, phosphorus, iron, zinc and copper.
CONTAINS a high amount of dietary fiber.

Cranberry Quinoa Porridge

If you're not organized enough to make hot cereal ahead of time, here's one you can enjoy in less than half an hour, start to finish, and that doesn't require any attention while it's cooking.

Makes 6 servings

Tip

Unless you have a stove with a true simmer, after reducing the heat to low I recommend placing a heat diffuser under the pot to prevent the mixture from boiling. This device also helps to ensure the grains will cook evenly and prevents hot spots, which might cause scorching, from forming. Heat diffusers are available at kitchen supply and hardware stores and are made to work on gas or electric stoves.

3 cups	water	750 mL
1 cup	quinoa, rinsed and drained	250 mL
½ cup	dried cranberries	125 mL
	Maple syrup or honey	
	Milk or non-dairy alternative, optional	

1. In a saucepan over medium heat, bring water to a boil. Stir in quinoa and cranberries and return to a boil. Reduce heat to low. Cover and simmer until quinoa is cooked (look for a white line around the seeds), about 15 minutes. Remove from heat and let stand, covered, about 5 minutes. Serve with maple syrup and milk or non-dairy alternative, if using.

Variations

Substitute dried cherries or blueberries or raisins for the cranberries.

Use red quinoa for a change.

Nutrients per serving

Calories	137
Protein	3.7 g
Carbohydrates	27.8 g
Fat (Total)	1.8 g
Saturated Fat	0.2 g
Monounsaturated Fat	0.5 g
Polyunsaturated Fat	0.7 g
Dietary Fiber	2.5 g
Sodium	8 mg
Cholesterol	0 mg

EXCELLENT SOURCE OF manganese.

GOOD SOURCE OF iron and magnesium.

SOURCE OF riboflavin, niacin, folate, pantothenic acid, phosphorus, zinc and copper.

CONTAINS a moderate amount of dietary fiber.

Cornmeal

Appetizers

Zucchini Fritters

Serve these fritters as part of an antipasti spread. They are great on their own or, if you like to gild the lily, even better with a bowl of tzatziki alongside. (Pictured with Corn Cakes, page 52.)

Makes about 2 dozen

Tips

To expedite preparation, shred zucchini and set aside to sweat while you prepare the remaining ingredients.

For ease of preparation use your food processor fitted with the shredding blade to shred the zucchini.

• Preheat oven to 200°F (100°C)

4 cups	shredded zucchini (about 3 medium)	1 L
1 tsp	coarse salt	5 mL
4 oz	feta, crumbled	125 g
6	green onions, white part with a bit of green, minced	6
½ cup	finely chopped fresh dill fronds	125 mL
2	cloves garlic, minced	2
2	eggs, beaten	2
½ cup	sorghum flour	125 mL
1 tbsp	cornstarch	15 mL
½ tsp	gluten-free baking powder	2 mL
¼ cup	vegetable oil (approx.)	60 mL

1. In a colander, placed over a sink, combine zucchini and salt. Toss well and set aside for 15 minutes to sweat. Using your hands, squeeze out as much water as possible. Spread on a clean tea towel and press to soak up as much liquid as possible, using a second tea towel, if necessary. (Zucchini should be as dry as possible; otherwise your fritters will be mushy.)

2. In a bowl, combine feta, green onions, dill and garlic. Add zucchini and eggs and mix well. Sprinkle sorghum flour, cornstarch and baking powder evenly over mixture and toss well.

3. In a large heavy skillet, heat oil over medium–high heat. Scoop out about 1 heaping tbsp (20 mL) of mixture at a time and drop into hot oil. Repeat until pan is full, leaving about 2 inches (5 cm) between fritters. Cook, turning once, until nicely golden, about 5 minutes per batch. Drain on paper towel–lined platter and keep warm in preheated oven while you complete the frying. Serve warm.

Nutrients per serving

Calories	42
Protein	1.7 g
Carbohydrates	3.2 g
Fat (Total)	2.7 g
Saturated Fat	1 g
Monounsaturated Fat	1.1 g
Polyunsaturated Fat	0.5 g
Dietary Fiber	0.3 g
Sodium	98 mg
Cholesterol	20 mg

SOURCE OF manganese.

Corn Cakes

VEGETARIAN FRIENDLY

These little cakes, which resemble corn-studded blini, are delicious on their own and quite divine topped with a dollop of your favorite salsa. (See photo page 51.)

Makes about 2 dozen

Tip

Use the second jalapeño for a spicier corn cake. If you are a true heat seeker, leave the veins and seeds in before chopping the pepper.

• Preheat oven to 200°F (100°C)

2 cups	corn kernels, preferably fresh, thawed if frozen	500 mL
½ cup	packed Italian flat-leaf parsley or cilantro leaves	125 mL
2 tbsp	finely chopped red bell pepper, optional	30 mL
1	shallot, chopped	1
2	cloves garlic, chopped	2
1 to 2	jalapeño peppers, seeded and coarsely chopped (see Tip, left)	1 to 2
1 tsp	salt	5 mL
½ tsp	freshly ground black pepper	2 mL
3 tbsp	sorghum flour	45 mL
1 tbsp	cornstarch	15 mL
3	eggs	3
2 tbsp	unsalted butter, divided	30 mL
2 tbsp	olive oil, divided	30 mL
	Salt, optional	

1. In a food processor fitted with metal blade, pulse corn, parsley, bell pepper, if using, shallot, garlic, jalapeño pepper(s), salt and pepper until finely chopped, about 15 times. Add flour and cornstarch and pulse 2 or 3 times to blend. Add eggs and process until smoothly blended, about 30 seconds.

2. In a large skillet, heat 1 tbsp (15 mL) each of the butter and oil over medium heat. Working in batches of about 6 cakes, drop 1 tbsp (15 mL) of batter per cake into pan. Cook until bottoms are brown, about 1 minute. Flip and cook until nicely browned on bottom, about 1 minute. Transfer to a baking sheet. Sprinkle with salt, if using, and keep warm in preheated oven. Repeat until all batter is used up, adding more butter and oil and adjusting heat between batches, as necessary.

Nutrients per serving

Calories	45
Protein	1.3 g
Carbohydrates	4.1 g
Fat (Total)	2.9 g
Saturated Fat	1 g
Monounsaturated Fat	1.4 g
Polyunsaturated Fat	0.3 g
Dietary Fiber	0.4 g
Sodium	106 mg
Cholesterol	26 mg

SOURCE OF folate.

Zesty Cheddar Crisps

These are great to nibble on pre-dinner with a glass of red wine. Mix up a batch during the holiday season and keep the dough in the refrigerator. Slice, bake and serve fresh from the oven, when guests arrive.

Makes about 3 dozen

Tip

Hot smoked paprika will lend a smoky, almost bacon-like flavor to these crisps, as well as heat. The flavor will be more intense and complex than that achieved with cayenne alone.

- Baking sheet, lined with parchment paper

1/3 cup	sorghum flour	75 mL
1/3 cup	fine brown rice flour	75 mL
2 tbsp	cornstarch	30 mL
1 tsp	gluten-free baking powder	5 mL
1 tsp	hot smoked paprika or 1/4 tsp (1 mL) cayenne pepper (see Tip, left)	5 mL
1/2 tsp	xanthan gum	2 mL
1/2 tsp	salt	2 mL
2 cups	shredded sharp (old) Cheddar cheese	500 ml
1/3 cup	unsalted butter, cubed	75 mL
1/4 cup	finely chopped pecans or walnuts	60 mL

1. In food processor fitted with metal blade, combine sorghum and brown rice flours, cornstarch, baking powder, paprika, xanthan gum and salt and pulse to blend, about 4 times. Add shredded cheese and butter and pulse until mixture resembles coarse crumbs, about 20 times. Turn out on a lightly floured board and knead until dough comes together. Shape into a roll about 1 inch (2.5 cm) in diameter. Spread nuts on a cutting board and roll dough in them until well coated. Wrap in plastic wrap and refrigerate until thoroughly chilled, for at least 3 hours or up to 1 week.

2. When you're ready to bake, preheat oven to 400°F (200°C). Cut dough into slices about 1/4 inch (0.5 cm) thick. Arrange on prepared baking sheet, at least 2 inches (5 cm) apart. Bake in preheated oven for 6 minutes. Remove from oven. Using a spatula, turn crisps over and bake until lightly browned, about 6 minutes more. Let cool in pan on rack for 2 minutes. Serve warm.

Nutrients per serving

Calories	57
Protein	1.9 g
Carbohydrates	2.6 g
Fat (Total)	4.4 g
Saturated Fat	2.5 g
Monounsaturated Fat	1.4 g
Polyunsaturated Fat	0.3 g
Dietary Fiber	0.2 g
Sodium	81 mg
Cholesterol	11 mg

SOURCE OF calcium and manganese.

Buckwheat Blini

Blini have luxurious overtones because they are traditionally served with the best caviar. While you can certainly top these with a dollop of beluga (if you're lucky enough to have some), they are also delicious with thin slices of smoked salmon, a squirt of fresh lemon juice, a spoonful of crème fraîche, liberal amounts of freshly ground black pepper and a sprinkling of finely snipped chives or paper-thin slices of red onion. If you're feeling the need for caviar, try substituting salmon caviar for the smoked salmon. The red bubbles look particularly pretty.

Makes about 36 blini

Tips

Although yeast does not contain gluten, a small percentage of people with celiac disease are sensitive to yeast. Most have no problem with active dry yeast, which is called for here. However, instant dry yeast is a different product and should be avoided by people with celiac disease.

Blini (the singular is blin) are best served immediately after cooking, but you can make them up to 1 day ahead. Cover and refrigerate cooked blini. Brush with extra virgin olive oil or melted butter and heat in 325°F (160°C) oven for about 10 minutes.

- **Preheat oven to 200°F (100°C)**
- **Nonstick skillet**

2 tsp	granulated sugar	10 mL
1¼ cups	warm whole milk (about 100°F/38°C)	300 mL
1 tsp	active dry yeast (see Tips, left)	5 mL
½ cup	sorghum flour	125 mL
½ cup	buckwheat flour	125 mL
1 tbsp	cornstarch	15 mL
½ tsp	salt	2 mL
1	egg, beaten	1
2 tbsp	melted unsalted butter	30 mL
	Oil	

1. In a bowl, combine sugar and warm milk. Stir to dissolve sugar. Sprinkle yeast evenly over top and set aside until frothy, about 10 minutes.

2. In another bowl, combine sorghum and buckwheat flours, cornstarch and salt. Stir well. Add yeast mixture and mix well. Add egg and butter and mix well. Cover with plastic wrap and set aside in a warm, draft-free place until mixture rises slightly and top is quite bubbly, about 1 hour.

3. Brush nonstick skillet lightly with oil and place over medium heat. Spoon 1 tbsp (15 mL) of batter per blin and cook until bubbles form on the top and underside is brown, about 30 seconds. Flip and cook until golden on the bottom, about 30 seconds. Transfer to a baking sheet as completed and keep warm in preheated oven. Grease skillet and adjust heat between batches, as necessary. Serve warm, with your favorite topping.

Nutrients per serving (1 blin)

Calories	26
Protein	0.9 g
Carbohydrates	3.3 g
Fat (Total)	1.2 g
Saturated Fat	0.6 g
Monounsaturated Fat	0.3 g
Polyunsaturated Fat	0.1 g
Dietary Fiber	0.1 g
Sodium	37 mg
Cholesterol	8 mg

SOURCE OF manganese.

Crêpes Parmentier

Although these potato pancakes are traditionally served with poached chicken in a cream sauce in France, their country of origin, they also work well like blini, as an appetizer base and as a gluten-free alternative to crostini or sliced baguette. They are delicious topped with pâté, smoked salmon and sour cream, salsa, tapenade or virtually any favorite spread.

Makes about 24 mini crepes

Tips

An easy way to cook the potatoes for this recipe is to microwave them. Place scrubbed potato in a microwave-safe dish. Add cold water to a depth of about ½ inch (1 cm), cover and microwave on High for 3 to 6 minutes or until potatoes are tender. Leave the lid on and let cool for at least 5 minutes before running under cold water and removing the skins.

If you have time, cook the potatoes ahead and refrigerate until you're ready to peel. They will be easier to shred.

Always check dairy products, such as cream, to make sure gluten has not been added.

- **Preheat oven to 200°F (100°C)**

8 oz	potatoes, boiled in their skins, cooled and peeled (see Tips, left)	250 g
2 tbsp	tapioca flour	30 mL
1 tsp	gluten-free baking powder	5 mL
½ tsp	salt	2 mL
	Freshly ground black pepper	
4	eggs	4
¼ cup	half-and-half (10%) cream	60 mL
2 tbsp	heavy or whipping (35%) cream (see Tips, left)	30 mL
2 tbsp	unsalted butter, divided	30 mL
2 tbsp	olive oil, divided	30 mL
	Salt	

1. In food processor fitted with shredding blade, shred potatoes. Transfer to a bowl and set aside.

2. Replace shredding blade with metal blade, add flour, baking powder, salt, and pepper to taste and pulse to blend. Add eggs and half-and-half and heavy creams and process until smoothly blended, about 30 seconds. Add potatoes and pulse to blend, about 5 times.

3. In a large skillet, preferably nonstick, heat half of the butter and half of the oil over medium heat. Working in batches, drop 1 tbsp (15 mL) of batter per crêpe into pan. Cook until top looks set and bottom is browned, about 2 minutes. Flip and cook on the second side until bottom is browned, about 1 minute. Sprinkle with salt. Transfer to a warm plate and keep warm in preheated oven. Repeat until all batter is used up, adding more butter and oil and adjusting heat between batches, as necessary.

Nutrients per serving (1 crêpe)

Calories	47
Protein	1.3 g
Carbohydrates	2.5 g
Fat (Total)	3.6 g
Saturated Fat	1.4 g
Monounsaturated Fat	1.6 g
Polyunsaturated Fat	0.3 g
Dietary Fiber	0.1 g
Sodium	72 mg
Cholesterol	36 mg

SOURCE OF selenium.

Yogurt Flatbread

Warm from the oven, these little flatbreads are yummy on their own or finished with some fresh herbs (see Variations, below). If you're so inclined you can also use them as a dipper or top with a dollop of salsa or chutney. They also make a good base for spreads.

Makes about 2½ dozen

Tips

Be sure to use good sea salt, such as *fleur de sel* to finish your bread. Refined table salt has a bitter acrid taste.

You can purchase za'atar in specialty spice shops or make your own. In a small bowl, combine 2 tbsp (30 mL) fresh thyme leaves, 1 tbsp (15 mL) toasted sesame seeds and 1 tsp (5 mL) each ground sumac and coarse sea salt. To toast sesame seeds, place in a dry skillet over medium heat and cook, stirring, just until they begin to brown. Immediately transfer to a bowl; once they start to brown they burn quickly.

Always check the labels of dairy products, such as yogurt, to make sure they are gluten-free.

- Preheat oven to 350°F (180°C)
- 2½-inch (6 cm) round cutter
- Baking sheets, lined with parchment paper

¾ cup	sorghum flour	175 mL
¾ cup	fine brown rice flour	175 mL
½ cup	tapioca flour	125 mL
1 tsp	xanthan gum	5 mL
1 tsp	gluten-free baking powder	5 mL
½ tsp	salt	2 mL
1 cup	plain yogurt (see Tips, left)	250 mL
2 tbsp	extra virgin olive oil	30 mL
	Course sea salt	

1. In a bowl, combine sorghum, brown rice and tapioca flours, xanthan gum, baking powder and salt. Add yogurt and, using a wooden spoon, mix as well as you can. Then use your hands to knead until a soft dough forms. Cover and let rest at room temperature for 1 hour.

2. Divide dough into quarters. Working with one piece at a time, on lightly floured board, roll out to a ⅛-inch (3 mm) thickness. Using cutter, cut into rounds and place about 2 inches (5 cm) apart on prepared sheets. Repeat until all the dough has been cut into circles, re-rolling scraps.

3. Bake in preheated oven until nicely puffed, about 15 minutes. Remove from oven and preheat broiler. Place flatbreads under broiler until lightly browned. Brush with olive oil and sprinkle with salt. Serve warm.

Variations

Za'atar-Spiked Flatbread: After the flatbreads have been brushed with olive oil, sprinkle with za'atar (see Tips, left).

Herb-Spiked Flatbread: In a small bowl, combine 1 tbsp (15 mL) minced fresh thyme leaves and 1 tsp (5 mL) finely grated lemon zest. After the flatbreads have been brushed with olive oil, sprinkle with the mixture, then finish with salt to taste.

Nutrients per serving (1 piece)

Calories	51
Protein	1 g
Carbohydrates	8.4 g
Fat (Total)	1.6 g
Saturated Fat	0.5 g
Monounsaturated Fat	0.9 g
Polyunsaturated Fat	0.2 g
Dietary Fiber	0.3 g
Sodium	56 mg
Cholesterol	1 mg

SOURCE OF manganese.

Polenta Crostini

Crostini made from polenta are a nice change from those made from bread. And they are gluten-free, to boot. They can be topped with almost anything you would use to top bread-based crostini, bearing in mind that polenta has a more assertive flavor than white bread. In general terms, you are probably safe with anything that is Italian in flavoring. See below right for some specific suggestions.

When cutting polenta crostini use your imagination. Round or fluted cookie cutters make particularly pretty crostini, but simple rectangles, squares or triangles work well, too. You can even cut animal shapes if you're serving crostini at a children's party.

Makes enough for about 36 average-size crostini

Tips

If you prefer, substitute vegetable or chicken stock for the water.

If you have trouble digesting cornmeal, look for an artisanal source to ensure it has not been genetically modified. Also, try soaking your cornmeal for at least 8 hours or overnight in warm non-chlorinated water (about 2 parts water to 1 part grain) with a spoonful or so of cider vinegar (preferably with the mother). Drain and rinse before cooking. Your polenta will be particularly creamy.

- Ovenproof saucepan
- 15- by 10-inch (37.5 by 25 cm) jelly roll pan, lined with plastic wrap

4½ cups	water (see Tips, left)	1.125 L
¼ tsp	salt	1 mL
1 cup	stone-ground cornmeal (see Tips, left)	250 mL
	Oil	

1. In a saucepan over medium heat, bring water and salt to a boil. Gradually stir in cornmeal in a steady stream. Cook, stirring constantly, until smooth and blended and mixture bubbles like lava, about 5 minutes.

2. Reduce heat to low (placing a heat diffuser under the pot if your stove doesn't have a true simmer). Continue cooking, stirring frequently, while mixture bubbles and thickens, until grains are tender and creamy, about 30 minutes, depending upon how finely it was ground.

3. Transfer to prepared dish or pan. Spread warm polenta evenly over the plastic. Cover completely with another piece of plastic and using the palm of your hand, flatten to level. (Don't worry if the edges are a bit uneven or if the polenta doesn't completely cover the bottom of the pan. You can trim it when you make the crostini.) Refrigerate, covered, for at least 6 hours, until chilled and set, or up to 2 days.

4. When you're ready to serve, preheat oven to 350°F (180°C).

5. Remove plastic and place polenta sheet on a large cutting board. Set aside until polenta reaches room temperature. Cut into desired shapes, using a sharp knife or cookie cutters. Brush top side of the shapes with olive oil. Place on a parchment paper–lined baking sheet and bake in preheated oven, for 10 minutes. Flip over, brush second side with olive oil and bake for 10 minutes, until edges begin to crisp. Let cool completely on pan on a wire rack before adding toppings.

Nutrients per serving (1 crostini)

Calories	12
Protein	0.2 g
Carbohydrates	2.6 g
Fat (Total)	0.1 g
Saturated Fat	0 g
Monounsaturated Fat	0 g
Polyunsaturated Fat	0.1 g
Dietary Fiber	0.5 g
Sodium	17 mg
Cholesterol	0 mg

Toppings for Polenta Crostini

Polenta crostini provide a great base for many delicious toppings. Here are some of my favorites.

Creamy Gorgonzola with Walnut Polenta Crostini: In a small bowl, combine equal parts gorgonzola and mascarpone cheese. Mix well. (Some cheese mongers sell a version of this already mixed; if you have access to it, by all means use it.) Spread on cooled polenta crostini to taste. Sprinkle finely chopped walnuts on top.

Fontina Cheese Polenta Crostini: Top cut crostini with thinly sliced Fontina cheese to taste. Bake in 350°F (180°C) oven until cheese is nicely melted, about 3 minutes. If you are grilling the crostini (see Variation, right), top with the cheese after turning once.

Roasted Garlic Polenta Crostini: Spread cooled polenta crostini with roasted garlic. To roast garlic, separate head into cloves but do not peel. Place in a small ovenproof container and toss with a bit of olive oil (about 2 tsp/10 mL) per head. Roast in 425°F (220°C) oven until softened, about 30 minutes. To serve, squeeze roasted garlic out of skins and spread over crostini.

Variations

Oven-Cooked Polenta: For a low-maintenance method of cooking polenta, use an ovenproof saucepan and after Step 1, cover saucepan and transfer to 350°F (180°C) oven (or if you don't have an ovenproof saucepan, transfer mixture to lightly greased 8-cup/2 L baking dish and cover with foil). Bake until cornmeal is tender and creamy, about 40 minutes.

Grilled Polenta Crostini: Complete Steps 1 though 3. Lightly grease the grates and preheat barbecue to High. Cut polenta into 36 squares (6 rows by 6 rows). Grill polenta squares until lightly charred, about 3 minutes per side. Remove from heat and add desired toppings.

Spinach and Mozzarella Polenta Crostini: In a skillet, melt 1 tbsp (15 mL) butter over medium heat. Add 1 clove of minced garlic and nutmeg to taste and cook, stirring, for 1 minute. Add 1 lb (500 g) fresh spinach leaves and cook, stirring, until nicely wilted, about 1 minute. Drain off liquid and season spinach to taste with salt and pepper. Stir in 4 oz (125 g) shredded fresh mozzarella (bocconcini). Spoon over polenta crostini. Serve warm or at room temperature. If you prefer, substitute Swiss chard for the spinach and Buffalo mozzarella for the bocconcini. Wash chard well and place in a heavy pot with just the water clinging to its leaves. Cook over low heat until nicely wilted, about 5 minutes.

Smoked Salmon and Grits Cakes

These savory squares are very easy to make and deliciously different. They are great finished with a small dollop of sour cream and a sprinkling of chives, as the recipe calls for. If you're looking for another flavor sensation, try topping each square with diced roasted red peppers, tossed in olive oil.

Makes about 64 squares

Tips

If you don't want to stir your grits frequently, use a nonstick saucepan. An occasional stir will be fine so long as the heat is low.

If you can't find stone-ground grits, use coarse stone-ground cornmeal. Do not use the finely ground grits that come in boxes. They are not whole grain (see Tips, page 58).

Always check dairy products such as whipping cream and sour cream to make sure they are gluten-free.

- 8-inch (20 cm) square pan, lightly greased

1½ cups	chicken or vegetable stock	375 mL
½ tsp	salt or to taste	2 mL
½ cup	white or yellow stone-ground corn grits (see Tips, left)	125 mL
¼ cup	heavy or whipping (35%) cream	60 mL
2 tbsp	unsalted butter	30 mL
1	egg, beaten	1
1 tsp	finely grated lemon zest	5 mL
2 tbsp	freshly squeezed lemon juice	30 mL
½ tsp	hot paprika	2 mL
4 oz	smoked salmon, diced	125 g
	Sour cream	
	Finely snipped chives	

1. In a saucepan over medium heat, bring stock and salt to a rapid boil. Add grits in a steady steam and cook, stirring frequently, until smoothly integrated. Stir in cream. Cover, reduce heat to low and simmer gently, stirring occasionally, until grits are soft and creamy, about 40 minutes. Remove from heat.

2. Add butter and egg and stir well with a wooden spoon. Add lemon zest, lemon juice and paprika and stir well. Stir in smoked salmon. Spread evenly in prepared pan and let cool.

3. Cut into 1-inch (2.5 cm) squares and using an inverted spatula remove from pan. Serve at room temperature, topped with a small dollop of sour cream and garnished with chives.

Nutrients per serving (1 piece)

Calories	18
Protein	0.6 g
Carbohydrates	1.1 g
Fat (Total)	1.3 g
Saturated Fat	0.5 g
Monounsaturated Fat	0.5 g
Polyunsaturated Fat	0.2 g
Dietary Fiber	0.1 g
Sodium	55 mg
Cholesterol	5 mg

Shrimp Tempura

In Japan and finer Japanese restaurants throughout the world, tempura batter is made from a very fine wheat flour that contains eggs. Good results can be achieved using brown rice flour, which is softer than all-purpose flour, along with sorghum flour, very cold soda water and fresh eggs. The cornstarch serves to lighten the batter.

Makes 9 to 12 servings

Tips

For best results, brine shrimp before cooking. Dissolve 2 tbsp (30 mL) kosher salt in 1 cup (250 mL) boiling water. Add ice cubes until cool to the touch. Add shrimp. Add water, if necessary, to cover and set aside at room temperature for 15 minutes. Drain and rinse thoroughly under cold running water. Pat dry.

Roasted Pepper and Salt: In a dry skillet, combine 1 tsp (5 mL) Szechuan peppercorns and 1 tsp (5 mL) coarse sea salt. Cook, stirring, over medium heat until pepper begins to pop. Immediately transfer to a mortar or spice grinder and grind.

Nutrients per serving

Calories	75
Protein	6.5 g
Carbohydrates	7 g
Fat (Total)	2.2 g
Saturated Fat	0.3 g
Monounsaturated Fat	1 g
Polyunsaturated Fat	0.7 g
Dietary Fiber	0.2 g
Sodium	47 mg
Cholesterol	51 mg

GOOD SOURCE OF selenium.
SOURCE OF vitamin E (alpha-tocopherol), niacin, phosphorus, iron, magnesium, manganese, zinc and copper.

- Candy/deep-fry thermometer

	Vegetable oil	
1	egg	1
½ cup	finely ground brown rice flour	125 mL
½ cup	sorghum flour	125 mL
½ cup	cornstarch, divided (approx.)	125 mL
1 cup	ice cold soda or sparkling mineral water	250 mL
1 lb	jumbo shrimp peeled and deveined (tails intact if you prefer), preferably brined (see Tips, left)	500 g
	Roasted Pepper and Salt (see Tips, left) or smoked sea salt, optional	

1. In a Dutch oven or wok, add oil to a depth of about 2 inches (5 cm). Heat over medium–high heat until temperature reaches 350°F (180°C).

2. Meanwhile, in a bowl, beat egg. Add brown rice and sorghum flours and ¼ cup (60 mL) of the cornstarch and mix until combined (it will be very lumpy). Add soda water and mix just until blended. Cover and refrigerate for 1 hour. Stir well before using.

3. Place remaining cornstarch in a resealable bag and add shrimp. Toss until well coated. Holding shrimp by the tail end, dip in batter one at a time. Add shrimp to hot oil in batches (about 6 at a time) and fry until crisp and golden, turning once, about 1 minute per side.

4. Transfer to a paper towel–lined plate to drain and sprinkle with Roasted Pepper and Salt, if using (see Tips, left).

Variation

Calamari Tempura: Substitute squid rounds (about ½ inch/ 2 mL thick) for the shrimp. Separate with a fork when adding to the batter to ensure all sides are coated.

Vegetable Tempura

Vegetables cosseted in batter and fried are absolutely delicious. They are a treat on their own with a sprinkling of good sea salt or Roasted Pepper and Salt (see Tips, page 62). Some, such as green onions and shiitake mushrooms, can be trimmed and added to the batter raw. Others require precooking. Sliced zucchini should be sweated in about 1 tsp (5 mL) of salt for 15 minutes, then patted dry; green beans should be trimmed and blanched for about 1 minute; carrots need to be cut into sticks (about ½- by 3-inches/1 by 7.5 cm) and blanched for about 2½ minutes; beets and potatoes should be sliced and parboiled (or microwaved) just until fork tender; and sweet potatoes should be sliced and roasted for about 30 minutes just until fork tender at 400°F (200°C). However, there are lots of other options. Use your imagination.

Makes 6 to 8 servings

Tip

Be sure to dry vegetables then dredge them in cornstarch before frying. Otherwise the batter won't adhere to the vegetables. The quantity of cornstarch is important. You want the vegetables to be lightly dusted. If you use too much, your tempura will be gluey.

Nutrients per serving

(Based on using two (8-ounce/250 g) sweet potatoes for frying)

Calories	112
Protein	1.5 g
Carbohydrates	21.1 g
Fat (Total)	2.4 g
Saturated Fat	0.2 g
Monounsaturated Fat	1.3 g
Polyunsaturated Fat	0.8 g
Dietary Fiber	2.2 g
Sodium	114 mg
Cholesterol	0 mg

EXCELLENT SOURCE OF vitamin A.

GOOD SOURCE OF manganese.

SOURCE OF vitamins C and E (alpha-tocopherol), thiamine, niacin, pantothenic acid, phosphorus, magnesium and copper.

CONTAINS a moderate amount of dietary fiber.

* Candy/deep-fry thermometer

Batter

¾ cup	cornstarch, divided (approx.)	175 mL
½ cup	finely ground brown rice flour	125 mL
1 tsp	gluten-free baking powder	5 mL
½ tsp	salt	2 mL
¾ cup	cold soda water or sparkling mineral water	175 mL
1 tsp	sesame oil	5 mL

Oil

Vegetables for frying (see Tips, left and Introduction, above)

Roasted Pepper and Salt (page 62), optional

1. In a bowl, combine ½ cup (125 mL) of the cornstarch, brown rice flour, baking powder and salt. Mix well. Add soda water and sesame oil and mix just until blended. (Don't overmix. It should be a bit lumpy.) Cover and refrigerate for 1 hour.

2. When you're ready to cook, in a Dutch oven or wok, add oil to a depth of about 2 inches (5 cm). Heat over medium–high heat until temperature reaches 350°F (180°C).

3. Spread remaining ¼ cup (60 mL) of cornstarch on a plate or place in a resealable bag and dredge vegetables in it. (Depending upon the quantity of vegetables you are using and their configuration, you may need to add more cornstarch.) Dip dredged vegetables in batter. Add to hot oil in batches (about 4 pieces at a time) and fry until crisp and golden, turning once, about 1 minute per side. Transfer to a paper towel–lined platter to drain. Sprinkle with Roasted Pepper and Salt, if using. Serve warm.

Variation

Dipping Sauce: To make a dipping sauce for vegetable tempura, combine ¼ cup (60 mL) gluten–free soy sauce, 2 tbsp (30 mL) each freshly squeezed lime juice and mirin and ½ tsp (2 mL) sambal oelek.

Millet

Soups

Fragrant Beef and Chinese "Barley" Soup with Shiitake Mushrooms

Here's an updated version of a classic soup — beef, barley and mushrooms — using gluten-free Job's tears in place of barley. The Chinese accents add intriguing flavors and give the soup a global spin without detracting from its traditional appeal. It's still a great cold weather pick-me-up — I can't imagine anything more perfect for après ski than a steaming bowl of this hearty brew.

Makes 6 main-course servings

Tips

Chinese 5-spice powder is available in the spice section of well-stocked supermarkets or in Asian markets. Check the label to make sure no gluten has been added.

If desired, use 1 box (1 quart/ 900 mL) ready-to-use reduced-sodium beef stock for this quantity but check the label to make sure it is gluten-free.

Nutrients per serving

Calories	237
Protein	15.1 g
Carbohydrates	27.1 g
Fat (Total)	8.1 g
Saturated Fat	1.9 g
Monounsaturated Fat	3.4 g
Polyunsaturated Fat	0.9 g
Dietary Fiber	2.4 g
Sodium	815 mg
Cholesterol	22 mg

EXCELLENT SOURCE OF zinc.

GOOD SOURCE OF riboflavin, niacin, pantothenic acid, phosphorus, iron and selenium.

SOURCE OF vitamin E (alpha-tocopherol), folate, thiamine, manganese, copper and magnesium.

CONTAINS a moderate amount of dietary fiber.

8	dried shiitake mushrooms	8
4 cups	hot water	1 L
1 tbsp	vegetable oil	15 mL
8 oz	stewing beef, trimmed and cut into bite-size pieces	250 g
2	onions, finely chopped	2
4	stalks celery, diced	4
8 oz	fresh shiitake mushrooms, stems removed and caps sliced	250 g
1 tbsp	minced garlic	15 mL
1 tbsp	minced gingerroot	15 mL
1/2 tsp	freshly ground black pepper	2 mL
1/2 tsp	Chinese 5-spice powder (see Tips, left)	2 mL
2/3 cup	Job's tears, rinsed and drained	150 mL
4 cups	reduced-sodium beef stock (see Tips, left)	1 L
1/4 cup	gluten-free reduced-sodium soy sauce (see Tip, page 79)	60 mL
	Finely chopped green onions, optional	

1. In a bowl, combine dried shiitake mushrooms with hot water. Let stand for 30 minutes. Strain through a coffee filter or a sieve lined with a damp paper towel, reserving liquid. Remove stems. Pat mushrooms dry and chop finely. Set mushrooms and liquid aside separately.

2. In a stockpot or Dutch oven, heat oil over medium heat for 30 seconds. Add beef, onions, celery, fresh mushrooms and reserved dry mushrooms and cook, stirring, for 1 minute. Reduce heat to low. Cover and cook until vegetables are softened, about 8 minutes. Add garlic, ginger, pepper and 5–spice powder and cook, stirring, for 1 minute. Add Job's tears and toss until well coated with mixture. Add stock and reserved mushroom soaking water and bring to a boil over high heat.

3. Reduce heat, loosely cover and simmer gently until Job's tears are tender, about 1 hour. Stir in soy sauce. Ladle into bowls and garnish with green onions, if using.

Fusion Corn Soup

Although the flavors are classic Middle Eastern, the hominy and corn add a "new world" spin, as well as depth of flavor and pleasing texture to this simple but delicious soup. The yogurt and lemon juice finish adds creaminess, as well as a pleasant hint of tartness.

Makes 6 servings

Tips

You can use rinsed, drained canned hominy or soak and cook dried hominy yourself (see page 18).

To clean leeks: Fill sink full of lukewarm water. Split leeks in half lengthwise and submerge in water, swishing them around to remove all traces of dirt. Transfer to a colander and rinse under cold water.

If, like me, you enjoy the taste of cumin, feel free to increase the quantity by as much as 2 tsp (10 mL).

If you are using prepared stock, check the label to make sure it doesn't contain gluten.

2 cups	drained cooked hominy (see Tips, left)	500 mL
1 tbsp	cumin seeds	15 mL
1 tbsp	olive oil	15 mL
2	leeks, white part only with just a hint of green, cleaned and thinly sliced (see Tips, left)	2
4	cloves garlic, minced	4
2 tsp	freshly grated lemon zest	10 mL
	Salt and freshly ground black pepper	
8 cups	Homemade Vegetable Stock with no-salt-added (see recipe, page 78) or reduced-sodium vegetable or chicken stock (see Tips, left)	2 L
¼ tsp	crumbled saffron threads, dissolved in 2 tbsp (30 mL) boiling water	1 mL
1½ cups	corn kernels, thawed if frozen	375 mL
⅓ cup	freshly squeezed lemon juice	75 mL
½ cup	finely chopped parsley	125 mL
	Plain yogurt	

1. In a dry stockpot or Dutch oven, toast cumin seeds over medium heat, stirring constantly, until fragrant, about 3 minutes. Transfer to a mortar or spice grinder and grind. Set aside.

2. Add oil to pot and heat over medium heat for 30 seconds. Add leeks and cook, stirring, until softened, about 5 minutes. Add garlic, lemon zest, salt and pepper to taste and reserved cumin and cook, stirring, for 1 minute. Add stock, saffron liquid and cooked hominy and bring to a boil.

3. Reduce heat to low. Cover and simmer until leeks are very tender, about 20 minutes. Add corn and return to a simmer, stirring often. Stir in lemon juice and parsley and adjust seasoning, if necessary. Cover and simmer until corn is tender and to blend flavors, for 5 minutes. To serve, ladle soup into bowls and top with a dollop of yogurt.

Nutrients per serving

Calories	122
Protein	2.4 g
Carbohydrates	18.5 g
Fat (Total)	5.4 g
Saturated Fat	0.7 g
Monounsaturated Fat	3.6 g
Polyunsaturated Fat	0.8 g
Dietary Fiber	2.5 g
Sodium	77 mg
Cholesterol	0 mg

EXCELLENT SOURCE OF folate.

SOURCE OF vitamins A, C and E (alpha-tocopherol), thiamine, niacin, zinc, phosphorus, iron, magnesium and manganese.

CONTAINS a moderate amount of dietary fiber.

Minestrone with Leafy Greens

Here's a hearty meal-in-a-bowl that makes a delicious lunch or light supper any time of the year. Leftovers make an excellent second meal, a great snack or a superb welcome home for hungry travelers.

Makes 6 main-course servings

Tips

When using leafy greens, such as kale or Swiss chard, be sure to remove the tough stems before chopping. Also, since they can be quite gritty, pay extra attention when washing.

To make crostini: Brush 8 to 10 slices of gluten-free baguette with olive oil on both sides. Toast under preheated broiler, turning once, until golden, about 2 minutes per side. Gluten-free baguettes are often available in specialty or natural foods stores.

Nutrients per serving

Calories	302
Protein	14.6 g
Carbohydrates	53.2 g
Fat (Total)	5.4 g
Saturated Fat	0.5 g
Monounsaturated Fat	1.8 g
Polyunsaturated Fat	0.8 g
Dietary Fiber	8.6 g
Sodium	84 mg
Cholesterol	0 mg

EXCELLENT SOURCE OF vitamins A and C, thiamine, folate, phosphorus, iron, magnesium, manganese and copper.

GOOD SOURCE OF vitamin E (alpha-tocopherol), niacin, riboflavin and calcium.

SOURCE OF pantothenic acid, zinc and selenium.

CONTAINS a very high amount dietary fiber.

2 cups	cooked white kidney beans or 1 can (14 to 19 oz/398 to 540 mL) beans, drained and rinsed (see Tips, page 85)	500 mL
4 cups	Homemade Vegetable Stock (see recipe, page 78) or reduced-sodium chicken stock (see Tips, page 70), divided	1 L
1 tbsp	olive oil	15 mL
2	onions, chopped	2
4	stalks celery, diced	4
4	cloves garlic, minced	4
2 tsp	dried Italian seasoning	10 mL
1/4 tsp	cayenne pepper	1 mL
1 cup	Job's tears, soaked, rinsed and drained	250 mL
1	can (14 oz/398 mL) no-salt-added diced tomatoes with juice (see Tip, page 100)	1
2 cups	water	500 mL
8 cups	coarsely chopped, trimmed kale or Swiss chard (see Tips, left)	2 L
	Salt and freshly ground black pepper	
	Gluten-free crostini, optional (see Tips, left)	
	Freshly grated Parmesan cheese or vegan alternative, optional (see Tips, pages 78 and 174)	
	Extra virgin olive oil	

1. In a food processor, combine beans with 1 cup (250 mL) of the stock and purée until smooth. Set aside.

2. In a large saucepan or a Dutch oven, heat oil over medium heat for 30 seconds. Add onions and celery and cook, stirring, until celery is softened, about 5 minutes. Add garlic, Italian seasoning and cayenne and cook, stirring, for 1 minute. Add Job's tears, tomatoes with juice, water, reserved bean mixture and remaining 3 cups (750 mL) of the stock and bring to a boil.

3. Reduce heat to low. Cover and simmer until Job's tears are almost tender, about 1 hour. Stir in kale. Cover and cook until kale is tender, about 15 minutes. Season to taste with salt and black pepper.

4. When ready to serve, ladle soup into bowls. Float 1 or 2 crostini in each bowl, if using. Sprinkle liberally with Parmesan, if using, and drizzle with olive oil.

Cockaleekie Soup

Traditionally made with barley, this prune-spiked chicken and leek soup is an old Scottish favorite. The prunes deepen the flavor and add a pleasant note of sweetness, but if you're averse to this image-challenged fruit, they may be omitted and the end result will be something along the lines of a classic chicken soup with barley but using gluten-free Job's tears.

Tips

To clean leeks: Fill sink full of lukewarm water. Split leeks in half lengthwise and submerge in water, swishing them around to remove all traces of dirt. Transfer to a colander and rinse under cold water.

If you are using prepared stock, check the label to make sure it doesn't contain gluten.

Nutrients per serving

Calories	320
Protein	28.1 g
Carbohydrates	31.9 g
Fat (Total)	9.2 g
Saturated Fat	1.8 g
Monounsaturated Fat	3.1 g
Polyunsaturated Fat	1.7 g
Dietary Fiber	3.1 g
Sodium	443 mg
Cholesterol	94 mg

EXCELLENT SOURCE OF vitamin A, niacin, phosphorus, iron and selenium.

GOOD SOURCE OF riboflavin, folate, pantothenic acid, zinc, magnesium and manganese.

SOURCE OF vitamins C and E (alpha-tocopherol), thiamine, copper and calcium.

CONTAINS a moderate amount of dietary fiber.

10	pitted prunes, finely chopped (about ½ cup/ 125 mL whole pitted prunes), optional	10
3 cups	water, divided	750 mL
1 tbsp	olive oil	15 mL
4	large leeks, white part with just a bit of green, cleaned and thinly sliced (see Tips, left)	4
4	stalks celery, diced	4
4	carrots, peeled and diced	4
1 tsp	dried thyme leaves, crumbled	5 mL
½ tsp	cracked black peppercorns	2 mL
4	whole cloves	4
1	piece cinnamon, about 1 inch (2.5 cm) long	1
1¼ cups	Job's tears, soaked, rinsed and drained	300 mL
2 lbs	skinless boneless chicken thighs, coarsely chopped	1 kg
4 cups	reduced-sodium chicken stock (see Tips, left)	1 L
½ cup	finely chopped parsley	125 mL

1. In a small bowl, combine prunes, if using, and 1 cup (250 mL) of the water. Stir well. Cover and set aside.

2. In a large saucepan, stockpot or Dutch oven, heat oil over medium heat for 30 seconds. Add leeks, celery and carrots and cook, stirring, until softened, about 7 minutes. Add thyme, peppercorns, cloves and cinnamon stick and cook, stirring, for 1 minute. Add Job's tears and toss until well coated with mixture. Add chicken, stock and 2 cups (500 mL) of water and bring to a boil.

3. Reduce heat to low. Cover and simmer until chicken is falling apart and Job's tears are tender, about 1 hour. Discard cloves and cinnamon stick.

4. Add prunes and soaking water, if using. Stir well. Cover and cook to allow flavors to meld, about 15 minutes. Ladle into bowls and garnish with parsley.

Slow Cooker Method: Complete Steps 1 and 2, reducing the quantity of water in Step 2 to 1 cup (250 mL). Transfer to slow cooker stoneware. Cover and cook on Low for 8 hours or on High for 4 hours, until Job's tears are tender. Add prunes and soaking water, if using. Cover and cook on High for 15 minutes, until heated through.

Scotch Broth

This hearty meal-in-a-bowl is the perfect dish for cold winter weekends. Serve steaming mugs after a brisk walk or a day on the slopes. To enhance the experience, make it in your slow cooker so it's ready and waiting when you come through the door, desperate for some heat-infusing sustenance. Add a tossed salad for a great light meal.

Makes 8 main-course servings

Tip

If you are using prepared stock, check the label to make sure it doesn't contain gluten.

Nutrient Tip

Parsnips don't usually spring to mind when thinking about vegetables, but they have a pleasantly sweet taste and provide fiber, folate and vitamin C, among other nutrients.

Nutrients per serving	
Calories	285
Protein	21.8 g
Carbohydrates	37.4 g
Fat (Total)	6 g
Saturated Fat	1.2 g
Monounsaturated Fat	2.3 g
Polyunsaturated Fat	0.6 g
Dietary Fiber	4.5 g
Sodium	717 mg
Cholesterol	41 mg

EXCELLENT SOURCE OF vitamin A, niacin, folate, phosphorus, iron, zinc and selenium.
GOOD SOURCE OF thiamine, riboflavin, manganese and magnesium.
SOURCE OF vitamins C and E (alpha-tocopherol), pantothenic acid, copper and calcium.
CONTAINS a high amount of dietary fiber.

1 to 2 tbsp	olive oil	15 to 30 mL
1 lb	boneless lamb shoulder or stewing beef, trimmed of fat and diced	500 g
3	leeks, white and light green parts only, cleaned and thinly sliced (see Tips, page 70)	3
4	stalks celery, diced	4
4	carrots, peeled and diced	4
2	parsnips, peeled and diced	2
2 tsp	dried thyme leaves, crumbled	10 mL
1/2 tsp	cracked black peppercorns	2 mL
1	bay leaf	1
1 1/4 cups	Job's tears, soaked, rinsed and drained	300 mL
8 cups	reduced-sodium beef stock (see Tip, left)	2 L
2 cups	water	500 mL
1 1/2 cups	green peas, thawed if frozen	375 mL
1/2 cup	finely chopped parsley	125 mL

1. In a large saucepan, stockpot or Dutch oven, heat 1 tbsp (15 mL) oil over medium-high heat for 30 seconds. Add lamb, in batches, and cook, stirring, until browned, about 1 minute per batch. Transfer to a plate as completed.

2. Reduce heat to medium. Add more oil to pot, if necessary. Add leeks, celery, carrots and parsnips and cook, stirring, until vegetables are softened, about 7 minutes. Add thyme, peppercorns and bay leaf and cook, stirring, for 1 minute. Add Job's tears and toss until well coated with mixture. Add stock, water and reserved lamb and bring to a boil.

3. Reduce heat to low. Cover and simmer until Job's tears are tender, about 1 hour. Add green peas and cook until tender, about 5 minutes. Discard bay leaf. Serve hot, liberally garnished with parsley.

Slow Cooker Method: Complete Steps 1 and 2, reducing the quantity of water in Step 2 to 1 cup (250 mL). Transfer mixture to slow cooker stoneware. Cover and cook on Low for 8 hours or on High for 4 hours, until Job's tears are tender. Add green peas. Cover and cook on High for 10 minutes, until tender. Garnish with parsley.

Curried Sweet Potato and Millet Soup

This soup is a lovely combination of flavors and texture. It has a mild curry taste, enhanced with the addition of orange and a hint of sweetness from the maple syrup. The toasted walnuts add taste and an appealing bit of crunch, while the optional yogurt provides a creamy finish. Although this is a great cold weather soup, it's light enough to be enjoyed any time of the year — perhaps even for dinner with the addition of salad.

Makes 6 servings

Tips

To get this quantity of puréed sweet potato, bake, peel and mash 2 medium sweet potatoes, each about 6 oz (175 g). You can also use a can (14 oz/398 mL) sweet potato purée.

Toasting brings out millet's pleasantly nutty flavor. To toast, heat in a dry skillet over medium heat, stirring constantly, until it crackles and releases its aroma, for 5 minutes.

Nutrients per serving

Calories	240
Protein	4.8 g
Carbohydrates	48.8 g
Fat (Total)	3.5 g
Saturated Fat	0.4 g
Monounsaturated Fat	1.6 g
Polyunsaturated Fat	1.2 g
Dietary Fiber	5.5 g
Sodium	46 mg
Cholesterol	0 mg

EXCELLENT SOURCE OF vitamin A and manganese.

GOOD SOURCE OF vitamin C, thiamine, folate, magnesium and zinc.

SOURCE OF vitamin E (alpha-tocopherol), riboflavin, niacin, pantothenic acid, calcium, phosphorus, iron and copper.

CONTAINS a high amount of dietary fiber.

1 tbsp	vegetable oil	15 mL
2	onions, finely chopped	2
2	carrots, peeled and diced	2
2	stalks celery, diced	2
2	cloves garlic, minced	2
2 tsp	minced gingerroot	10 mL
2 tsp	curry powder (see Tips, page 132)	10 mL
1 tsp	freshly grated orange zest	5 mL
2 cups	sweet potato purée (see Tips, left)	500 mL
6 cups	Homemade Vegetable Stock (see recipe, page 78) or reduced-sodium chicken stock (see Tip, page 71)	1.5 L
¾ cup	millet, toasted (see Tips, left)	175 mL
1 cup	freshly squeezed orange juice	250 mL
¼ cup	pure maple syrup	60 mL
	Salt and freshly ground black pepper	
	Toasted chopped walnuts or sliced almonds	
	Plain yogurt, optional	

1. In a large saucepan or stockpot, heat oil over medium heat for 30 seconds. Add onions, carrots and celery and cook, stirring, until carrots have softened, about 7 minutes.

2. Add garlic, ginger, curry powder and orange zest and cook, stirring, for 1 minute. Add sweet potato and stock and stir well. Bring to a boil. Stir in millet. Reduce heat to low. Cover and simmer until millet is tender and flavors have blended, about 30 minutes.

3. Add orange juice and maple syrup and heat through. Season to taste with salt and pepper. Ladle into bowls and garnish with toasted walnuts and a drizzle of yogurt, if using.

Variation

Curried Sweet Potato and Quinoa Soup: Substitute an equal quantity of quinoa for the millet. Do not toast it, but rinse thoroughly before adding to the soup.

Fennel-Scented Tomato and Wild Rice Soup

If, like me, you get cravings for tomatoes, this soup is for you. It's especially welcome in the winter when delicious fresh tomatoes are hard to find. When made with fire-roasted tomatoes (see Tips, below), it provides a real tomato hit. The fennel brings intriguing licorice flavor, which complements the tomatoes, and the wild rice adds texture and nutrients such as dietary fiber to make this soup particularly enjoyable.

Makes 8 servings

Tips

For a slightly more intense tomato flavor, substitute 2 cans (each 14 oz/398 mL) fire-roasted tomatoes with juice for the crushed tomatoes. Check the label to make sure that gluten has not been added.

Toasting fennel seeds intensifies their flavor. To toast fennel seeds, stir them in a dry skillet over medium heat until fragrant, about 3 minutes. Transfer to a mortar or spice grinder and grind.

Nutrients per serving

Calories	123
Protein	4.5 g
Carbohydrates	23.9 g
Fat (Total)	2.3 g
Saturated Fat	0.3 g
Monounsaturated Fat	1.3 g
Polyunsaturated Fat	0.4 g
Dietary Fiber	4.3 g
Sodium	50 mg
Cholesterol	0 mg

EXCELLENT SOURCE OF manganese.

GOOD SOURCE OF folate, iron, magnesium and copper.

SOURCE OF vitamins A, C and E (alpha-tocopherol), thiamine, riboflavin, niacin, pantothenic acid, calcium, phosphorus and zinc.

CONTAINS a high amount of dietary fiber.

1 tbsp	olive oil	15 mL
2	leeks, white part only with just a hint of green, cleaned and sliced (see Tips, page 70)	2
1	bulb fennel, base and leafy stems discarded, bulb thinly sliced on the vertical	1
3	cloves garlic, sliced	3
1 tsp	fennel seeds, toasted and ground (see Tips, left)	5 mL
½ tsp	salt, optional	2 mL
½ tsp	freshly ground black pepper	2 mL
5 cups	Homemade Vegetable Stock (see recipe, page 78) or reduced-sodium chicken stock (see Tip, page 71), divided	1.25 L
1	can (28 oz/796 mL) crushed tomatoes (see Tips, page 126)	1
¾ cup	wild rice, rinsed and drained	175 mL
	Heavy or whipping (35%) cream, optional	
	Finely chopped parsley	

1. In a large saucepan or stockpot, heat oil over medium heat for 30 seconds. Add leeks and fennel and cook, stirring, until vegetables are softened, about 7 minutes. Add garlic, fennel seeds, salt, if using, and pepper and cook, stirring, for 1 minute. Stir in 2 cups (500 mL) of the stock and tomatoes. Remove from heat. Using an immersion blender, purée soup. (You can also do this, in batches, in a food processor, and return to the pot.) Return to medium heat. Add remaining stock and wild rice and bring to a boil.

2. Reduce heat to low. Cover and cook until rice is tender and grains have begun to split, about 1 hour. (Cooking times for wild rice vary. Expect your grains to be cooked anywhere between 50 minutes to more than 1 hour.) Ladle into bowls, drizzle with cream, if using, and garnish with parsley.

Slow Cooker Method: Complete Step 1, reducing the quantity of stock to 4 cups (1 L). Transfer contents of saucepan to slow cooker stoneware. Cover and cook on Low for 8 hours or on High for 4 hours, until rice is tender.

Southwestern Turkey Chowder

This soup is so good I can't wait to finish the celebratory turkey and get it started. I think it's the best way to use up leftover turkey. If you're planning to eat lightly following a holiday, it makes a perfect dinner with the addition of salad.

Makes 8 main-course servings

Tips

For the best flavor, toast and grind whole cumin seeds rather than buying ground cumin. Simply stir seeds in a dry skillet over medium heat until fragrant, about 3 minutes. Immediately transfer to a spice grinder or mortar and grind.

Use any combination of long-cooking gluten-free whole grains in this soup, such as Job's tears, hominy, brown, red or wild rice. All will be delicious.

Nutrients per serving

Calories	320
Protein	21.4 g
Carbohydrates	48 g
Fat (Total)	6.6 g
Saturated Fat	1.5 g
Monounsaturated Fat	2.6 g
Polyunsaturated Fat	1.8 g
Dietary Fiber	8.3 g
Sodium	107 mg
Cholesterol	51 mg

EXCELLENT SOURCE OF niacin, phosphorus, iron, magnesium, manganese, zinc and selenium.

GOOD SOURCE OF vitamin A, folate, thiamine, riboflavin, pantothenic acid and copper.

SOURCE OF vitamins C and E (alpha-tocopherol) and calcium.

CONTAINS a very high amount of dietary fiber.

10 cups	turkey stock (see recipe, below)	2.5 L
1 tbsp	olive oil	15 mL
3	onions, diced	3
4	stalks celery, diced	4
1 tbsp	ground cumin (see Tips, left)	15 mL
2 tsp	dried oregano leaves	10 mL
4	cloves garlic, minced	4
½ tsp	cracked black peppercorns	2 mL
1½ cups	long-cooking gluten-free whole grains, soaked, rinsed and drained (see Tips, left)	375 mL
1	can (28 oz/796 mL) no-salt-added diced tomatoes with juice (see Tips, page 126)	1
2 to 3	ancho, guajillo or mild New Mexico dried chiles	2 to 3
1 cup	loosely packed fresh cilantro leaves	250 mL
2 cups	diced cooked turkey	500 mL
2 cups	corn kernels	500 mL

1. In a stockpot, heat oil over medium heat for 30 seconds. Add onions and celery and cook, stirring, until vegetables are softened, about 5 minutes. Add cumin, oregano, garlic and peppercorns and cook, stirring, for 1 minute. Add whole grains and toss until coated. Add tomatoes with juice and stock and bring to a boil.

2. Reduce heat to low. Cover and simmer until grains are tender, about 1 hour.

3. In a heatproof bowl, 30 minutes before grains have finished cooking, combine dried chiles and 2 cups (500 mL) boiling water. Set aside for 30 minutes, weighing chiles down with a cup to ensure they remain submerged. Drain, discarding soaking liquid and stems and chop coarsely. Transfer to a blender. Add cilantro and ½ cup (125 mL) of stock from the chowder. Purée. Add to stockpot along with the turkey and corn. Cover and cook until corn is tender and flavors meld, about 20 minutes.

TURKEY STOCK

To make turkey stock, break the carcass into manageable pieces and place in a stockpot. Add 2 each carrots, celery stalks and onions, quartered, plus 8 whole peppercorns. Add water to cover. Bring to a boil over medium-high heat. Reduce heat to low. Cover and simmer for 3 hours. Strain, reserving liquid and discarding solids.

Gingery Chicken and Wild Rice Soup

The addition of a flavorful whole grain, leeks and a hint of ginger is a particularly delicious spin on classic chicken and rice soup. I like to make the stock a day ahead so it can be refrigerated, which makes easy work of skimming off the fat. This makes a great light dinner accompanied by a tossed salad.

Makes 6 main-course servings

Tip

For best results, make the stock and cook the chicken the day before you plan to serve the soup. Cover and refrigerate stock and chicken separately. The fat will rise to the surface of the stock and can be easily removed. It will be easy to remove the skin and chop the cold chicken. Save the excess chicken to make sandwiches or a salad.

Nutrients per serving

Calories	269
Protein	21.8 g
Carbohydrates	27 g
Fat (Total)	8.3 g
Saturated Fat	1.9 g
Monounsaturated Fat	3.9 g
Polyunsaturated Fat	1.7 g
Dietary Fiber	2.4 g
Sodium	276 mg
Cholesterol	79 mg

EXCELLENT SOURCE OF niacin, phosphorus and manganese.
GOOD SOURCE OF thiamine, folate, pantothenic acid, magnesium, zinc and selenium.
SOURCE OF vitamin E (alpha-tocopherol), riboflavin, iron and copper.
CONTAINS a moderate amount dietary fiber.

1	whole chicken (about 3 lbs/1.5 kg), cut into pieces	1
1	onion, coarsely chopped	1
2	carrots, peeled and diced	2
2	stalks celery, diced	2
4	sprigs parsley	4
1	clove garlic	1
1	bay leaf	1
½ tsp	salt	2 mL
½ tsp	cracked black peppercorns	2 mL
12 cups	water	3 L
1 tbsp	olive oil	15 mL
2	large leeks, white part only, cleaned and sliced (see Tips, page 70)	2
2	cloves garlic, minced	2
2 tbsp	minced gingerroot	30 mL
1 cup	brown and wild rice mixture, rinsed and drained (see Tips, page 91)	250 mL

1. In a stockpot, combine chicken, onion, carrots, celery, parsley, whole garlic, bay leaf, salt, peppercorns and water. Bring to a boil over high heat. Using a slotted spoon, skim off foam. Reduce heat to medium-low and simmer, uncovered, until chicken is falling off the bone, about 1½ hours. Drain, reserving chicken and liquid separately. Let cool. Cut the chicken into bite-size pieces, discarding skin and bones. Skim off fat from the stock (see Tip, left).

2. Measure 2 cups (500 mL) of chicken and set aside in the refrigerator. (Refrigerate remainder for other uses, see Tip, left.) In a large saucepan or stockpot, heat oil over medium heat for 30 seconds. Add leeks and cook, stirring, until softened, about 5 minutes. Add minced garlic and ginger and cook, stirring, for 1 minute. Add rice and toss to coat. Add reserved stock and bring to a boil. Reduce heat and simmer, uncovered, until rice is quite tender, about 1 hour. Add reserved chicken. Cover and simmer until chicken is heated through, about 15 minutes.

Variation

Substitute an equal quantity of rinsed wild rice for the mixture. You may need to increase the cooking time, depending upon the size of the grains.

Hearty Miso-Spiked Vegetable Soup

Here's a hearty vegetable soup that's the perfect antidote to a blustery day. The addition of miso adds robustness and a hint of complexity, which is often lacking in simple vegetable soups. Serve this with your favorite sandwich for a delicious soup and sandwich meal.

Makes 6 main-course servings

Tips

If you have fresh thyme, use 2 sprigs, stem and all. Remove and discard before serving.

I haven't added salt because the miso is quite salty. Taste and adjust seasoning when the soup is completed, if necessary.

Brown rice miso is gluten-free.

Stir in freshly grated Parmesan for a hint of creaminess and additional flavor, if desired.

1 tbsp	olive oil	15 mL
2	onions, finely chopped	2
4	carrots, peeled and diced	4
4	stalks celery, diced	4
1 tsp	dried thyme (see Tips, left)	5 mL
	Freshly ground black pepper (see Tips, left)	
1 cup	Job's tears, soaked, rinsed and drained	250 mL
8 cups	Homemade Vegetable Stock (see recipe, below)	2 L
2 cups	sliced green beans	500 mL
¼ cup	brown rice miso (see Tips, left)	60 mL
½ cup	finely chopped parsley	125 mL
	Freshly grated Parmesan cheese or vegan alternative, optional (see Tips, left and page 174)	

1. In a large saucepan or stockpot, heat oil over medium heat for 30 seconds. Add onions, carrots and celery and cook, stirring, until carrots are softened, about 7 minutes. Stir in thyme and season to taste with pepper. Add Job's tears and toss until well coated with mixture. Add stock and bring to a boil.

2. Reduce heat to low. Cover and simmer until Job's tears are tender, about 1 hour. Add green beans and miso. Cover and cook until beans are tender and flavors meld, about 15 minutes. Stir in parsley and serve. Garnish with Parmesan, if using.

Nutrients per serving

Calories	211
Protein	7.8 g
Carbohydrates	35.2 g
Fat (Total)	5.1 g
Saturated Fat	0.5 g
Monounsaturated Fat	1.8 g
Polyunsaturated Fat	0.7 g
Dietary Fiber	4.2 g
Sodium	482 mg
Cholesterol	0 mg

EXCELLENT SOURCE OF vitamin A.

GOOD SOURCE OF thiamine, folate, phosphorus, iron and manganese.

SOURCE OF vitamins C and E (alpha-tocopherol), riboflavin, niacin, calcium, magnesium, zinc and copper.

CONTAINS a high amount of dietary fiber.

HOMEMADE VEGETABLE STOCK

You can dramatically reduce your sodium intake by making your own vegetable stock with no salt added. You can also be certain that your homemade version doesn't contain gluten. In a stockpot, combine 12 cups (3 L) water, 6 sprigs parsley, 3 bay leaves, 10 black peppercorns and 1 tsp (5 mL) dried thyme leaves with 3 onions and 3 cloves garlic, coarsely chopped. Add 8 carrots and 6 stalks celery, scrubbed and coarsely chopped. Bring to a boil over high heat. Reduce heat to low. Cover and simmer for 2 hours. Strain and discard solids. Cover and refrigerate for up to 5 days or freeze in an airtight container. If you prefer, make the stock in your slow cooker. Cover and cook on Low for 8 hours or on High for 4 hours.

Thai-Inspired Peanut and Wild Rice Soup

If your taste buds have grown tired of the same old thing, here's a delightfully different soup to wake them up. With basic flavors that are reminiscent of Thai peanut sauce and the addition of classic North American wild rice, this soup qualifies as fusion cooking. It makes a great lunch, or even a light dinner accompanied by a platter of stir-fried bok choy.

Makes 6 servings

Tip

Tamari is a type of soy sauce that shouldn't contain wheat. However, check the label

Nutrient Tip

Although this soup is relatively high in fat, it is very low in saturated fat. Virtually all of the fat comes from the peanuts and most is the heart-healthy unsaturated kind. Moreover, peanuts have a very high antioxidant content.

Nutrients per serving	
Calories	365
Protein	15.8 g
Carbohydrates	30.5 g
Fat (Total)	22.9 g
Saturated Fat	3.2 g
Monounsaturated Fat	10.9 g
Polyunsaturated Fat	7.4 g
Dietary Fiber	4 g
Sodium	326 mg
Cholesterol	0 mg

EXCELLENT SOURCE OF niacin, folate, phosphorus, magnesium, manganese, zinc and copper.

GOOD SOURCE OF vitamins A and E (alpha-tocopherol), thiamine, riboflavin and iron.

SOURCE OF vitamin C, pantothenic acid, calcium and selenium.

CONTAINS a high amount of dietary fiber.

2 cups	cooked wild rice (see cooking instructions, page 32)	500 mL
2	stalks lemongrass, smashed and chopped	2
4	cloves garlic, minced	4
2 tbsp	minced gingerroot	30 mL
3	dried red chile peppers, crumbled	3
2 tbsp	tomato paste	30 mL
6 cups	Homemade Vegetable Stock (see recipe, page 78) or reduced-sodium chicken stock (see Tips, page 71)	1.5 L
2 cups	unsalted roasted peanuts	500 mL
3 tbsp	rice vinegar	45 mL
2 tbsp	gluten-free soy sauce (see Tip, left)	30 mL
1 tbsp	liquid honey	15 mL
	Finely grated zest and juice of 1 lime	
	Finely chopped cilantro	
	Finely chopped fresh chile peppers, optional	

1. In a large saucepan or stockpot, combine lemongrass, garlic, ginger, dried chile peppers, tomato paste and stock. Bring to a boil over medium heat. Reduce heat to low. Cover and simmer for 30 minutes. Strain, discarding solids. Return liquid to pot.

2. In a food processor or blender, combine peanuts, rice vinegar, soy sauce, honey and lime zest. Process until mixture is the consistency of chunky peanut butter. Stir into liquid. Add wild rice and bring to a boil over medium heat. Reduce heat to low. Cover and simmer to allow flavors to meld, about 20 minutes. Stir in lime juice. Ladle into bowls and garnish with cilantro and chile peppers, if using.

Congee with Chinese Greens and Barbecued Pork

If you live near a Chinatown, where freshly cooked barbecued pork is readily available, this delicious soup is a snap to make. Just make sure your source does not cook with MSG. At our house, it's a favorite weekend lunch. I put the rice on in the morning and it's done by the time we're ready to eat. All I need to do is add the pork and Chinese greens and purée the soup.

Makes 6 servings

Tips

If you are using prepared stock, check the label to make sure it doesn't contain gluten.

Chinese broccoli, also known as *gai lan*, is available in Asian markets. If you can't find it, substitute an equal quantity of shredded bok choy.

Unless you have a stove with a true simmer, after reducing the heat to low I recommend placing a heat diffuser under the pot to prevent the mixture from boiling.

4 cups	reduced-sodium chicken stock (see Tips, left)	1 L
4 cups	water	1 L
¾ cup	short-grain brown rice, rinsed and drained	175 mL
4 cups	shredded Chinese broccoli (see Tips, left)	1 L
4 oz	shredded boneless Chinese barbecued pork	125 g
¼ cup	thinly sliced green onions, white part with a bit of green	60 mL
	Chopped fresh chile pepper, optional	
	Gluten-free soy sauce, optional	

1. In a saucepan, combine stock, water and rice. Bring to a boil over medium–high heat. Reduce heat to low and simmer until rice has almost dissolved and is creamy, about 2½ hours.

2. Add broccoli and cook, stirring, until greens are wilted, about 5 minutes. Remove from heat. Using an immersion blender, purée soup. (You can also do this, in batches, in a food processor.) Return to element, stir in pork and cook until heated through, about 5 minutes. Garnish with green onions and chile pepper, if using. Season to taste with soy sauce, if using.

Variation

Duck Congee: Substitute an equal quantity of Chinese barbecued duck for the pork.

Nutrients per serving

Calories	150
Protein	8.9 g
Carbohydrates	23.1 g
Fat (Total)	2.6 g
Saturated Fat	0.8 g
Monounsaturated Fat	1.1 g
Polyunsaturated Fat	0.5 g
Dietary Fiber	3.1 g
Sodium	576 mg
Cholesterol	12 mg

EXCELLENT SOURCE OF manganese.

GOOD SOURCE OF vitamin C, thiamine and magnesium.

SOURCE OF vitamin A, niacin, pantothenic acid, phosphorus, iron, zinc and copper.

CONTAINS a moderate amount of dietary fiber.

Mushroom-Scented Quinoa Congee with Zucchini

It took me a long time to appreciate congee, the bland rice porridge traditionally served for breakfast in Asia. It wasn't until a Chinese friend took me to his favorite restaurant in Vancouver and introduced me to a delicious version made with scallops and a delicate fish broth that I understood the appeal. Although the ingredients and flavors are very different, this thick creamy soup has the same comforting texture and subtle flavoring. I like to serve this for Sunday lunch, but it also makes a great snack any time of the day.

Makes 6 main-course servings

Tips

I like to use dried portobello, porcini or mixed wild mushrooms in this soup.

White mushrooms work well in this soup, but if you prefer a stronger mushroom taste, use cremini or portobello mushrooms.

Nutrients per serving

Calories	143
Protein	4.4 g
Carbohydrates	24.9 g
Fat (Total)	3.7 g
Saturated Fat	0.5 g
Monounsaturated Fat	2 g
Polyunsaturated Fat	0.8 g
Dietary Fiber	3.9 g
Sodium	201 mg
Cholesterol	0 mg

EXCELLENT SOURCE OF copper and manganese.

GOOD SOURCE OF niacin, folate, pantothenic acid, magnesium, phosphorus and iron.

SOURCE OF vitamins A, C and E (alpha-tocopherol), thiamine, riboflavin, zinc and selenium.

CONTAINS a moderate amount of dietary fiber.

1	package (½ oz/14 g) dried mushrooms (see Tips, left)	1
1 cup	hot water	250 mL
1 tbsp	olive oil	15 mL
2	onions, chopped	2
2	cloves garlic, minced	2
1 tsp	dried oregano leaves, crumbled	5 mL
½ tsp	salt	2 mL
½ tsp	freshly ground black pepper	2 mL
8 oz	fresh mushrooms, chopped (see Tips, left)	250 g
¾ cup	quinoa, rinsed and drained	175 mL
4 cups	cubed (½-inch/1 cm) zucchini	1 L
6 cups	Homemade Vegetable Stock (see recipe, page 78) or reduced-sodium chicken stock (see Tips, page 71)	1.5 L

1. In a heatproof bowl, soak mushrooms in hot water for 30 minutes. Strain through a coffee filter or a sieve lined with a damp paper towel, reserving liquid. Pat mushrooms dry and chop finely. Set mushrooms and liquid aside separately.

2. In a stockpot or large saucepan, heat oil over medium heat for 30 seconds. Add onions and cook, stirring, until softened, about 3 minutes. Add garlic, oregano, salt, pepper and reserved dried mushrooms and cook, stirring, for 1 minute. Add fresh mushrooms and cook, stirring, until well coated with mixture. Add quinoa and cook, stirring until coated. Add zucchini, stock and reserved mushroom soaking liquid and bring to a boil.

3. Reduce heat to low. Cover loosely and simmer until zucchini is tender and quinoa is cooked, about 15 minutes. Remove from heat. Using an immersion blender, purée soup. (You can also do this, in batches, in a food processor.) Serve immediately.

Variation

Mushroom-Scented Millet Congee with Zucchini: Substitute an equal quantity of toasted millet for the quinoa. Cook a bit longer, about 25 minutes.

Kasha

Salads

Asian-Style Quinoa Salad with Chili-Orange Dressing

Perhaps surprisingly, since quinoa is a "new world" grain, it takes very well to Asian ingredients such as water chestnuts. This is a nice light salad that is perfect for summer dining or a buffet. It's an ideal accompaniment to grilled meat or fish.

Makes 6 side servings

Tip

The chili sauce adds a pleasant bit of zest, but if you're heat averse you can omit it. Heat seekers can increase the quantity to taste.

3 cups	cooked quinoa, cooled (see cooking instructions, page 26)	750 mL

CHILI-ORANGE DRESSING

1 tsp	finely grated orange zest	5 mL
1/4 cup	freshly squeezed orange juice	60 mL
1 tbsp	gluten-free reduced-sodium soy sauce	15 mL
1 tbsp	liquid honey or agave nectar	15 mL
2 tsp	sesame oil	10 mL
1/2 tsp	Asian chili sauce, such as sambal oelek (see Tip, left)	2 mL
	Freshly ground black pepper	
1	can (8 oz/227 g) water chestnuts, drained and chopped	1
1	red bell pepper, seeded and chopped	1
1 1/2 cups	chopped snow peas, cooked until tender-crisp and cooled	375 mL
4	green onions, white part with a bit of green, thinly sliced	4

1. *Chili-Orange Dressing:* In a small bowl, whisk together orange zest and juice, soy sauce, honey, sesame oil, chili sauce and pepper to taste. Set aside.
2. In a serving bowl, combine quinoa, water chestnuts, bell pepper, snow peas and green onions. Add dressing and toss until combined. Chill thoroughly.

Variation

Asian-Style Millet Salad with Chili-Orange Dressing: Substitute 3 cups (750 mL) cooked toasted millet (see cooking instructions, page 22) for the quinoa.

Nutrients per serving

Calories	166
Protein	5.3 g
Carbohydrates	30 g
Fat (Total)	3.3 g
Saturated Fat	0.4 g
Monounsaturated Fat	1.1 g
Polyunsaturated Fat	1.4 g
Dietary Fiber	3.7 g
Sodium	121 mg
Cholesterol	0 mg

EXCELLENT SOURCE OF vitamin C, iron and manganese.

GOOD SOURCE OF magnesium and copper.

SOURCE OF vitamins A and E (alpha-tocopherol), folate, thiamine, riboflavin, niacin, pantothenic acid, phosphorus and zinc.

CONTAINS a moderate amount of dietary fiber.

Southwestern Bean and Chinese "Barley" Salad with Roasted Peppers

Ingredients traditionally associated with the American Southwest, such as beans, corn and peppers, combine with hearty Job's tears to produce this deliciously robust salad. Packed with nutrients, it is particularly high in dietary fiber. It makes a great addition to a buffet or potluck dinner.

Makes 8 side servings

Tips

Beans do not contain gluten, but canned beans may be processed in a facility where gluten is present. Check the label.

Poblano peppers are a mild chile pepper. If you are a heat seeker, add an extra one, or even a minced jalapeño pepper for some real punch. The suggested quantity produces a mild result. If you're heat averse, use bell peppers, instead.

Nutrients per serving	
Calories	330
Protein	9.6 g
Carbohydrates	39.2 g
Fat (Total)	16 g
Saturated Fat	1.9 g
Monounsaturated Fat	10.2 g
Polyunsaturated Fat	1.7 g
Dietary Fiber	4.5 g
Sodium	154 mg
Cholesterol	0 mg

EXCELLENT SOURCE OF vitamin C and folate.
GOOD SOURCE OF vitamin E (alpha-tocopherol), iron, phosphorus, magnesium and manganese.
SOURCE OF vitamin A, thiamine, riboflavin, niacin, zinc and copper.
CONTAINS a high amount of dietary fiber.

3 cups	cooked Job's tears, cooled (see cooking instructions, page 20)	750 mL
DRESSING		
3 tbsp	red wine vinegar	45 mL
½ tsp	salt	2 mL
	Freshly ground black pepper	
½	clove garlic, finely grated	½
½ cup	extra virgin olive oil	125 mL
2 cups	cooked red kidney beans or 1 can (14 to 19 oz/398 to 540 mL) kidney beans, drained and rinsed (see Tips, left)	500 mL
2 cups	cooked cooled corn kernels	500 mL
2	roasted poblano or roasted red bell peppers, peeled, seeded and diced (see Tips, left)	2
2	whole sun-dried tomatoes, packed in olive oil, finely chopped	2
1	small red onion, diced	1
¼ cup	finely chopped parsley	60 mL

1. *Dressing:* In a small bowl, combine vinegar, salt and pepper to taste, stirring until salt dissolves. Stir in garlic. Gradually whisk in olive oil. Set aside.

2. In a serving bowl, combine Job's tears, kidney beans, corn, roasted peppers, sun-dried tomatoes and onion. Add dressing and toss well. Garnish with parsley. Chill until ready to serve.

BELL PEPPERS

Bell peppers are members of the capsicum family, which includes chile peppers, such as the poblano peppers featured in this salad. Bell peppers make a wonderful addition to dishes because they add both color and nutrients. A medium-size bell pepper has about 32 calories and is a rich source of powerful antioxidants, such as beta-carotene and vitamin C, which help to keep your immune system healthy, among other benefits. Vitamin C helps our bodies fight free radical damage and may help to prevent age-related aliments, such as heart disease and diabetes.

Asian-Style Beef and Chinese "Barley" Salad with Arugula

When my friend Andrew Chase had his Toronto restaurant Youki Asian Bar and Bistro, I went there as often as I could just to eat his Asian beef salad, which was to die for. The memory of that fabulous dish dominates my mind every time I make my own simplified and nutritionally enhanced version, which includes nutrient-rich Job's tears. It makes a great summer meal.

Makes 4 servings

Tips

Tamari soy sauce should be gluten-free. Check the label.

Use any hot Asian chili sauce, such as sambal oelek, but if you are heat averse, pay close attention to the quantity. You may want to start with ½ tsp (2 mL) and increase the amount if it suits your taste.

Nutrients per serving	
Calories	351
Protein	25.6 g
Carbohydrates	25.3 g
Fat (Total)	16.5 g
Saturated Fat	3.3 g
Monounsaturated Fat	9.7 g
Polyunsaturated Fat	1.4 g
Dietary Fiber	2 g
Sodium	348 mg
Cholesterol	42 mg

EXCELLENT SOURCE OF niacin, iron, phosphorus, selenium and zinc.

GOOD SOURCE OF vitamins C and E (alpha-tocopherol), folate, riboflavin and magnesium.

SOURCE OF vitamin A, thiamine, pantothenic acid, calcium, manganese and copper.

CONTAINS a moderate amount of dietary fiber.

1½ cups	cooked Job's tears, cooled (see cooking instructions, page 20)	375 mL
1 cup	cubed (½-inch/1 cm) peeled cucumber	250 mL
6	green onions, white part only, thinly sliced	6
2	tomatoes, seeded and diced	2
DRESSING		
2 tbsp	rice vinegar	30 mL
1 tbsp	gluten-free reduced-sodium soy sauce (see Tips, left)	15 mL
1	Thai or long red chile pepper, seeded and minced, optional	1
3 tbsp	extra virgin olive oil	45 mL
DRIZZLE		
3 tbsp	freshly squeezed lime juice	45 mL
1 tbsp	gluten-free fish sauce	15 mL
1 tsp	hot Asian chili sauce or to taste, optional (see Tips, left)	5 mL
4 cups	arugula leaves	1 L
12 oz	New York strip sirloin, grilled to desired degree of doneness and thinly sliced on the bias	375 g

1. In a bowl, combine Job's tears, cucumber, green onions and tomatoes.

2. *Dressing:* In a small bowl, combine rice vinegar, soy sauce and chile pepper, if using. Gradually whisk in olive oil. Add to Jobs' tears mixture and toss well.

3. *Drizzle:* In another small bowl, combine lime juice, fish sauce and chili sauce, if using. Set aside.

4. Line a serving bowl or deep platter with arugula. Spread evenly with grain mixture and lay beef strips evenly over top. Sprinkle with half of the drizzle. Pour remainder into a small serving bowl and pass at the table.

Variation

Asian-Style Beef and Rice Salad with Arugula: Substitute 2 cups (500 mL) cooked cooled long–grain brown rice for the Job's tears. To keep the grains of rice separate, rinse the hot cooked rice thoroughly under cold running water. Drain well and let cool.

Cold Soba Noodles

This is one of my favorite summer dishes. I love to serve it when we're dining in the garden on a warm evening. In fact, it's a key component of one of my preferred al fresco dinners, served alongside grilled fish or chicken and a salad of cooled baby beets and sliced red onions tossed in a garlicky vinaigrette. Yum.

Makes 6 side servings

Tips

Most soba noodles contain some wheat flour, so make sure to check the label. The wheat free versions are most readily available at natural foods stores or Japanese markets.

Tamari is a type of soy sauce that shouldn't contain wheat. However, check the label.

If you don't have a fresh chile pepper, substitute ¼ tsp (1 mL) or more (depending upon how much you like heat) of an Asian chili paste such as sambal oelek.

8 oz	dried 100% buckwheat soba noodles (see Tips, left)	250 g
1 tsp	sesame oil	5 mL

DRESSING

3 tbsp	gluten-free reduced-sodium soy sauce (see Tips, left)	45 mL
2 tbsp	rice wine vinegar	30 mL
½ tsp	salt	2 mL
1	long red chile pepper, seeded and finely chopped (see Tips, left)	1
1 tbsp	minced gingerroot	15 mL
2 tbsp	extra virgin olive oil	30 mL
1 tbsp	sesame oil	15 mL
½ cup	thinly sliced green onions, white part with a bit of green	125 mL
	Freshly ground black pepper	
2 tbsp	toasted sesame seeds	30 mL

1. In a large pot of boiling salted water, cook noodles until tender to the bite, about 7 minutes. Drain, rinse well in cold running water and drain again. Toss with sesame oil and chill until ready to serve.

2. *Dressing:* In a small bowl, combine soy sauce, vinegar, salt, chile pepper and ginger. Whisk in olive oil and sesame oil.

3. In a serving bowl, combine chilled noodles and green onions. Add dressing and toss well. Season to taste with black pepper. Sprinkle with sesame seeds.

Nutrients per serving

Calories	225
Protein	7.9 g
Carbohydrates	30.7 g
Fat (Total)	9.4 g
Saturated Fat	1.3 g
Monounsaturated Fat	5.2 g
Polyunsaturated Fat	2.5 g
Dietary Fiber	2.2 g
Sodium	711 mg
Cholesterol	0 mg

EXCELLENT SOURCE OF manganese.

GOOD SOURCE OF vitamin C.

SOURCE OF vitamins A and E (alpha-tocopherol), thiamine, niacin, folate, pantothenic acid, phosphorus, iron, magnesium, zinc and copper.

CONTAINS a moderate amount of dietary fiber.

Wild Rice and Smoked Turkey Salad with Dried Cherries

This is one of my daughter's favorite salads. When she was away at university, I'd try to have some on hand for those times she arrived home late at night in a famished state. Serve this over a bed of leaf lettuce for a light main course. It also makes a great buffet dish.

Makes 6 side servings

Tips

Dijon mustard is a robust blend of mustard seeds, white wine, herbs and seasonings and it should not contain gluten. However, gluten has made its way into other condiments, so check the label.

Deli meats may contain gluten, so purchase a brand that is labeled gluten-free.

Nutrients per serving	
Calories	246
Protein	8.6 g
Carbohydrates	27.9 g
Fat (Total)	12.1 g
Saturated Fat	1.6 g
Monounsaturated Fat	8.3 g
Polyunsaturated Fat	1.8 g
Dietary Fiber	3.4 g
Sodium	559 mg
Cholesterol	9 mg

EXCELLENT SOURCE OF manganese.
GOOD SOURCE OF vitamin E (alpha-tocopherol), folate, phosphorus and magnesium.
SOURCE OF vitamins A and C, thiamine, riboflavin, niacin, calcium, iron, zinc, copper and selenium.
CONTAINS a moderate amount of dietary fiber.

2 cups	cooked brown and wild rice mixture, rinsed in cold water and drained (see Tips, page 91 and cooking instructions, page 32)	500 mL

DRESSING

1 tbsp	red wine vinegar	15 mL
1 tbsp	Dijon mustard (see Tips, left)	15 mL
½ tsp	salt	2 mL
	Freshly ground black pepper	
¼ cup	extra virgin olive oil	60 mL
2 tbsp	finely chopped parsley	30 mL
1½ cups	diced smoked turkey (about 6 oz/175 g) (see Tips, left)	375 mL
2	stalks celery, diced	2
4	green onions, white part with a bit of green, thinly sliced	4
½ cup	dried cherries	125 mL
1	small head leaf lettuce	1
¼ cup	toasted sliced almonds	60 mL

1. *Dressing:* In a bowl, whisk together vinegar, mustard, salt and pepper to taste. Gradually whisk in olive oil. Whisk in parsley and set aside.

2. In a bowl, combine rice, turkey, celery, green onions and cherries. Add dressing and toss well.

3. Arrange lettuce in a shallow serving bowl or deep platter. Arrange rice mixture over top. Sprinkle with toasted almonds.

Quinoa and Radish Salad with Avocado Dressing

VEGAN FRIENDLY

Quinoa has a delicate texture and produces a salad that is refreshingly light. I love to make this salad in summer when tomatoes and radishes are abundant and at their peak. I put any leftovers in the fridge and enjoy them for snacks the following day.

Makes 6 side servings

Tips

The bit of walnut oil adds appealing but subtle flavor along with beneficial omega-3 fats to this pleasantly mild vinaigrette, but if you don't have it, just use an extra tablespoon (15 mL) olive oil. When buying walnut oil, look for a cold-pressed version and, because it's highly perishable, be sure to keep it refrigerated and use it up quickly.

If field tomatoes aren't in season, halved or quartered cherry tomatoes also work well in this salad.

Nutrients per serving

Calories	239
Protein	5.1 g
Carbohydrates	26.4 g
Fat (Total)	13.5 g
Saturated Fat	1.7 g
Monounsaturated Fat	7.6 g
Polyunsaturated Fat	3.3 g
Dietary Fiber	5.5 g
Sodium	216 mg
Cholesterol	0 mg

EXCELLENT SOURCE OF magnesium and manganese.
GOOD SOURCE OF vitamins C and E (alpha-tocopherol), folate, iron and copper.
SOURCE OF vitamin A, thiamine, riboflavin, niacin, pantothenic acid, phosphorous and zinc.
CONTAINS a high amount of dietary fiber.

3 cups	cooked quinoa, cooled (see cooking instructions, page 26)	750 mL
AVOCADO DRESSING		
1	avocado, pitted and peeled	1
2 tbsp	extra virgin olive oil	30 mL
2 tbsp	white wine vinegar	30 mL
1 tbsp	walnut oil (see Tips, left)	15 mL
½ tsp	salt	2 mL
	Freshly ground black pepper	
2 cups	diced, cored tomatoes (see Tips, left)	500 mL
2 cups	thinly sliced radishes (see Variations, below)	500 mL

1. *Avocado Dressing:* In a food processor or blender, combine avocado, olive oil, vinegar, walnut oil, salt and pepper to taste. Process until smooth and blended.

2. In a serving bowl, combine tomatoes, radishes and quinoa. Add dressing and toss until combined. Chill until ready to serve.

Variations

Millet and Radish Salad with Avocado Dressing: Substitute 3 cups (750 mL) cooked toasted millet (see cooking instructions, page 22) for the quinoa.

If you don't have radishes, substitute ½ cup (125 mL) finely chopped red onion.

Rice Salad Niçoise

This refreshing salad, with a mostly Mediterranean spin, is a perfect dinner solution for those summer days when it's too hot to cook and you can't bear the thought of a heavy meal. Just cook the rice in your rice cooker, rinse and drain. Complete Steps 1 and 2 and chill overnight. The salad is ready to eat whenever you are.

Tips

Lundberg makes a brown and wild rice mixture, which works well in this salad. If you prefer, combine equal quantities of plain brown and wild rice.

Rinsing cooked rice reduces stickiness. Place the cooked rice in a strainer and rinse under cold running water. Drain thoroughly before using.

Nutrient Tip

Virtually all of the fat in this salad comes from the olives, olive oil and the tuna, and is heart-healthy unsaturated fat.

Nutrients per serving

Calories	345
Protein	13.5 g
Carbohydrates	26.9 g
Fat (Total)	21.3 g
Saturated Fat	3.1 g
Monounsaturated Fat	14.2 g
Polyunsaturated Fat	3.2 g
Dietary Fiber	3.9 g
Sodium	940 mg
Cholesterol	11 mg

EXCELLENT SOURCE OF vitamins C and E (alpha-tocopherol), niacin, manganese and selenium.
GOOD SOURCE OF vitamin A, magnesium and phosphorus.
SOURCE OF thiamine, riboflavin, folate, pantothenic acid, iron, zinc and copper.
CONTAINS a moderate amount of dietary fiber.

2 cups	cooked brown and wild rice mixture, rinsed in cold water and drained (see Tips, left and cooking instructions, page 32)	500 mL
1	can (6 oz/170 g) tuna, preferably Italian, packed in olive oil, drained	1
2	roasted red peppers, chopped	2
½ cup	chopped drained marinated artichoke hearts	125 mL
½ cup	pitted black olives, sliced	125 mL
½ cup	pitted green olives, sliced	125 mL
	Chopped hot pickled peppers, optional	

DRESSING

2 tbsp	red wine vinegar	30 mL
½ tsp	salt	2 mL
¼ tsp	freshly ground black pepper	1 mL
¼ cup	extra virgin olive oil	60 mL
	Leafy lettuce, optional	
	Hard-cooked eggs, quartered, optional	

1. In a serving bowl, combine rice, tuna, red peppers, artichoke hearts, black and green olives and hot pepper, if using.

2. *Dressing:* In a small bowl, combine vinegar, salt and black pepper, stirring until salt dissolves. Gradually whisk in olive oil. Add to rice mixture and toss well. Chill thoroughly.

3. Just before serving, spread over a bed of lettuce, if using. Garnish with eggs, if using.

TUNA

Tuna is one of the best sources of heart-healthy omega-3 fats, yet watchdogs such as the FDA have advised that tuna (along with other large fish, such as shark and swordfish) be consumed with caution because it is likely to contain high levels of mercury. The quantity of tuna in this salad easily falls within the guidelines for safe consumption, even for pregnant or nursing women (6 ounces/170 g per week), but if you're concerned, look for tins of tuna labeled "skipjack," rather than albacore. Albacore tuna have about three times more mercury than these smaller fish, which are a healthier alternative.

Kasha and Beet Salad with Celery and Feta

I love the robust flavors of this hearty salad. Beets, parsley and feta are the perfect balance for assertive buckwheat. It's a great combination and a wonderful buffet dish.

Makes 6 to 8 side servings

Tip

Buckwheat groats that are already toasted are known as kasha. If you prefer a milder buckwheat flavor, use groats rather than kasha in this dish. Just place them in a dry skillet over medium-high heat and cook, stirring constantly, until they are nicely fragrant, about 4 minutes. In the process they will darken from a light shade of sand to one with a hint of brown. Groats you toast yourself have a milder flavor than store-bought kasha.

	Nutrients per serving	
Calories		177
Protein		5.4 g
Carbohydrates		23.3 g
Fat (Total)		8.1 g
Saturated Fat		2.5 g
Monounsaturated Fat		4.4 g
Polyunsaturated Fat		0.8 g
Dietary Fiber		3.7 g
Sodium		571 mg
Cholesterol		10 mg

EXCELLENT SOURCE OF manganese.

GOOD SOURCE OF folate and magnesium.

SOURCE OF vitamins A, C and E (alpha-tocopherol), thiamine, riboflavin, niacin, pantothenic acid, calcium, phosphorus, iron, zinc, copper and selenium.

CONTAINS a moderate amount of dietary fiber.

2 cups	vegetable or chicken stock (see Tips, page 104)	500 mL
2	cloves garlic, minced	2
1 cup	kasha or buckwheat groats (see Tip, left)	250 mL

DRESSING

1/4 cup	red wine vinegar	60 mL
1 tsp	Dijon mustard (see Tips, page 89)	5 mL
1/2 tsp	salt	2 mL
1/2 tsp	freshly ground black pepper	2 mL
3 tbsp	extra virgin olive oil	45 mL
2 cups	diced peeled cooked beets	500 mL
4	stalks celery, diced	4
6	green onions, white part only, thinly sliced	6
1/2 cup	finely chopped parsley	125 mL
3 oz	crumbled feta cheese	90 g

1. In a saucepan over medium-high heat, bring stock and garlic to a boil. Gradually add kasha, stirring constantly to prevent clumping. Reduce heat to low. Cover and simmer until all the liquid is absorbed and kasha is tender, about 10 minutes. Remove from heat. Fluff up with a fork and transfer to a serving bowl and let cool slightly.

2. *Dressing:* In a small bowl, combine vinegar, mustard, salt and pepper, stirring until salt dissolves. Gradually whisk in olive oil until blended. Add to kasha and toss well.

3. Add beets, celery and green onions to kasha and toss again. Chill until ready to serve. Just before serving, garnish with parsley and sprinkle feta over top.

Variation

Rice and Beet Salad with Celery and Feta: Substitute 3 cups (750 mL) cooked long-grain brown rice for the cooked kasha.

Corn and Sausage Salad with Shredded Hearts of Romaine

This is an absolutely delicious combination of ingredients. Serve it on a buffet table or bring it to a potluck and expect that it will quickly disappear. It also makes a great brown-bag lunch. Leave the shredded romaine on top and toss the salad just before you're ready to serve so the lettuce doesn't wilt.

Makes 8 side servings

Tips

You can use drained, rinsed canned hominy, or cook your own (see page 18).

I like to use very hot pickled peppers, such as Tabasco, in this salad, but if you're heat averse, milder ones, such as pepperoncini or banana peppers, taste good, too.

Check the label to make sure your kielbasa is gluten-free.

To shred lettuce, peel off the outer leaves of romaine and slice across the heart very thinly using a chef's knife.

Nutrients per serving	
Calories	215
Protein	9.8 g
Carbohydrates	13.6 g
Fat (Total)	14.3 g
Saturated Fat	4.5 g
Monounsaturated Fat	7.2 g
Polyunsaturated Fat	1.9 g
Dietary Fiber	2.5 g
Sodium	608 mg
Cholesterol	33 mg

EXCELLENT SOURCE OF vitamin A and folate.
GOOD SOURCE OF phosphorus.
SOURCE OF vitamins C and E (alpha-tocopherol), thiamine, riboflavin, niacin, calcium, iron, magnesium, manganese and zinc.
CONTAINS a moderate amount of dietary fiber.

1½ cups	drained cooked hominy (see Tips, left)	375 mL
1½ cups	cooled cooked corn kernels	375 mL
DRESSING		
2 tbsp	red wine vinegar	30 mL
2 tsp	Dijon mustard	10 mL
½ tsp	salt	2 mL
	Freshly ground black pepper	
1	clove garlic, finely grated or put through a press	1
¼ cup	extra virgin olive oil	60 mL
1 tbsp	minced drained pickled hot peppers (see Tips, left)	15 mL
8 oz	turkey kielbasa (see Tips, left), diced	250 g
4 oz	Asiago cheese, diced	125 g
4	stalks celery, diced	4
1	small red onion, diced	1
6 cups	shredded hearts of romaine (see Tips, left)	1.5 L

1. *Dressing:* In a small bowl, combine vinegar, mustard, salt and black pepper to taste, stirring until salt dissolves. Stir in garlic. Gradually whisk in olive oil until blended. Stir in hot peppers and set aside.

2. In a serving bowl, combine cooked hominy and corn, kielbasa, Asiago, celery and red onion. Add dressing and toss well. Arrange shredded lettuce on top. Cover and chill thoroughly. When ready to serve, toss well.

Variations

Substitute 1½ cups (375 mL) cooked cooled Job's tears for the hominy.

For a more robust flavor, substitute an equal quantity of smoked Cheddar for the Asiago cheese.

Cranberry Pecan Millet Salad

This salad has a delectable combination of flavors and textures — the slightly tart cranberries and orange are beautifully balanced by the crunchy pecans and mildly nutty flavor of the millet. It's exotic enough to liven up any buffet and makes a particularly delicious and delightfully different accompaniment to poultry.

Makes 8 side servings

Tip

Toasting the millet enhances its pleasantly nutty flavor.

Nutrient Tip

I often use a fair bit of parsley in my recipes for two reasons: its very tasty and its loaded with nutrients such as vitamin K, which among other benefits may play an important role in bone health.

1 cup	millet	250 mL
1½ cups	water	375 mL
	Salt, optional	
DRESSING		
¼ cup	freshly squeezed orange juice	60 mL
½ tsp	balsamic vinegar	2 mL
½ tsp	salt	2 mL
Pinch	freshly grated nutmeg	Pinch
	Freshly ground black pepper	
¼ cup	extra virgin olive oil	60 mL
1	red bell pepper, seeded and diced	1
½ cup	finely chopped parsley	125 mL
½ cup	dried cranberries	125 mL
½ cup	toasted chopped pecans	125 mL
2 tsp	finely grated orange zest	10 mL

1. In a saucepan over medium heat, toast millet, stirring, until it crackles and releases its aroma, about 5 minutes. Transfer to a bowl. Add water to saucepan and bring to a boil. Stir in millet and return to a boil. Reduce heat to low. Cover and simmer until water is absorbed, about 25 minutes. Remove from heat and let stand, covered, for 10 minutes. Transfer to a serving bowl and fluff with a fork. Set aside and let cool.

2. *Dressing:* In a small bowl, combine orange juice, vinegar and salt, stirring until salt dissolves. Add nutmeg and pepper to taste. Whisk in olive oil. Set aside.

3. In a serving bowl, combine bell pepper, parsley, cranberries, pecans and orange zest. Add fluffed millet and toss. Add dressing and toss until combined. Chill thoroughly before serving.

Nutrients per serving

Calories	234
Protein	3.7 g
Carbohydrates	28 g
Fat (Total)	12.6 g
Saturated Fat	1.5 g
Monounsaturated Fat	7.9 g
Polyunsaturated Fat	2.6 g
Dietary Fiber	3.8 g
Sodium	149 mg
Cholesterol	0 mg

EXCELLENT SOURCE OF
vitamin C and manganese.

GOOD SOURCE OF
magnesium.

SOURCE OF vitamins A and E (alpha-tocopherol), thiamine, riboflavin, niacin, folate, iron, zinc, copper and phosphorus.

CONTAINS a moderate amount of dietary fiber.

Millet Salad with Lemony Chickpeas and Tomatoes

Although I enjoy this salad all year round, I especially like making it in winter when its light airy texture and Mediterranean flavors remind me that summer will come again. It makes a great addition to a buffet table, an interesting dish for a potluck and is an excellent side served with grilled fish or roast chicken. You can even use it as an appetizer — just put out hearts of romaine to use as dippers.

Makes 10 side servings

Tips

If field tomatoes are in season, substitute an equal quantity of seeded diced tomatoes for the cherry tomatoes.

Chickpeas do not contain gluten, but canned chickpeas may be processed in a facility where gluten is present. It is always a good idea to check the label and, if necessary, contact the manufacturer. For this quantity of chickpeas, soak and cook 1 cup (250 mL) dried chickpeas.

1 cup	millet	250 mL
2 cups	water or vegetable stock	500 mL
DRESSING		
1/4 cup	freshly squeezed lemon juice	60 mL
1/2 tsp	salt	2 mL
Pinch	cayenne pepper, optional	Pinch
	Freshly ground black pepper	
6 tbsp	extra virgin olive oil	90 mL
1/4 cup	finely chopped parsley or dill	60 mL
2 cups	halved cherry tomatoes (see Tips, left)	500 mL
2 cups	cooked chickpeas or 1 can (14 to 19 oz/398 to 540 mL) chickpeas, drained and rinsed (see Tips, left)	500 mL
8	green onions, white part only, finely chopped	8
2 cups	thinly sliced radishes	500 mL
	Hearts of romaine, optional	

1. In a saucepan over medium heat, toast millet, stirring, until it crackles and releases its aroma, about 5 minutes. Transfer to a bowl. Add water to saucepan and bring to a boil. Stir in millet and return to a boil. Reduce heat to low. Cover and simmer until water is absorbed, about 25 minutes. Remove from heat and let stand, covered, for 10 minutes. Transfer to a serving bowl and fluff with a fork. Set aside and let cool.

2. *Dressing:* Meanwhile, in a small bowl, combine lemon juice, salt, cayenne, if using, and pepper to taste, stirring until salt dissolves. Whisk in olive oil. Add parsley. Set aside.

3. Add tomatoes, chickpeas, green onions and radishes to millet and toss. Add dressing and toss well. Cover and chill. If using lettuce, line a serving bowl with hearts of romaine and add salad. Or serve salad as an appetizer and use romaine as dippers.

Variations

To add variety to your grain consumption, use half quinoa and half millet. Cook the grains together as per Step 1.

Quinoa Salad with Lemony Chickpeas and Tomatoes: Substitute quinoa for millet. Reduce the cooking time to 15 minutes.

Nutrients per serving

Calories	217
Protein	5.8 g
Carbohydrates	27.5 g
Fat (Total)	9.7 g
Saturated Fat	1.3 g
Monounsaturated Fat	6.3 g
Polyunsaturated Fat	1.6 g
Dietary Fiber	4.3 g
Sodium	130 mg
Cholesterol	0 mg

EXCELLENT SOURCE OF folate and manganese.

GOOD SOURCE OF magnesium.

SOURCE OF vitamins A, C and E (alpha-tocopherol), thiamine, riboflavin, niacin, phosphorous, iron, zinc and copper.

CONTAINS a high amount of dietary fiber.

Everyday Tuna and Red Rice Salad

The use of Bhutanese red rice or more delicate brown Kalijira rice, both of which cook in less than 30 minutes, allows you to make this very tasty and nutritious rice salad for a weekday meal. This salad is very flexible. It is designed for convenience, which includes using ingredients you're likely to have on hand — that way, you can prepare a nutritious meal when you haven't had time to shop.

Makes 4 main-course servings

Tips

Bhutanese red and Kalijira rice are available at specialty stores or Whole Foods. They are often sold under the Lotus Foods label.

Use a fine Microplane grater to grate garlic or put it through a press.

1½ cups	water	375 mL
¾ cup	Bhutanese red or Kalijira brown rice, rinsed and drained (see Tips, left)	175 mL
DRESSING		
1 tbsp	white wine vinegar	15 mL
1 tsp	Dijon mustard	5 mL
½ tsp	salt	2 mL
	Freshly ground black pepper	
3 tbsp	extra virgin olive oil	45 mL
1	small shallot, minced, or 2 tbsp (30 mL) finely chopped green onion, white part only	1
½	clove garlic, finely grated	½
1	can (6 oz/170 g) albacore tuna, drained	1
1 cup	cooked sliced green beans, cooled, optional	250 mL
½	red bell pepper, seeded and diced	½
¼ cup	sliced pitted black olives or 1 tbsp (15 mL) diced capers	60 mL
4	green onions, white part only, thinly sliced, or ¼ cup (60 mL) finely chopped red onion	4
1	sun-dried tomato, packed in olive oil, finely chopped, or ½ cup (125 mL) quartered cherry or grape tomatoes	1
2 tbsp	finely chopped parsley	30 mL
	Lettuce leaves or hearts of romaine, optional	

Nutrients per serving

Calories	296
Protein	12.1 g
Carbohydrates	29.8 g
Fat (Total)	14.8 g
Saturated Fat	2.1 g
Monounsaturated Fat	9.1 g
Polyunsaturated Fat	2.4 g
Dietary Fiber	3.1 g
Sodium	515 mg
Cholesterol	11 mg

EXCELLENT SOURCE OF vitamin C, niacin and selenium.

GOOD SOURCE OF vitamin E (alpha-tocoperol).

SOURCE OF vitamin A, folate, phosphorous, iron, magnesium and copper.

CONTAINS a moderate amount of dietary fiber.

1. In a heavy saucepan with a tight-fitting lid, bring water to a rapid boil. Stir in rice and return to a boil. Reduce heat to low. Cover and simmer until liquid is absorbed and rice is tender, about 25 minutes. (If liquid remains, remove lid and return to element for a few minutes until it evaporates.) Fluff up with a fork.

2. *Dressing:* In a small bowl, combine vinegar, mustard and salt, stirring until salt dissolves. Season to taste with pepper. Gradually whisk in olive oil. Stir in shallot and garlic.

3. In a bowl, combine tuna, beans, if using, pepper, olives, onions, sun-dried tomato and parsley. Toss until blended.

4. *To serve:* Spoon warm rice onto plates and top with tuna mixture. Or, line a platter with leafy lettuce or hearts of romaine and spoon rice onto lettuce and top with tuna mixture.

Red Rice

Poultry

Arroz con Pollo

This Spanish approach to chicken and rice is a great one-dish meal, delicious enough to serve to guests. I love this version, which has quite a bit of liquid, because I enjoy spooning the luscious sauce over the chicken as I eat. If you prefer a drier version, reduce the quantity of chicken stock by 1 cup (250 mL) and/or omit the wine. A tossed green salad is all you need to add.

Makes 6 servings

Tip

When using prepared products such as sausage, stock and canned tomatoes, check the label. Gluten may suddenly appear in a previously gluten-free product, due to changes in manufacturing process.

Nutrient Tip

Most of the fat in this recipe comes from the chorizo and the chicken skin. If you're concerned about the quantity of fat, remove the skin from the chicken and reduce the quantity of sausage.

Nutrients per serving

Calories	477
Protein	34.3 g
Carbohydrates	35.4 g
Fat (Total)	21.5 g
Saturated Fat	6.3 g
Monounsaturated Fat	9.9 g
Polyunsaturated Fat	3.7 g
Dietary Fibre	3.9 g
Sodium	715 mg
Cholesterol	93 mg

EXCELLENT SOURCE OF vitamin C, thiamine, niacin, phosphorus, magnesium, manganese and selenium.
GOOD SOURCE OF vitamin A, pantothenic acid, riboflavin, zinc, iron and copper.
SOURCE OF vitamin E (alpha-tocopherol), folate and calcium.
CONTAINS a modern amount of dietary fiber.

- **Preheat oven to 350°F (180°C)**

1 tbsp	olive oil	15 mL
4 oz	soft chorizo sausage, removed from casings (see Tip, left)	125 g
2 lbs	skin-on bone-in chicken pieces, cut into serving-size pieces, rinsed and patted dry	1 kg
2	onions, finely chopped	2
1	red bell pepper, seeded and diced	1
4	cloves garlic, minced	4
2 tsp	sweet paprika	10 mL
1/2 tsp	salt or to taste	2 mL
	Freshly ground black pepper	
1 cup	long-grain brown rice, rinsed and drained	250 mL
1/2 cup	dry white wine	125 mL
1/4 tsp	crumbled saffron threads, dissolved in 2 tbsp (30 mL) boiling water	1 mL
2 cups	reduced-sodium chicken stock (see Tip, left)	500 mL
1	can (14 oz/398 mL) no-salt-added diced tomatoes with juice	1
1 cup	cooked green peas, optional	250 mL

1. In a Dutch oven or large ovenproof saucepan with a tight-fitting lid, heat oil over medium–high heat for 30 seconds. Add chorizo and cook, stirring and breaking up with a spoon, until cooked through, about 2 minutes. Using a slotted spoon, transfer cooked sausage to a plate. Add chicken, in batches, and cook, turning once, until nicely browned, about 5 minutes per batch. Set sausage and chicken aside. Drain off all but 1 tbsp (15 mL) fat from pan.

2. Reduce heat to medium. Add onions, bell pepper and garlic and cook, stirring, until vegetables are softened, about 5 minutes. Add paprika, salt and black pepper to taste and cook, stirring, for 1 minute. Add rice and cook, stirring, for 1 minute. Add white wine and saffron liquid and bring to a boil. Boil for 1 minute. Add stock and tomatoes with juice and bring to a boil. Boil for 2 minutes. Return sausage and chicken to pan.

3. Cover and cook in preheated oven until rice is tender and chicken is no longer pink inside, about 1 hour. Stir in green peas, if using, and cook until heated through.

Coconut Chicken with Quinoa

This delightfully different chicken is a potpourri of mouthwatering flavors and beneficial nutrients. Keep the accompaniments simple. Steamed green beans make a nice finish.

Makes 4 servings

Tip

You can substitute already-ground spices for the cumin seeds and allspice and skip the toasting step. I'd use 1 tsp (5 mL) ground cumin and ½ tsp (2 mL) ground allspice in this recipe.

Nutrient Tip

The crispy chicken skin adds texture and flavor to this dish, but it also adds fat. If you want to reduce the quantity of fat, remove the skin. Most of the saturated fat comes from the chicken skin and the coconut milk.

Nutrient per serving

Calories	477
Protein	34.5 g
Carbohydrates	32.4 g
Fat (Total)	23.8 g
Saturated Fat	9.5 g
Monounsaturated Fat	8.4 g
Polyunsaturated Fat	3.9 g
Dietary Fiber	4.3 g
Sodium	597 mg
Cholesterol	86 mg

EXCELLENT SOURCE OF vitamin C, niacin, phosphorus, iron, magnesium, manganese and selenium.

GOOD SOURCE OF vitamin A, riboflavin, folate, pantothenic acid and zinc.

SOURCE OF vitamin E (alpha-tocopherol), thiamine, copper and calcium.

CONTAINS a high amount of dietary fiber.

2 tsp	cumin seeds (see Tip, left)	10 mL
1 tsp	whole allspice (see Tip, left)	5 mL
1 tbsp	olive oil	15 mL
1½ lbs	skin-on bone-in chicken breasts, rinsed and patted dry	750 g
1	onion, finely chopped	1
1	red bell pepper, seeded and diced	1
1	green bell pepper, seeded and diced	1
6	cloves garlic, minced	6
½ to 1	chile pepper, seeded and minced, optional	½ to 1
1 tsp	curry powder (see Tips, page 132)	5 mL
½ tsp	salt	2 mL
½ tsp	freshly ground black pepper	2 mL
¾ cup	quinoa, rinsed and drained	175 mL
1½ cups	reduced-sodium chicken stock (see Tips, page 104)	375 mL
½ cup	coconut milk (see Tip, page 122)	125 mL

1. In a dry large skillet over medium heat, combine cumin seeds and allspice. Toast, stirring constantly, until fragrant, about 4 minutes. Immediately transfer to a mortar or a spice grinder and grind. Set aside.

2. In same skillet, heat oil over medium heat for 30 seconds. Add chicken, in batches, skin side down, and brown well, about 4 minutes. Turn over, cover and cook for 10 minutes. Remove from pan and keep warm. Drain all but 1 tbsp (15 mL) fat from pan.

3. Add onion, bell peppers, garlic and chile pepper, if using, and cook, stirring, until vegetables are softened, about 5 minutes. Add curry powder, salt, black pepper, reserved ground spices and quinoa and cook, stirring, until quinoa is well integrated into mixture, about 1 minute. Add stock and coconut milk and bring to a boil. Lay chicken, skin side up, over mixture. Reduce heat to low. Cover and cook until chicken is no longer pink inside, about 30 minutes.

Chinese-Style Chicken Fried Rice

This flavorful stir-fry, rich in the appetizing flavors of soy sauce, ginger and shiitake mushrooms, is a great weeknight dinner that is relatively speedy to make so long as you have cooked the rice ahead of time. A plate of steamed or stir-fried bok choy makes a perfect finish.

Makes 4 servings

Tips

Tamari is a type of soy sauce that shouldn't contain wheat. However, check the label.

If you prefer, use leftover cooked chicken to make this recipe. Combine with the marinade and set aside for 15 minutes. Skip Steps 1 and 4. Drain off excess liquid and add to the pan along with the mushrooms.

2 cups	cooked brown rice (see cooking instructions, page 28)	500 mL
3 tbsp	gluten-free reduced-sodium soy sauce, divided (see Tips, left)	45 mL
1 tbsp	Shaoxing wine, sake, dry vermouth or vodka	15 mL
1 tbsp	minced gingerroot	15 mL
2	cloves garlic, minced	2
	Freshly ground black pepper	
8 oz	skinless boneless chicken breast, thinly sliced (see Tips, left)	250 g
4	dried shiitake mushrooms	4
2 tbsp	reduced-sodium chicken stock	30 mL
1 tbsp	mushroom soaking liquid	15 mL
1 tbsp	gluten-free oyster sauce	15 mL
1 tsp	sesame oil	5 mL
2 tbsp	olive oil, divided	30 mL
2	eggs, lightly beaten	2
6	green onions, white part with a bit of green, thinly sliced	6
1 cup	barely cooked green peas	250 mL

1. In a bowl, combine 2 tbsp (30 mL) of the soy sauce, Shaoxing wine, ginger, garlic and pepper to taste. Add sliced chicken and toss to combine. Cover and set aside for 30 minutes.

2. Meanwhile, in a small bowl, combine dried mushrooms with hot water to cover. Ensuring they remain submerged, set aside until mushrooms are tender, about 30 minutes. Drain, reserving 1 tbsp (15 mL) of the mushroom soaking liquid. Remove stems, if necessary, and slice caps thinly. Set aside.

3. In another small bowl, combine stock, reserved mushroom soaking liquid, oyster sauce and sesame oil. Set aside.

4. In a wok or large skillet, heat 1 tbsp (15 mL) of the olive oil over medium-high heat for 30 seconds. Add chicken with marinade and cook, stirring, until no longer pink, about 3 minutes. Transfer to a plate and set aside. Wipe pan clean.

5. Add remaining 1 tbsp (15 mL) oil to pan. Add eggs and cook until scrambled, about 30 seconds. Add mushrooms and green onions and cook, stirring, for 30 seconds. Add peas and toss well. Add reserved chicken and rice and toss well. Add reserved sauce and cook, stirring, until heated through, about 1 minute.

Nutrient per serving

Calories	379
Protein	23 g
Carbohydrates	45.3 g
Fat (Total)	12.5 g
Saturated Fat	2.3 g
Monounsaturated Fat	7.1 g
Polyunsaturated Fat	2.1 g
Dietary Fiber	5.6 g
Sodium	712 mg
Cholesterol	126 mg

EXCELLENT SOURCE OF riboflavin, niacin, pantothenic acid, magnesium, manganese, zinc, copper and selenium.
GOOD SOURCE OF folate, thiamine, phosphorus and iron.
SOURCE OF vitamins A, C and E (alpha-tocopherol) and calcium.
CONTAINS a high amount of dietary fiber.

Peppery Chicken Quinoa

Not only is this dish pretty to look at, it's very easy to make. Enjoy this when peppers are in season. It makes a great one-dish weeknight meal.

Makes 4 servings

Tips

If you are using prepared stock, check the label to make sure it doesn't contain gluten.

Harissa is a North African chili paste. Prepared versions may contain gluten, so check the label. If you don't have it, pass your favorite hot pepper sauce at the table to satisfy any heat seekers in the group.

3 cups	reduced-sodium chicken stock (see Tips, left), divided	750 mL
1 tbsp	harissa, optional (see Tips, left)	15 mL
1 cup	quinoa, rinsed and drained	250 mL
3 tbsp	extra virgin olive oil, divided	45 mL
½ tsp	cracked black peppercorns	2 mL
1 lb	skinless boneless chicken breasts, thinly sliced	500 g
4	cloves garlic, thinly sliced	4
3	red bell peppers, seeded and cut into thin strips	3
2 tbsp	sherry vinegar	30 mL
¼ cup	finely chopped parsley	60 mL

1. In a saucepan over medium heat, bring 2 cups (500 mL) of the stock to a boil. Stir in harissa, if using. Add quinoa in a steady steam, stirring constantly, and return to a boil. Reduce heat to low. Cover and simmer until tender, about 15 minutes. Remove from heat and let stand for 5 minutes. Fluff with a fork.

2. Meanwhile, in a large skillet or wok, heat 1 tbsp (15 mL) of the olive oil over medium–high heat. Add black peppercorns and stir well. Add chicken and cook, stirring, until it turns white and almost cooks through, about 5 minutes. Transfer to a plate.

3. Add remaining 2 tbsp (30 mL) of oil to pan. Add garlic and cook, stirring, just until it begins to turn golden, about 2 minutes. Add bell peppers and cook, stirring, until they begin to shimmer, about 2 minutes. Add remaining 1 cup (250 mL) of stock and sherry vinegar and cook until mixture is reduced by half, about 8 minutes. Return chicken to pan and toss until heated through. Remove from heat.

4. *To serve:* Spread cooked quinoa over a deep platter and scoop out an indentation in the middle. Fill with chicken mixture and garnish with parsley.

Variation

Instead of quinoa, serve this over brown or red rice.

Nutrient per serving

Calories	418
Protein	34.6 g
Carbohydrates	37.5 g
Fat (Total)	14.7 g
Saturated Fat	2.1 g
Monounsaturated Fat	8.7 g
Polyunsaturated Fat	2.5 g
Dietary Fiber	4.5 g
Sodium	530 mg
Cholesterol	67 mg

EXCELLENT SOURCE OF vitamins A and C, niacin, iron, magnesium, manganese and selenium.
GOOD SOURCE OF riboflavin, pantothenic acid, zinc, phosphorus and copper.
SOURCE OF vitamin E (alpha-tocopherol), folate, thiamine and calcium.
CONTAINS a high amount of dietary fiber.

Italian-Style Chicken and Rice

This mouthwatering combination of chicken and rice, accented with pancetta and hints of lemon and chile peppers, is comfort food, Italian-style. Finish this with a drizzle of your best extra virgin olive oil and, in season, add a tomato and bocconcini salad garnished with fresh basil.

Makes 6 servings

Tip

If you can't find pancetta, you can substitute an equal quantity of bacon. When using deli meats, always check the label to make sure they are gluten-free.

Nutrient Tip

The nutrient analysis on this recipe was done using 2 oz (60 g) of bacon, which contributes 8.5 g of fat per serving. If you're concerned about your intake of fat, reduce the quantity of bacon or pancetta and remove the skin from the chicken, but be aware that the dish won't be nearly as tasty.

Nutrient per serving

Calories	521
Protein	32.4 g
Carbohydrates	44.6 g
Fat (Total)	23.2 g
Saturated Fat	8.6 g
Monounsaturated Fat	12.6 g
Polyunsaturated Fat	4.8 g
Dietary Fiber	4.8 g
Sodium	486 mg
Cholesterol	89 mg

EXCELLENT SOURCE OF niacin, phosphorus, magnesium, manganese and selenium.
GOOD SOURCE OF pantothenic acid, thiamine, riboflavin, zinc and iron.
SOURCE OF vitamins A and C, folate and copper.
CONTAINS a high amount of dietary fiber.

- Preheat oven to 350°F (180°C)
- Covered 10-cup (2.5 L) baking dish

1 cup	short-grain brown rice	250 mL
2½ cups	reduced-sodium chicken stock (see Tips, page 104) or water	625 mL
1 tbsp	olive oil	15 mL
2 lbs	skin-on bone-in chicken breasts, cut into serving-size pieces, rinsed and patted dry	1 kg
2 oz	chunk of pancetta, finely chopped (see Tip, left)	60 g
2	onions, thinly sliced on the vertical	2
4	cloves garlic, minced	4
2	dried red cayenne peppers	2
1 tbsp	finely grated lemon zest	15 mL
1½ tsp	dried Italian seasoning	7 mL
	Coarse sea salt	
	Freshly ground black pepper	
2 tbsp	freshly squeezed lemon juice	30 mL
	Extra virgin olive oil	

1. In a heavy saucepan with a tight-fitting lid, combine rice and stock. Bring to a rapid boil over high heat. Reduce heat to low. Cover and simmer for 15 minutes. Remove from heat and set aside.

2. Meanwhile, in a large skillet, heat oil over medium–high heat for 30 seconds. Add chicken, in batches, and cook, turning once, until nicely browned, about 5 minutes per batch. Transfer to a plate and set aside. Drain off all but 1 tbsp (15 mL) fat from pan.

3. Reduce heat to medium. Add pancetta and cook, stirring, for 2 minutes. Add onions and cook, stirring, until softened, about 3 minutes. Add garlic, dried peppers, lemon zest and Italian seasoning and cook, stirring, for 1 minute. Add reserved rice with liquid and bring to a boil.

4. Transfer to baking dish. Arrange chicken over top. Cover and bake in preheated oven until chicken is no longer pink inside and rice is tender, about 45 minutes. Remove and discard cayenne peppers.

5. Sprinkle chicken with sea salt and pepper to taste. Drizzle with lemon juice and olive oil.

Jambalaya

This is a great dish for a family dinner or a casual evening with friends. The robust flavors are delicious any time of the year, but particularly appreciated on a chilly night. All you need to add is warm whole-grain rolls, a big salad and, if you're feeling festive, some robust red wine.

Makes 6 servings

Tips

If you like heat, use hot Italian sausage and/or add a diced chile pepper with the bell peppers.

Cajun seasoning should be simply a blend of spices, which are gluten-free, but some brands add wheat starch so be sure to check the label.

If you don't have Cajun seasoning, substitute 1 tsp (5 mL) of any variety of paprika — sweet, hot or smoked, depending on your taste.

	Nutrient per serving	
Calories		341
Protein		27.3 g
Carbohydrates		29.2 g
Fat (Total)		12.6 g
Saturated Fat		3.3 g
Monounsaturated Fat		4.8 g
Polyunsaturated Fat		1.9 g
Dietary Fiber		2.9 g
Sodium		667 mg
Cholesterol		80 mg

EXCELLENT SOURCE OF vitamin C, niacin, phosphorus, iron and selenium.

GOOD SOURCE OF thiamine, riboflavin and zinc.

SOURCE OF vitamins A and E (alpha-tocopherol) folate, pantothenic acid, magnesium, manganese, copper and calcium.

CONTAINS a moderate amount of dietary fiber.

3 cups	reduced-sodium chicken stock (see Tips, page 104)	750 mL
¾ cup	Job's tears, soaked, rinsed and drained	175 mL
1 tbsp	olive oil	15 mL
8 oz	Italian sausage, removed from casings (see Tips, left and page 136)	250 g
1 lb	skinless boneless chicken thighs, cut into bite-size pieces	500 g
2	onions, finely chopped	2
2	stalks celery, diced	2
2	bell peppers, such as 1 green and 1 red, seeded and diced	2
1	chile pepper, seeded and diced, optional (see Tips, left)	1
4	cloves garlic, minced	4
2 tsp	Cajun seasoning (see Tips, left)	10 mL
1 tsp	dried thyme leaves	5 mL
1	can (28 oz/796 mL) no-salt-added diced tomatoes with juice	1
8 oz	medium shrimp, cooked, peeled and deveined, optional	250 g

1. In a heavy saucepan with a tight-fitting lid, bring stock to a boil. Add Job's tears and return to a boil. Reduce heat to low. Cover and simmer for 30 minutes. (The Job's tears will not be fully cooked and liquid won't be completely absorbed.)

2. Meanwhile, in a Dutch oven, heat oil over medium heat for 30 seconds. Add sausage and cook, breaking up with a spoon, until no longer pink, about 4 minutes. Add chicken and cook, stirring, until very lightly browned, about 2 minutes. Transfer to a bowl. Drain off all but 1 tbsp (15 mL) fat from pan, if necessary.

3. Add onions, celery, bell peppers and chile pepper, if using, and cook, stirring, until softened, about 5 minutes. Add garlic, Cajun seasoning and thyme and cook, stirring, for 1 minute. Add tomatoes with juice and bring to a boil. Stir in partially cooked Job's tears with liquid and return sausage and chicken to pot. Stir well.

4. Reduce heat to low. Cover and simmer until Job's tears are tender and liquid is absorbed, about 30 minutes. Stir in shrimp, if using, and cook until heated through, about 10 minutes.

Creole Chicken with Red Rice

I love the lively Cajun flavors of this dish. Served on a deep platter, surrounded by colorful rice and sprinkled with flecks of toasted sliced almonds, it's pretty enough to serve to guests.

Makes 6 servings

Tips

I like to use red rice in this recipe for its visual effect, but the dish is equally delicious made with long-grain brown rice. Put the rice on to cook before you start the chicken and it will be ready when you are.

While most Worcestershire sauce is gluten-free, some brands contain malt vinegar, which is not. Check the label.

Nutrient Tip

One serving of this dish is relatively high in calories because it is a fairly large portion. Keep the sides to a minimum.

Nutrient per serving	
Calories	446
Protein	28.9 g
Carbohydrates	40.8 g
Fat (Total)	18.3 g
Saturated Fat	3.9 g
Monounsaturated Fat	9.2 g
Polyunsaturated Fat	3.4 g
Dietary Fiber	4.2 g
Sodium	107 mg
Cholesterol	76 mg

EXCELLENT SOURCE OF selenium and niacin.
GOOD SOURCE OF vitamins C and E (alpha-tocopherol), pantothenic acid, phosphorus, magnesium, iron and manganese.
SOURCE OF vitamin A, thiamine, riboflavin, folate, calcium, zinc and copper.
CONTAINS a high amount of dietary fiber.

3 cups	cooked red rice (see Tips, left)	750 mL
2 tbsp	sorghum flour	30 mL
2 tbsp	cornstarch	30 mL
1 tsp	cayenne pepper	5 mL
1 tsp	cracked black peppercorns	5 mL
2 lbs	skin-on bone-in chicken breasts, cut into serving-size pieces, rinsed and patted dry	1 kg
2 tbsp	olive oil	30 mL
2	onions, chopped	2
2	stalks celery, diced	2
1	green bell pepper, seeded and diced	1
2	cloves garlic, minced	2
1	bay leaf	1
1	can (14 oz/398 mL) no-salt-added diced tomatoes with juice	1
1 cup	gluten-free beer	250 mL
2 tsp	gluten-free Worcestershire sauce (see Tips, left)	10 mL
	Salt	
¼ cup	toasted sliced almonds	60 mL

1. In a plastic bag, combine sorghum flour, cornstarch, cayenne and black peppercorns. Add chicken, in batches, tossing until well coated with mixture. Discard excess.

2. In a skillet, heat oil over medium–high heat. Add chicken, in batches, and brown, turning once, about 5 minutes per batch. Transfer to a plate and keep warm. Drain off all but 2 tbsp (30 mL) fat from pan.

3. Add onions, celery and bell pepper and cook, stirring, until softened, about 7 minutes. Add garlic and bay leaf and cook, stirring, for 1 minute. Add tomatoes with juice, beer and Worcestershire sauce and bring to a boil. Season to taste with salt. Return chicken to pan, skin side up. Cover and simmer, turning once or twice, until chicken is tender and no longer pink inside, about 45 minutes.

4. *To serve:* On a deep platter, arrange rice in a ring around the edge, leaving the center hollow. Arrange chicken in the hollow and garnish with almonds.

Southwestern-Style Chile Chicken with Wehani Rice

Bathed in a luscious sauce and served on a bed of robust red rice, perfectly braised chicken is home cooking at its finest. Complete this meal with warm tortillas and a tossed green salad.

Makes 8 servings

Tips

If you are using prepared stock, check the label to make sure it doesn't contain gluten.

Wehani rice, which is grown by Lundberg Family Farms, is one of my favorite varieties of rice. It is robust and chewy and is widely available in well-stocked supermarkets or natural foods stores. Bhutanese, Thai or Camargue red rice can be substituted, although the cooking times vary. If you prefer, cook the rice in a rice cooker.

Nutrient per serving

Calories	395
Protein	31.5 g
Carbohydrates	27.6 g
Fat (Total)	17.7 g
Saturated Fat	4.3 g
Monounsaturated Fat	8 g
Polyunsaturated Fat	3.5 g
Dietary Fiber	4 g
Sodium	305 mg
Cholesterol	85 mg

EXCELLENT SOURCE OF niacin and selenium.
GOOD SOURCE OF vitamin A, riboflavin, phosphorus, iron and magnesium.
SOURCE OF vitamins C and E (alpha-tocopherol), thiamine, folate, pantothenic acid, manganese, copper and zinc.
CONTAINS a high amount of dietary fiber.

3 cups	reduced-sodium chicken stock (see Tips, left), divided	750 mL
1 cup	Wehani rice, rinsed and drained (see Tips, left)	250 mL
4	dried ancho, mild New Mexico or guajillo chiles	4
2 cups	boiling water	500 mL
1 cup	packed coarsely chopped cilantro (stems and leaves)	250 mL
2 tbsp	red wine vinegar	30 mL
1 tbsp	extra virgin olive oil (approx.)	15 mL
3 lbs	skin-on bone-in chicken breasts, cut into serving-size pieces, rinsed and patted dry	1.5 kg
2	onions, finely chopped	2
4	cloves garlic, minced	4
1 tbsp	ground cumin (see Tips, right)	15 mL
1 tsp	dried oregano leaves, preferably Mexican	5 mL
1/2 tsp	cracked black peppercorns	2 mL
	Salt, optional	
	Finely chopped cilantro	

1. In a saucepan with a tight-fitting lid over medium–high heat, bring 2 cups (500 mL) of the stock to a boil. Add rice and stir well. Return to a rapid boil. Reduce heat to low (see Tips, right). Cover and cook until liquid is absorbed and rice is tender, about 45 minutes.

2. Meanwhile, in a heatproof bowl, soak dried chiles in boiling water for 30 minutes, weighing down with a cup to ensure they remain submerged. Drain, discarding soaking liquid and stems. Pat dry, chop finely and transfer to a blender. Add remaining 1 cup (250 mL) of stock, cilantro and vinegar. Purée and set aside.

3. Meanwhile, in a Dutch oven, heat oil over medium–high heat for 30 seconds. Add chicken, in batches, and cook, turning once, until skin is browned and crispy, about 10 minutes per batch, adding more oil, if necessary. Transfer to a plate and set aside. Drain off all but 1 tbsp (15 mL) fat from pan. Reduce heat to medium.

Tips

For the best flavor, toast and grind whole cumin seeds rather than buying ground cumin. Simply stir seeds in a dry skillet over medium heat until fragrant, about 3 minutes. Immediately transfer to a spice grinder or mortar and grind.

Unless you have a stove with a true simmer, after reducing the heat to low I recommend placing a heat diffuser under the pot to prevent the mixture from boiling.

4. Add onions to pan and cook, stirring, until softened, about 3 minutes. Add garlic, cumin, oregano and peppercorns and cook, stirring, for 1 minute. Stir in reserved chile mixture. Add salt to taste, if using. Return chicken to pan, skin side up, and spoon a little sauce over each piece. Reduce heat to low. Cover and simmer until chicken is no longer pink inside, about 30 minutes, turning the chicken over to cook in the sauce for the last 5 minutes of cooking.

5. *To serve:* On a deep platter, arrange rice in a ring around the edge, leaving the center hollow. Spoon chicken and sauce into the center and garnish with additional cilantro.

OLIVE OIL

I always use extra virgin olive oil when making salads because I love the flavor. I also love the fact that it is extremely good for you. Over the years, numerous studies have shown a link between the consumption of olive oil and a reduced rate of heart disease. Thus encouraged, the FDA allowed the following health claim in 2004: "Limited and not conclusive scientific evidence suggests that eating about 2 tablespoons (23 grams) of olive oil daily may reduce the risk of coronary heart disease due to the monounsaturated fat in olive oil. To achieve this possible benefit, olive oil is to replace a similar amount of saturated fat and not increase the total number of calories you eat in a day." But recent research suggests that olive oil does more than keep your heart healthy. Greek researchers have shown that it can help to keep your blood pressure under control and a study published in the *British Journal of Nutrition* linked the consumption of olive oil with improved bone health. Moreover, it's not just the monounsaturated fats that create health benefits. Olive oil is rich in oleic acid, which caused aggressive breast cancer cells to self-destruct in one laboratory study, and oleocanthal, a natural anti-inflammatory that acts like low-dose ibuprofen in the body. Researchers believe that keeping inflammation at bay may have multiple health benefits, such as reducing the risk of heart disease, stroke and certain types of cancer.

Italian-Style Chicken in White Wine with Olives and Polenta

This is a fairly straightforward recipe for chicken cooked in white wine, distinguished by the addition of fresh sage and sliced green olives, which add pleasant acidity to the sauce. Served over polenta, it makes a delicious one-dish meal.

Makes 8 servings

Tips

Have your butcher cut chicken breasts into quarters.

Corn flour is dried corn that has been ground into flour. It is available in natural foods stores. Check to make sure it has been produced in a gluten-free facility. Do not confuse it with cornstarch. In some parts of the world (not North America) cornstarch is called corn flour.

If you are using prepared stock, check the label to make sure it doesn't contain gluten.

Nutrient per serving

Calories	365
Protein	29.7 g
Carbohydrates	19.7 g
Fat (Total)	17.8 g
Saturated Fat	4.4 g
Monounsaturated Fat	8.6 g
Polyunsaturated Fat	3.5 g
Dietary Fiber	3.8 g
Sodium	498 mg
Cholesterol	85 mg

EXCELLENT SOURCE OF vitamin A, niacin, phosphorus and selenium.
GOOD SOURCE OF pantothenic acid, magnesium, manganese and zinc.
SOURCE OF vitamins C and E (alpha-tocopherol), riboflavin, thiamine, folate, iron and copper.
CONTAINS a moderate amount of dietary fiber.

- **Preheat oven to 350°F (180°C)**

1	batch Creamy Polenta (see Variations, page 183)	1
1 tbsp	olive oil	15 mL
3 lbs	skin-on bone-in chicken breasts, cut into serving-size pieces, rinsed and patted dry	1.5 kg
2	onions, finely chopped	2
2	carrots, peeled and diced	2
2	stalks celery, diced	2
2	cloves garlic, minced	2
2 tsp	dried Italian seasoning	10 mL
6	fresh sage leaves, chopped, or ½ tsp (2 mL) dried sage	6
½ tsp	freshly ground black pepper	2 mL
¼ tsp	cayenne pepper	1 mL
	Salt	
2 tbsp	corn flour (see Tips, left)	30 mL
1 cup	dry white wine	250 mL
1 cup	reduced-sodium chicken stock (see Tips, left)	250 mL
	Salt and freshly ground black pepper	
1 cup	sliced pitted green olives	250 mL
1 tbsp	freshly squeezed lemon juice	15 mL

1. In a Dutch oven, heat oil over medium heat for 30 seconds. Add chicken, in batches, and brown, turning once, about 6 minutes per batch. Transfer to a plate as completed and set aside.

2. Add onions, carrots and celery to pan and cook, stirring, until vegetables are softened, about 7 minutes. Add garlic, Italian seasoning, sage, black pepper, cayenne and salt to taste and cook, stirring, for 1 minute. Add corn flour and cook, stirring, until mixture congeals, for 1 minute. Add wine and stock and bring to a boil. Cook, stirring, until mixture thickens, about 3 minutes. Return chicken to pot. Cover and bake in preheated oven until chicken is no longer pink inside, about 45 minutes. Stir in olives and lemon juice.

3. *To serve:* Spread polenta over a deep platter and top with chicken and sauce.

Moroccan-Style Chicken Stew with Chickpeas and Rice

Chicken, lemon and olives are a classic Moroccan combination and are quite heavenly. This luscious stew, which is very easy to make, is a great dish for Sunday dinner or casual entertaining. It's a great one-dish meal, but you can add some sautéed bitter greens, such as rapini, or a tossed green salad. If you're a heat seeker, pass harissa at the table.

Makes 4 servings

Tips

When using any canned product, such as tomatoes or chicken stock, check the label to make sure ingredients containing gluten have not been added.

You can buy preserved lemons at Middle Eastern food stores. It's also very easy to make your own. If you don't have a preserved lemon, substitute 1 tbsp (15 mL) freshly squeezed lemon juice.

Nutrient per serving

Calories	348
Protein	27.7 g
Carbohydrates	40.3 g
Fat (Total)	9.3 g
Saturated Fat	1.5 g
Monounsaturated Fat	5.2 g
Polyunsaturated Fat	1.7 g
Dietary Fiber	6.4 g
Sodium	493 mg
Cholesterol	50 mg

EXCELLENT SOURCE OF niacin, folate, iron, magnesium, manganese, copper and selenium.
GOOD SOURCE OF vitamin E (alpha-tocopherol), thiamine, pantothenic acid, phosphorus and zinc.
SOURCE OF vitamins A and C, riboflavin and calcium.
CONTAINS a very high amount of dietary fiber.

2 cups	cooked short-grain brown rice (see cooking instructions, page 28)	500 mL
1 tbsp	olive oil	15 mL
2	onions, finely chopped	2
12 oz	skinless boneless chicken breasts or thighs, cut into 1/2-inch (1 cm) cubes	375 g
4	cloves garlic, minced	4
2 tbsp	minced gingerroot	30 mL
1 tbsp	turmeric	15 mL
1/2 tsp	freshly ground black pepper	2 mL
1	can (14 oz/398 mL) no-salt-added diced tomatoes with juice (see Tips, left)	1
1 cup	reduced-sodium chicken stock	250 mL
	Salt, optional	
1 cup	cooked chickpeas	250 mL
1	preserved lemon, rinsed and chopped (see Tips, left)	1
1/2 cup	pitted green olives, chopped	125 mL
	Harissa, optional (see below)	

1. In a large saucepan or Dutch oven, heat oil over medium–high heat for 30 seconds. Add onions and cook, stirring, until softened, about 3 minutes. Add chicken and cook, stirring, just until onions begin to turn golden, about 5 minutes. Add garlic, ginger, turmeric and pepper and cook, stirring, for 1 minute. Add tomatoes with juice and stock and bring to a boil. Add salt to taste, if using.

2. Stir in rice and chickpeas. Reduce heat to low. Cover and simmer until chicken is no longer pink inside and flavors meld, about 30 minutes. Stir in preserved lemon and simmer for 5 minutes. Garnish with olives. Pass harissa at the table, if using.

HARISSA

Harissa is a traditional North African chili paste, often added to soups or stews to add heat. Not all brands are gluten-free so check the label. If you don't have it, and crave a bit of fire, substitute your favorite hot pepper sauce.

Southwestern Turkey Stew with Cornmeal Dumplings

This stew captures the best of the Southwest — the seductive flavors of chiles, combined with luscious chunks of turkey in a tomato-based broth. Comforting cornmeal dumplings complete the theme.

Makes 6 servings

Tips

Check the label to make sure your chili powder doesn't contain gluten. Strictly speaking, it should be just a blend of spices.

Corn flour is finely ground cornmeal. Do not confuse it with cornstarch, which is a refined product, used in this case to lighten the dumplings.

Nutrient per serving	
Calories	302
Protein	23.8 g
Carbohydrates	34.9 g
Fat (Total)	8 g
Saturated Fat	1.6 g
Monounsaturated Fat	4.1 g
Polyunsaturated Fat	1.8 g
Dietary Fiber	5 g
Sodium	687 mg
Cholesterol	42 mg

EXCELLENT SOURCE OF niacin, phosphorus and manganese.
GOOD SOURCE OF riboflavin, zinc, iron, magnesium and calcium.
SOURCE OF vitamins A, C and E (alpha-tocopherol), pantothenic acid, thiamine, folate, copper and selenium.
CONTAINS a high amount of dietary fiber.

1 tbsp	olive oil	15 mL
2	onions, finely chopped	2
4	stalks celery, chopped	4
4	cloves garlic, minced	4
1	jalapeño pepper, seeded and minced	1
1	chipotle pepper in adobo sauce, minced (see Tips, page 127)	1
1 tbsp	chili powder (see Tips, left)	15 mL
½ tsp	cracked black peppercorns	2 mL
1 lb	skinless boneless turkey breast, cut into ½-inch (1 cm) cubes	500 g
2 tbsp	corn flour (see Tips, left)	30 mL
1	can (14 oz/398 mL) no-salt-added diced tomatoes with juice	1
2½ cups	reduced-sodium chicken stock (see Tips, page 114)	625 mL
2 cups	sliced green beans	500 mL
DUMPLINGS		
¾ cup	stone-ground cornmeal	175 mL
⅓ cup	sorghum flour	75 mL
1 tbsp	cornstarch	15 mL
2 tsp	gluten-free baking powder	10 mL
½ tsp	salt	2 mL
1 cup	buttermilk	250 mL
1 tbsp	olive oil	15 mL

1. In a skillet, heat oil over medium heat for 30 seconds. Add onions and celery and cook, stirring, until celery softens, about 5 minutes. Add garlic, jalapeño and chipotle peppers, chili powder and peppercorns and cook, stirring, for 1 minute. Add turkey and cook, stirring, until surface whitens, about 2 minutes. Add corn flour and cook, stirring, for 1 minute. Add tomatoes with juice and stock and bring to a boil. Reduce heat to low and simmer, stirring occasionally, until flavors meld, about 15 minutes. Stir in green beans.

2. *Dumplings:* In a bowl, combine cornmeal, sorghum flour, cornstarch, baking powder and salt. Make a well in the center. In a measuring cup, combine buttermilk and oil, mixing well. Pour into well and stir just until mixture is evenly moistened. Ensure stew is at a simmer and drop dough by heaping tablespoons (15 mL) onto simmering liquid. Cover tightly and steam until dumplings are puffed and tender, about 20 minutes.

Turkey Cutlets in Gingery Lemon Gravy with Cranberry Rice

Delicious and easy to make, this is a great weeknight dinner so long as you allow time for cooking the rice. It's hard to believe that anything so flavorful is so easy to make. The cranberries and the hint of orange complement the nutty, slightly earthy flavor of the rice, and the luscious lemon ginger gravy unites it all. To complete the meal, the only thing you need is a steamed vegetable, such as green beans or carrots.

Makes 4 servings

Tips

If you are using prepared stock, check the label to make sure it doesn't contain gluten.

If you prefer a bit of heat, use hot rather than sweet paprika when dredging the turkey.

Nutrient Tip

In addition to adding flavor to the gravy, the ginger in this recipe is very good for your digestion.

Nutrient per serving

Calories	374
Protein	23.5 g
Carbohydrates	42.3 g
Fat (Total)	12.6 g
Saturated Fat	3.5 g
Monounsaturated Fat	6.8 g
Polyunsaturated Fat	1.7 g
Dietary Fiber	2.8 g
Sodium	233 mg
Cholesterol	51 mg

EXCELLENT SOURCE OF niacin, phosphorus, magnesium and manganese.

GOOD SOURCE OF zinc and selenium.

SOURCE OF vitamins A, C and E (alpha-tocopherol), thiamine, riboflavin, folate, pantothenic acid, iron and copper.

CONTAINS a moderate amount of dietary fiber.

CRANBERRY RICE

1¼ cups	water or reduced-sodium chicken stock (see Tips, left)	300 mL
2 tbsp	freshly squeezed orange juice	30 mL
¾ cup	long-grain brown rice, rinsed and drained	175 mL
⅓ cup	dried cranberries	75 mL
1 tsp	grated orange zest	5 mL

TURKEY CUTLETS

2 tbsp	sorghum flour	30 mL
1 tbsp	cornstarch	15 mL
1 tsp	paprika	5 mL
½ tsp	freshly ground black pepper	2 mL
4	turkey cutlets (about 12 oz/375 g in total)	4
2 tbsp	olive oil, divided	30 mL
1 tbsp	butter, divided	15 mL
2	cloves garlic, minced	2
1 tbsp	minced gingerroot	15 mL
1 cup	reduced-sodium chicken stock	250 mL
1 tbsp	freshly squeezed lemon juice	15 mL

1. *Cranberry Rice:* In a heavy saucepan with a tight-fitting lid over medium heat, bring water and orange juice to a boil. Stir in rice and return to a boil. Reduce heat to low. Cover and simmer until rice is tender and water has been absorbed, about 50 minutes. Remove from heat and fluff with a fork. Stir in cranberries and orange zest and keep warm.

2. *Turkey Cutlets:* On a plate or in a plastic bag, combine sorghum flour, cornstarch, paprika and pepper. Add turkey and toss until well coated with mixture. Reserve any excess.

3. In a large skillet, heat 1 tbsp (15 mL) of the oil and 1½ tsp (7 mL) of the butter over medium–high heat until butter has melted. Add 2 cutlets and cook until browned, about 2 minutes. Turn and cook until no longer pink inside, about 2 minutes more. Transfer to a warm platter and keep warm. Repeat with remaining cutlets, oil and butter. Reduce heat to medium.

4. Add garlic and ginger to pan and cook, stirring, for 1 minute. Add reserved flour mixture and cook, stirring, for 1 minute. Add stock, lemon juice and any turkey juices that have accumulated on the platter and cook, stirring, until thickened, about 2 minutes. Pour over cutlets. Serve on a bed of Cranberry Rice.

Variation

Chicken Cutlets in Gingery Lemon Gravy with Cranberry Rice: Substitute an equal quantity of chicken cutlets for the turkey.

TURKEY

Turkey is one of the best sources of complete protein because once the skin is removed, it is a very lean meat. In addition to being protein rich, turkey is also a good source of important B vitamins — niacin, B_6 and B_{12} — as well as zinc, an immune system protector that can be challenging to obtain from dietary sources. The body can utilize the zinc in turkey and other meats more readily than that from non-meat sources. Turkey is also a good source of the trace mineral selenium, an antioxidant that supports a number of bodily functions. Research indicates that selenium intake may reduce the risk of coronary artery disease and protect the body from prostate, colorectal and lung cancers. However, a recent study published in the *Annals of Internal Medicine* found that taking selenium supplements actually increased the risk of developing Type-2 diabetes. Since recent evidence suggests that taking antioxidants as supplements may not have positive health benefits, the safest strategy is to focus on obtaining these phytonutrients by eating nutrient dense whole foods.

Black Rice

Fish and Seafood

Salmon and Wild Rice Cakes with Avocado-Chili Topping

With the addition of a big salad or an abundance of veggies, these tasty burgers make a light weeknight meal. For convenience, cook the rice ahead. The salmon mixture is quickly assembled.

Makes 4 servings (see Tips, below)

Tips

With additions such as salad, one burger makes a light meal for most people. However, hungry people might want an extra half or whole one.

I prefer to leave the salmon bones in as they add calcium, but if you prefer, remove them.

Tamari is a type of soy sauce that shouldn't contain wheat.

When mixed, the cakes are very wet and not easily shaped into patties. However, they dry out and solidify quickly on cooking.

Nutrients per serving

Calories	279
Protein	15.3 g
Carbohydrates	21.1 g
Fat (Total)	15.6 g
Saturated Fat	2.7 g
Monounsaturated Fat	9 g
Polyunsaturated Fat	2.5 g
Dietary Fiber	4.9 g
Sodium	559 mg
Cholesterol	66 mg

EXCELLENT SOURCE OF niacin, manganese and selenium.
GOOD SOURCE OF vitamin E (alpha-tocopherol), folate, riboflavin, pantothenic acid, phosphorus, magnesium and zinc.
SOURCE OF vitamins A and C, thiamine, calcium, iron and copper.
CONTAINS a high amount of dietary fiber.

1½ cups	cooked brown and wild rice mixture, cooled	375 mL
1	can (7.5 oz/213 g) salmon, drained (see Tips, left)	1
1	egg	1
4	green onions, white part only with a bit of green, chopped	4
1 tbsp	gluten-free soy sauce (see Tips, left)	15 mL
	Freshly ground black pepper	
1 tbsp	olive oil	15 mL

AVOCADO-CHILI TOPPING

1	avocado, mashed	1
1 tbsp	freshly squeezed lemon juice	15 mL
¼ tsp	salt	1 mL
	Freshly ground black pepper	
½ tsp	Asian chili sauce, such as sambal oelek	2 mL

1. In a food processor, combine salmon, egg, green onions, soy sauce and pepper to taste. Process until smooth. Add rice and pulse to blend.

2. In a skillet, heat oil over medium heat for 30 seconds. Using a large spoon, drop salmon mixture into the pan in 4 blobs (see Tips, left). Cook until crispy outside and hot in the center, about 5 minutes per side.

3. *Avocado-Chili Topping:* Meanwhile, in a bowl, combine avocado, lemon juice, salt, pepper to taste and Asian chili sauce. Mix well.

4. Serve burgers warm with a large dollop of Avocado–Chili Topping.

PAN-FRIED FISH

If, like me, you enjoy a piece of fresh-caught fish, pan-fried, but can no longer tolerate it being dredged in flour, here is the perfect gluten-free solution. Simply mix together 3 parts sorghum flour and 1 part cornstarch. Dredge fish fillets in the mixture and skillet-fry in oil or clarified butter. The result will be as delicious as any traditional renditions you remember.

Indonesian-Style Shrimp Fried Rice

Serve this one-dish meal when you're in the mood for a slightly different weekday dinner. The shrimp chips are a fun and flavorful addition that should be prepared before you start the dish. Although the fried egg adds cholesterol, in my opinion, it really enhances the dish.

Makes 4 servings

Tips

Indonesian shrimp chips are available in Asian markets. They should be made from rice flour and be gluten-free, but check the label. When deep-fried, they puff up, adding flavor and texture to the fried rice.

Ketjap manis is available in Asian markets. Check the label to make sure it is gluten-free. If you can't find it, use 1 tbsp (15 mL) gluten-free soy sauce combined with 1 tbsp (15 mL) pure maple syrup in this recipe.

Nutrients per serving

Calories	415
Protein	28.7 g
Carbohydrates	39.7 g
Fat (Total)	15.2 g
Saturated Fat	2.6 g
Monounsaturated Fat	7.5 g
Polyunsaturated Fat	4 g
Dietary Fiber	3.1 g
Sodium	490 mg
Cholesterol	352 mg

EXCELLENT SOURCE OF niacin, phosphorus, iron, magnesium, manganese, zinc and selenium.
GOOD SOURCE OF vitamins A and E (alpha-tocopherol), thiamine, riboflavin, folate, pantothenic acid and copper.
SOURCE OF vitamin C and calcium.
CONTAINS a moderate amount of dietary fiber.

FRIED SHRIMP CHIPS, OPTIONAL

	Oil for deep-frying	
	Shrimp chips (see Tips, left)	
3 cups	cooked long-grain brown rice, cooled (see cooking instructions, page 28)	750 mL
2 tbsp	oil (approx.)	30 mL
12 oz	shrimp, peeled and deveined, thawed if frozen	375 g
4	eggs	4
	Salt and freshly ground black pepper	
2 tsp	Thai red curry paste (see Tips, page 150)	10 mL
2 cups	shredded Napa cabbage	500 mL
2 tbsp	ketjap manis (see Tips, left)	30 mL
4	green onions, white part with a bit of green, thinly sliced	4

1. *Fried Shrimp Chips (optional):* In a wok or saucepan, pour oil to about a 1-inch (2.5 cm) depth and heat until hot but not smoking. (If the oil is too hot, the chips will curl up and cook unevenly.) Add shrimp chips, 2 at a time, and fry, turning constantly with tongs, until they are puffed all over, about 20 seconds. Transfer to a paper towel to drain.

2. In a wok or a skillet, heat 1 tbsp (15 mL) of the oil over medium-high heat for 30 seconds. Add shrimp and cook, stirring, until they turn pink and opaque, 3 to 5 minutes. Transfer to a plate. Add remaining 1 tbsp (15 mL) oil to the pan and heat just until hot but not smoking. Break an egg into the pan and season lightly with salt and pepper. Cook until edges begin to brown. Then, using a spatula, flip and continue cooking until the yolk sets, about 1 minute. Transfer to plate and repeat until all eggs are cooked. Remove wok from heat and let cool for 1 to 2 minutes.

3. Reduce heat to low. Return cooled wok to heat, adding a bit more oil, if necessary, and add curry paste. Cook, stirring, until fragrant and paste begins to separate from oil, about 5 minutes. Add cabbage and stir well until coated. Using your fingers to break up any clusters, add rice to wok. Cook, stirring constantly, until thoroughly coated with curry–cabbage mixture. Add shrimp and cook, stirring, until heated through. Add ketjap manis and stir well. Garnish with green onions.

4. *To serve:* Spoon rice onto plates and top each serving with a fried egg. Serve shrimp chips alongside, if using.

Saffron-Scented Shrimp with Chile Rice

This dish has so much going for it, it's hard to believe it's so easy to make. Stir-fried shrimp, in a creamy sauce with a hint of saffron, are surrounded by a ring of slightly spicy rice. A garnish of toasted almonds adds texture and completes the visual effect.

Makes 6 servings

Tip

Coconut milk should be a healthy product that is suitable for people who are allergic to gluten. However, some brands contain guar gum, which although it does not contain gluten, is not recommended for people with celiac disease. Also the product may be processed in a facility where gluten is present. Check the label and, if necessary, follow up with the manufacturer.

Nutrients per serving

Calories	377
Protein	21.9 g
Carbohydrates	41.1 g
Fat (Total)	15.1 g
Saturated Fat	6.3 g
Monounsaturated Fat	4.9 g
Polyunsaturated Fat	2.9 g
Dietary Fiber	5.7 g
Sodium	412 mg
Cholesterol	147 mg

EXCELLENT SOURCE OF niacin, phosphorus, iron, magnesium, manganese, copper and selenium.

GOOD SOURCE OF vitamins A, C and E (alpha-tocopherol), thiamine, folate and zinc.

SOURCE OF riboflavin, pantothenic acid and calcium.

CONTAINS a high amount of dietary fiber.

1	batch Chile Rice (see recipe, page 176)	1
2 tbsp	olive oil, divided	30 mL
1 tbsp	minced gingerroot	15 mL
1 tsp	turmeric	5 mL
1 lb	shrimp, peeled and deveined, thawed if frozen	500 g
	Freshly ground black pepper	
1	onion, finely chopped	1
2	cloves garlic, minced	2
1	long green or red chile, seeded and minced	1
1	stick cinnamon, about 2 inches (5 cm) long	1
4	green cardamom pods, crushed	4
½ tsp	salt	2 mL
⅛ tsp	crumbled saffron threads, dissolved in 2 tbsp (30 mL) boiling water	0.5 mL
¾ cup	coconut milk (see Tip, left)	175 mL
	Toasted slivered almonds	

1. In a skillet, heat 1 tbsp (15 mL) of the oil over medium–high heat for 30 seconds. Add ginger and turmeric and stir well. Add shrimp and cook, stirring, until they turn pink and opaque, 3 to 5 minutes. Season to taste with pepper. Transfer to a plate and set aside.

2. Reduce heat to medium. Add remaining 1 tbsp (15 mL) of oil to pan. Add onion and cook, stirring, until softened, about 3 minutes. Add garlic, chile, cinnamon, cardamom and salt and cook, stirring, for 1 minute. Add saffron liquid and coconut milk and bring to a boil. Reduce heat and simmer until flavors meld, about 5 minutes. Stir in reserved shrimp and cook until heated through, about 2 minutes.

3. *To serve:* On a deep platter, arrange rice in a ring around the edge, leaving the center hollow. Pour shrimp mixture into the hollow and garnish with toasted almonds. Serve immediately.

Mussels in Spicy Lemongrass Broth with Chinese Black Rice

This dish was inspired by a favorite recipe from New World Noodles *by Bill Jones and Stephen Wong. If you're organized, you can make this for a great weeknight dinner. Prepare the broth and rice ahead of time and refrigerate overnight. Just add a salad, such as sliced tomatoes tossed in vinaigrette. If you're entertaining, this makes a smashing first course for as many as eight people.*

Makes 4 servings

Tips

To cook Chinese black rice, bring 1¾ cups (425 mL) water to a rapid boil. Stir in 1 cup (250 mL) rice and return to a rapid boil. Reduce heat to low and simmer until rice is tender and water is absorbed, about 30 minutes. Remove from heat and let stand, covered, for 5 minutes.

For convenience, cook the broth to the 25-minute mark in Step 2 and refrigerate for up to 2 days. The flavors will improve with standing. Strain out the solids and reheat broth when you're ready to finish the dish.

Nutrients per serving	
Calories	254
Protein	12.1 g
Carbohydrates	38 g
Fat (Total)	6 g
Saturated Fat	0.6 g
Monounsaturated Fat	2.5 g
Polyunsaturated Fat	1.5 g
Dietary Fiber	0.3 g
Sodium	150 mg
Cholesterol	19 mg

EXCELLENT SOURCE OF iron, manganese and selenium.
GOOD SOURCE OF niacin, thiamine, folate and phosphorus.
SOURCE OF vitamins A, C and E (alpha-tocopherol), riboflavin, pantothenic acid, magnesium, copper and zinc.

2 cups	cooked Chinese black rice (see Tips, left)	500 mL
1 tbsp	olive oil	15 mL
1	onion, chopped	1
2	cloves garlic, minced	2
1 tbsp	minced gingerroot	15 mL
2 tsp	coriander seeds	10 mL
1	stick cinnamon, about 2 inches (5 cm) long	1
2	stalks lemongrass, coarsely chopped	2
½ tsp	cracked black peppercorns	2 mL
¼ tsp	hot pepper flakes	1 mL
¼ cup	tomato paste (see Tips, 140)	60 mL
4 cups	reduced-sodium vegetable stock (see Tip, page 126)	1 L
2 lbs	mussels, cleaned	1 kg
	Finely chopped cilantro	

1. In a large saucepan, heat oil over medium heat for 30 seconds. Add onion and cook, stirring, until softened, about 3 minutes. Add garlic, ginger, coriander seeds, cinnamon stick, lemongrass, peppercorns and hot pepper flakes and cook, stirring, for 1 minute. Add tomato paste and stock and bring to a boil. Reduce heat to low. Cover and simmer until flavors meld, about 25 minutes (see Tips, left). Strain through a fine mesh strainer and, to maximize the flavor, gently press out the liquid using a wooden spoon. Discard solids.

2. Transfer strained broth to a large saucepan and bring to a boil. Add cooked rice and mussels. Cover and cook until mussels open. Discard any that do not open. Ladle mussels and broth into bowls. Garnish with cilantro and serve.

Variation

Substitute any non-glutinous rice for the Chinese black rice. Italian Black Venere, Kalijira brown or long-grain brown rice would work well in this recipe.

Salmon Stew with Corn and Quinoa

This tasty stew is easy to make and, with the addition of licorice-flavored Pernod, has a uniquely sophisticated flavor. Add a simple green salad to expand the range of nutrients and bump up the amount of fiber you consume.

Makes 8 servings

Nutrient Tip

Salmon is one of the best sources of omega-3 fatty acids, which are essential to good health. Studies show that an adequate supply of omega-3 fatty acids can reduce the risk of coronary artery disease, slightly lower blood pressure and strengthen the immune system, among other benefits.

Nutrients per serving

Calories	373
Protein	24.1 g
Carbohydrates	26.5 g
Fat (Total)	18.6 g
Saturated Fat	5.8 g
Monounsaturated Fat	6.7 g
Polyunsaturated Fat	4.4 g
Dietary Fiber	2.8 g
Sodium	488 mg
Cholesterol	67 mg

EXCELLENT SOURCE OF thiamine, niacin, folate, pantothenic acid, phosphorus, magnesium, manganese and selenium.
GOOD SOURCE OF riboflavin, iron, zinc and copper.
SOURCE OF vitamins A, C and E (alpha-tocopherol) and calcium.
CONTAINS a moderate amount of dietary fiber.

1 tbsp	olive oil	15 mL
2 tbsp	finely chopped pancetta or bacon	30 mL
3	leeks, white part only, cleaned and thinly sliced (see Tips, page 70)	3
1/2 tsp	dried thyme leaves	2 mL
1/2 tsp	cayenne pepper	2 mL
1	bay leaf	1
1/2 tsp	salt	2 mL
1 cup	dry white wine	250 mL
6 cups	fish stock or 3 cups (750 mL) bottled clam juice diluted with 3 cups (750 mL) water	1.5 L
2 cups	corn kernels	500 mL
1 cup	quinoa, rinsed and drained (see Tips, page 136)	250 mL
1 1/2 lbs	salmon fillets, skin removed and cut into 1-inch (2.5 cm) pieces	750 g
1/2 cup	heavy or whipping (35%) cream or half-and-half (10%) cream	125 mL
1/4 cup	Pernod, optional	60 mL
1/2 cup	finely chopped chives	125 mL

1. In a Dutch oven, heat oil over medium heat for 30 seconds. Add pancetta and cook, stirring, until it begins to brown, about 3 minutes. (If you're using bacon, cook until crisp and drain off all but 1 tbsp/15 mL fat from pan before proceeding with recipe.)

2. Reduce heat to medium. Add leeks and cook, stirring, until softened, about 5 minutes. Add thyme, cayenne, bay leaf and salt and cook, stirring, for 1 minute. Add wine, bring to boil and boil until reduced by half, about 5 minutes. Add stock and corn and return to a boil. Stir in quinoa. Reduce heat to low. Cover and cook until quinoa is almost tender, about 15 minutes.

3. Add salmon and simmer until opaque and flakes easily with a fork, about 6 minutes. Stir in whipping cream and cook until heated through, about 2 minutes. Stir in Pernod, if using. Garnish with chives.

Peppery Shrimp with Quinoa

Quinoa cooked with tomatoes, onion, a bell pepper and a bit of saffron provides a bed for sautéed shrimp in this elegant dish. Simple and delicious, this is easy enough to serve on weeknights.

Makes 4 servings

Tip

When using any canned product, such as tomatoes or vegetable stock, check the label to make sure ingredients containing gluten have not been added.

Nutrient Tip

North Americans consume too much salt, largely because most of it (77%) is hidden in processed foods and restaurant meals. That's why I recommend using canned tomatoes with no salt added and reduced-sodium stocks or, even better, making your own with no salt added.

Nutrients per serving	
Calories	355
Protein	25.8 g
Carbohydrates	37.4 g
Fat (Total)	10.2 g
Saturated Fat	1.4 g
Monounsaturated Fat	5.7 g
Polyunsaturated Fat	1.9 g
Dietary Fiber	5.9 g
Sodium	240 mg
Cholesterol	166 mg

EXCELLENT SOURCE OF vitamins A and C, niacin, phosphorus, iron, manganese, magnesium, copper and selenium.
GOOD SOURCE OF vitamin E (alpha-tocopherol), thiamine, folate and zinc.
SOURCE OF riboflavin, pantothenic acid and calcium.
CONTAINS a high amount of dietary fiber.

2 tbsp	olive oil, divided	30 mL
1	onion, diced	1
1	green bell pepper, seeded and diced	1
¼ tsp	crumbled saffron threads, dissolved in 2 tbsp (30 mL) boiling water	1 mL
½ cup	water or reduced-sodium vegetable stock	125 mL
1	can (14 oz/398 mL) no-salt-added diced tomatoes with juice (see Tip, left)	1
¾ cup	quinoa, rinsed and drained	175 mL
12 oz	shrimp, peeled and deveined, thawed if frozen	375 g
4	cloves garlic, minced	4
1 tsp	finely grated lemon zest	5 mL
¼ tsp	cayenne pepper	1 mL
	Freshly ground black pepper	
½ cup	dry white wine	125 mL
2 tbsp	freshly squeezed lemon juice	30 mL
1 cup	cooked green peas	250 mL
	Salt, optional	

1. In a saucepan, heat 1 tbsp (15 mL) of the oil over medium heat for 30 seconds. Add onion and bell pepper and cook, stirring, until softened, about 5 minutes. Add saffron liquid, water and tomatoes with juice and bring to a boil. Stir in quinoa. Reduce heat to low. Cover and cook until quinoa is tender, about 15 minutes. Remove from heat and let stand, covered, for 5 minutes. Fluff with a fork.

2. In a skillet, heat remaining 1 tbsp (15 mL) of oil over medium–high heat. Add shrimp and cook, stirring, just until they turn pink and opaque, 3 to 5 minutes. Add garlic, lemon zest, cayenne and black pepper to taste. Cook, stirring, for 1 minute. Add white wine and lemon juice and bring to a boil. Stir in peas until heated through. Season to taste with salt, if using.

3. *To serve:* On a deep platter, arrange quinoa in a ring around the edge, leaving the center hollow. Arrange shrimp in the center.

Variation

Peppery Shrimp with Millet: Substitute an equal quantity of millet for the quinoa. For the best flavor, before using in the recipe toast the rinsed millet in a dry skillet, stirring until fragrant, about 5 minutes. Stir the millet into tomato mixture (Step 1) and return to a boil. Cover and simmer over low heat for 20 minutes, then remove from heat and let stand for 10 minutes.

Peppery Quinoa Stew with Corn and Crispy Snapper

This zesty stew is chock-full of lip-smacking flavor. It's a meal-in-a-bowl, although you may want to add some gluten-free bread to soak up the tasty broth.

Makes 6 servings

Tips

Chipotle peppers are dried smoked jalapeño peppers. Not all brands of chipotle peppers in abodo sauce are gluten-free so be sure to check the label.

Chipotle peppers pack a lot of wallop. If you're not a heat seeker, err on the side of caution and use half of one here. You can always add a little hot sauce if you find the result too tame.

Nutrients per serving

Calories	340
Protein	29.6 g
Carbohydrates	37.9 g
Fat (Total)	8.3 g
Saturated Fat	1.2 g
Monounsaturated Fat	4.2 g
Polyunsaturated Fat	1.9 g
Dietary Fiber	4.8 g
Sodium	103 mg
Cholesterol	42 mg

EXCELLENT SOURCE OF vitamin C, phosphorus, iron, magnesium, manganese and selenium.

GOOD SOURCE OF vitamins A and E (alpha-tocopherol), thiamine, niacin, folate, pantothenic acid, copper and zinc.

SOURCE OF riboflavin and calcium.

CONTAINS a high amount of dietary fiber.

2 tbsp	olive oil, divided	30 mL
2	onions, finely chopped	2
4	stalks celery, diced	4
1	red bell pepper, seeded and chopped	1
1	green bell pepper, seeded and chopped	1
2	cloves garlic, minced	2
2 tsp	ground cumin (see Tips, page 111)	10 mL
1 tsp	dried oregano leaves	5 mL
	Salt and freshly ground black pepper	
½ to 1	chipotle pepper in adobo sauce, minced (see Tips, left)	½ to 1
4 cups	reduced-sodium vegetable or chicken stock	1 L
1	can (14 oz/398 mL) no-salt-added diced tomatoes with juice (see Tip, page 126)	1
1 cup	corn kernels	250 mL
1 cup	quinoa, rinsed and drained	250 mL
3 tbsp	sorghum flour	45 mL
1 tbsp	cornstarch	15 mL
1 tsp	chili powder	5 mL
1½ lbs	skinless snapper or other firm white fish fillets, cut into 1-inch (2.5 cm) cubes	750 g
	Finely chopped cilantro	

1. In a stockpot, heat 1 tbsp (15 mL) of the oil over medium heat. Add onions, celery, bell peppers and garlic and stir well. Reduce heat to low. Cover and cook until vegetables are softened, about 10 minutes. Increase heat to medium. Add cumin, oregano, and salt and black pepper to taste and cook, stirring, for 1 minute. Add chipotle pepper, stock, tomatoes with juice and corn and bring to a boil. Stir in quinoa. Reduce heat to low. Cover and simmer until quinoa is tender, about 15 minutes. Remove from heat and set aside.

2. On a plate or in a plastic bag, combine sorghum flour, cornstarch and chili powder. Add snapper and roll until coated. Discard excess flour. In a skillet, heat remaining 1 tbsp (15 mL) of oil over medium–high heat for 30 seconds. Add dredged snapper and sauté until fish is nicely browned on both sides and cooked to desired doneness, about 4 minutes.

3. *To serve:* Ladle stew into soup plates and layer snapper on top. Garnish with cilantro.

Mexican-Style Seafood Stew with Hominy

This rustic dish has an abundance of flavors that combine in intriguing ways. The chiles add depth with a hint of heat, and the hominy and clams add robustness. I like to finish this with a garnish of avocado cubes drizzled with lime juice, which inserts creaminess and a hit of acidity into the mix.

Makes 6 servings

Tips

Fish stock provides the best flavor base, but you can substitute an equal quantity of vegetable stock or equal parts bottled clam juice and water.

If you prefer, use 1½ cups (375 mL) drained home-cooked hominy. For soaking and cooking instructions, see page 18.

If using the avocado, cut it a few minutes ahead and toss with about 1 tbsp (15 mL) lime juice, which will prevent browning.

Nutrients per serving	
Calories	219
Protein	25.8 g
Carbohydrates	15.5 g
Fat (Total)	5.9 g
Saturated Fat	1 g
Monounsaturated Fat	2.4 g
Polyunsaturated Fat	1.4 g
Dietary Fiber	3.3 g
Sodium	480 mg
Cholesterol	66 mg

EXCELLENT SOURCE OF niacin, iron, folate, phosphorus, manganese and selenium.
GOOD SOURCE OF vitamin A, riboflavin, pantothenic acid, magnesium, zinc and copper.
SOURCE OF vitamins C and E (alpha-tocopherol), thiamine and calcium.
CONTAINS a moderate amount of dietary fiber.

2	dried ancho, guajillo or mild New Mexico chiles	2
1 cup	packed cilantro leaves	250 mL
4 cups	fish stock, divided (see Tips, left)	1 L
1 tbsp	olive oil	15 mL
2	onions, finely chopped	2
3	cloves garlic, minced	3
1 tsp	ground cumin	5 mL
1 tsp	dried oregano leaves, preferably Mexican	5 mL
1	can (14 oz/398 mL) diced tomatoes with juice	1
1	can (15 oz/412 mL) hominy, drained and rinsed (see Tips, left)	1
	Salt and freshly ground black pepper	
12	clams, thoroughly scrubbed and rinsed	12
12 oz	skinless snapper fillets or other firm white fish, cut into bite-size pieces	375 g
6 oz	medium shrimp, peeled and deveined	175 g
	Finely chopped cilantro	
	Avocado cubes, optional (see Tips, left)	
	Lime wedges	

1. In a heatproof bowl, soak chiles in boiling water for 30 minutes, weighing down with a cup to ensure they remain submerged. Drain, discarding soaking liquid and stems, and chop coarsely. Transfer to a blender. Add cilantro and 1 cup (250 mL) of the stock. Purée and set aside.

2. In a large saucepan or stockpot, heat oil over medium heat for 30 seconds. Add onions and cook, stirring, until softened, about 3 minutes. Add garlic, cumin and oregano and cook, stirring, for 1 minute. Add tomatoes with juice, reserved chile mixture, remaining stock and hominy. Season to taste with salt and pepper and bring to a boil. Reduce heat to low. Cover and simmer until flavors meld, about 30 minutes.

3. Increase heat to medium–high. Return mixture to a full boil. Add clams. Cover and cook, shaking the pot, until all the clams open, about 5 minutes. Discard any that do not open. Add snapper and shrimp and cook, stirring, until fish is tender and shrimp turn pink and are cooked through, 3 to 5 minutes.

4. *To serve:* Ladle stew into soup plates. Garnish with cilantro and avocado, if using. Pass lime wedges at the table.

Mexican-Style Millet and Shrimp

If you're tired of simple stir-fries, try this for a welcome change of pace. The millet pilaf, lightly flavored with chipotle pepper, forms a bed for tasty stir-fried shrimp bathed in gently warmed tomatoes and avocado, and finished with a liberal sprinkling of cilantro.

Nutrient Tip

Although avocados are high in calories, ounce for ounce, they are extremely nutritious. Moreover, avocados help your body make better use of antioxidants, such as the lycopene in tomatoes. For instance, one recent study showed that when avocado was added to tomato salsa, lycopene absorption was increased by 4.4 times.

1 cup	millet, rinsed and drained	250 mL
2 tbsp	olive oil, divided	30 mL
1	onion, diced	1
4	cloves garlic, minced	4
1 tsp	dried oregano leaves, preferably Mexican	5 mL
	Freshly ground black pepper	
½ to 1	chipotle pepper in adobo sauce, minced	½ to 1
2 cups	reduced-sodium vegetable or chicken stock	500 mL
½ cup	water	125 mL
1 lb	shrimp, peeled and deveined, thawed if frozen	500 g
2 cups	diced tomatoes	500 mL
2 tbsp	freshly squeezed lime juice	30 mL
1	avocado, diced	1
	Salt	
¼ cup	finely chopped cilantro	60 mL

1. In a saucepan over medium heat, toast millet, stirring constantly, until it crackles and releases its aroma, about 5 minutes. Transfer to a bowl and set aside.

2. In same saucepan, heat 1 tbsp (15 mL) of the oil over medium heat for 30 seconds. Add onion and cook, stirring, until softened, about 3 minutes. Add garlic, oregano and black pepper to taste and cook, stirring, for 1 minute. Add chipotle pepper and stir well. Add stock and water and bring to a boil. Stir in millet. Return to a boil. Reduce heat to low. Cover tightly and simmer until liquid is absorbed, about 25 minutes. Set aside. Just before you're ready to serve, fluff millet with a fork and spread over a deep platter.

3. In a wok, heat remaining 1 tbsp (15 mL) of the oil over medium–high heat for 30 seconds. Add shrimp and cook, stirring, until they turn pink and opaque, 2 to 5 minutes. Using tongs, arrange shrimp over top of millet. Add tomatoes and lime juice to pan and toss well. Add avocado and cook until heated through. Season to taste with salt and pepper. Arrange mixture over shrimp and garnish with cilantro.

Variation

Mexican-Style Quinoa and Shrimp: Substitute an equal quantity of quinoa for the millet. Omit water and reduce cooking time to about 20 minutes.

Nutrients per serving

Calories	319
Protein	21.1 g
Carbohydrates	33.6 g
Fat (Total)	11.5 g
Saturated Fat	1.8 g
Monounsaturated Fat	7 g
Polyunsaturated Fat	2 g
Dietary Fiber	6.5 g
Sodium	185 mg
Cholesterol	147 mg

EXCELLENT SOURCE OF niacin, iron, magnesium, manganese and selenium.
GOOD SOURCE OF vitamin E (alpha-tocopherol), folate, thiamine, zinc, phosphorus and copper.
SOURCE OF vitamins A and C, riboflavin, pantothenic acid and calcium.
CONTAINS a very high amount of dietary fiber.

Job's Tears

Meat

Beef Biriyani

This is a classic Indian dish made with layers of basmati rice, a curry filling and yogurt. It makes a large quantity and is perfect to add interest to a buffet. If you're cooking for your family, it's a great Sunday dinner with the addition of puréed spinach or a salad. Don't be daunted by the quantity if you're cooking for fewer people — just cut the recipe in half.

Makes 10 servings

Tips

I prefer to toast and grind cumin and coriander seeds myself and it produces better flavor. However, if you prefer, you can substitute 2 tsp (10 mL) ground cumin and 1½ tsp (7 mL) ground coriander and skip the toasting.

Check to make sure your curry powder doesn't contain gluten. Some blends may contain wheat or are processed in a facility where wheat is present, thus being potentially contaminated.

Nutrients per serving

Calories	361
Protein	26.7 g
Carbohydrates	39.1 g
Fat (Total)	10.5 g
Saturated Fat	3.6 g
Monounsaturated Fat	4.3 g
Polyunsaturated Fat	0.9 g
Dietary Fiber	3.4 g
Sodium	219 mg
Cholesterol	49 mg

EXCELLENT SOURCE OF niacin, phosphorus, magnesium, manganese and zinc.
GOOD SOURCE OF riboflavin, thiamine, pantothenic acid and iron.
SOURCE OF vitamins A and C, folate, calcium and copper.
CONTAINS a moderate amount of dietary fiber.

MARINADE

1 tbsp	cumin seeds (see Tips, left)	15 mL
2 tsp	coriander seeds	10 mL
2	onions, finely chopped	2
2 tbsp	minced gingerroot	30 mL
2 tbsp	minced garlic	30 mL
1 cup	plain yogurt (minimum 4% M.F.)	250 mL
2 lbs	trimmed stewing beef, cut into bite-size pieces	1 kg

FILLING

1 tbsp	olive oil	15 mL
2	onions, thinly sliced on the vertical	2
2 tsp	curry powder (see Tips, left)	10 mL
½ tsp	cracked black peppercorns	2 mL
¼ tsp	cayenne pepper, optional	1 mL
½ tsp	crumbled saffron threads, dissolved in ½ cup (125 mL) boiling water	2 mL
	Salt	
2 cups	reduced-sodium beef stock (see Tips, right)	500 mL
2 cups	water	500 mL
1	stick cinnamon, about 2 inches (5 cm) long	1
2 cups	brown basmati or brown long-grain rice, rinsed and drained	500 mL
1 to 2	long red or green chiles, seeded and minced	1 to 2
1 cup	plain yogurt (minimum 4% M.F.) (see Tips, page 153)	250 mL

1. In a dry skillet over medium heat, toast cumin and coriander seeds, stirring constantly, until fragrant, about 3 minutes. Transfer to a mortar or a spice grinder and grind. Set aside.

2. *Marinade:* In a bowl, combine onions, ginger, garlic, yogurt and reserved spices. Add beef and toss well. Cover and marinate in the refrigerator for at least 2 hours (see Tips, right).

3. *Filling:* Using a slotted spoon, remove beef from marinade and pat dry. Set marinade aside. In a skillet, heat oil over medium–high heat for 30 seconds. Add beef, in batches, and cook, stirring, until browned, about 4 minutes per batch. Transfer to a plate and set aside.

Tips

When using any canned product, such as tomato sauce or beef stock, check the label to make sure ingredients containing gluten have not been added.

You can marinate the meat for up to 2 days ahead of cooking, if you prefer. Or you can make the components ahead and assemble just before you're ready to serve. Complete Steps 1 through 4. Cover and refrigerate meat mixture for up to 2 days. Complete Step 5. Transfer cooked rice to a shallow container and let cool slightly. Immediately cover and refrigerate separate from the meat mixture for up to 2 days.

4. Add onions to pan and cook, stirring, until golden, about 15 minutes. Add curry powder, peppercorns and cayenne, if using, and cook, stirring for 1 minute. Return beef and any accumulated juices to pan and stir well. Add reserved marinade and saffron liquid. Stir well and bring to a boil. Season to taste with salt. Reduce heat to low. Cover and simmer, watching carefully and stirring occasionally to ensure mixture doesn't scorch, until beef is fork tender, about 45 minutes.

5. Meanwhile, in a heavy pot with a tight-fitting lid over medium-high heat, bring stock, water and cinnamon stick to a boil. Add rice and return to a boil. Reduce heat to low. Cover and simmer until rice is tender and liquid has been absorbed, about 50 minutes. Remove cinnamon stick and stir in chiles.

6. *Assembly:* Fifteen minutes before you're ready to bake, preheat oven to 350°F (180°C). Spread approximately one third of rice evenly over bottom of baking dish, ensuring it's completely covered. Add beef mixture. Spread one third of rice over beef and spread yogurt over rice. Spread remaining rice evenly over yogurt. Cover and bake in preheated oven until piping hot, about 30 minutes.

Variation

Lamb Biriyani: Substitute an equal quantity of stewing lamb for the beef. Eliminate the beef stock and cook the rice in 4 cups (1 L) water.

MAGNESIUM

One serving of this recipe is an excellent source of magnesium, a mineral that supports every major system in our bodies. Among its most important functions, magnesium helps to keep bones strong, and an insufficient intake of this mineral may increase the risk of osteoporosis in older women. It also supports the nervous system, working with calcium to help keep nerves relaxed and healthy. Without an adequate supply of magnesium, muscles may react, triggering cramps and spasms. Muscle tension, anxiety and heart disease are among the ailments linked with a magnesium deficiency.

Savory Lamb Shanks with Eggplant

Here's a rich, delicious Mediterranean-inspired stew that will warm the cockles of your heart on a chilly night. Although lamb shanks are fatty, they are succulent and the dish is loaded with nutrients. If you're watching your weight, treat it as a dietary splurge. Lamb shanks are at their best when cooked slowly in moist heat, so if you have a slow cooker, by all means use it to make this dish.

Makes 8 servings

Tips

Have your butcher slice the shanks for you. Depending on their size, you'll get from 2 to 4 pieces from each shank.

After adding the lamb to the casserole, make sure you arrange it so all the meat is submerged in the cooking liquid. If using a slow cooker, complete Steps 1, 2 and 3. Transfer to stoneware, cover and cook on Low for 10 hours, until the meat is falling off the bone.

Nutrients per serving

Calories	392
Protein	30.3 g
Carbohydrates	30.3 g
Fat (Total)	17.1 g
Saturated Fat	5.7 g
Monounsaturated Fat	8 g
Polyunsaturated Fat	1.5 g
Dietary Fiber	3.6 g
Sodium	346 mg
Cholesterol	62 mg

EXCELLENT SOURCE OF niacin, folate, phosphorus, iron, zinc and selenium.
GOOD SOURCE OF manganese.
SOURCE OF vitamins A, C and E (alpha-tocopheral) thiamine, riboflavin, pantothenic acid, magnesium, copper and calcium.
CONTAINS a moderate amount of dietary fiber.

1	large eggplant, peeled, cut into 2-inch (5 cm) cubes	1
4 lbs	sliced lamb shanks (see Tips, left)	2 kg
½ tsp	salt	2 mL
½ tsp	cracked black peppercorns	2 mL
2 tbsp	olive oil (approx.), divided	30 mL
2	onions, thinly sliced on the vertical	2
4	cloves garlic, minced	4
2	bay leaves	2
1 tbsp	finely grated lemon zest	15 mL
1	stick cinnamon, about 2 inches (5 cm) long	1
1 cup	Job's tears, soaked, drained and rinsed	250 mL
1 cup	red wine	250 mL
1	can (28 oz/796 mL) no-salt-added tomatoes with juice (see Tips, page 133)	1
¼ cup	finely chopped parsley	60 mL

1. Sprinkle the eggplant pieces with salt and set aside in a colander for 1 to 2 hours. (If time is short, blanch them in heavily salted water.) In either case, rinse thoroughly in fresh cold water and, using your hands, squeeze out the excess moisture. Pat dry with paper towels.

2. Preheat oven to 325°F (160°C). Pat shanks dry with paper towel and season with salt and peppercorns. In a Dutch oven, heat 1 tbsp (15 mL) of the oil over medium–high heat for 30 seconds. Add lamb shanks, in batches, and brown well on all sides, about 4 minutes per batch. Transfer to a plate as completed and set aside. Drain off all but 2 tbsp (30 mL) fat from pan, if necessary. (If your lamb is very lean, you may not have enough oil left in the pan and may need to add a bit here.)

3. Add eggplant, in batches, and cook, stirring, until lightly browned, adding more oil, if needed. Remove and set aside. Add onions to pan and cook, stirring, until lightly browned, about 7 minutes. Add garlic, bay leaves, lemon zest and cinnamon stick and cook, stirring, for 1 minute. Add Job's tears and toss to coat. Add wine and tomatoes with juice, reserved lamb shanks and any accumulated juices and eggplant and bring to a boil.

4. Cover and bake in preheated oven until meat is tender and falling off the bone, about 2½ hours. Garnish with parsley.

Sloppy Joes Zucchini

There's so much tasty filling in these zucchini, they remind me of Sloppy Joe burgers spilling out of a bun. They aren't fancy, but they make a delicious weeknight meal and are particularly good to make in the late summer and fall when zucchini are abundant.

Makes 6 servings

Nutrient Tip

This recipe is relatively high in sodium, virtually all of which comes from three sources: the regular canned tomatoes (279 mg), the added salt (172 mg) and last, but certainly not least, the feta cheese (279 mg). If you're watching your sodium intake, you can omit the added salt, use canned tomatoes with no salt added, and/or substitute low-salt feta cheese for the regular version.

Nutrients per serving	
Calories	325
Protein	18.9 g
Carbohydrates	37.1 g
Fat (Total)	12.7 g
Saturated Fat	5.6 g
Monounsaturated Fat	4.6 g
Polyunsaturated Fat	1.3 g
Dietary Fiber	6.2 g
Sodium	882 mg
Cholesterol	44 mg

EXCELLENT SOURCE OF vitamins A and C, riboflavin, niacin, phosphorus, iron, magnesium, manganese, copper and zinc.
GOOD SOURCE OF folate, thiamine, pantothenic acid, selenium and calcium.
SOURCE OF vitamin E (alpha-tocopherol).
CONTAINS a very high amount of dietary fiber.

- Preheat oven to 375°F (190°C)
- 13- by 9-inch (3 L) baking dish

2 cups	reduced-sodium beef stock (see Tips, page 133)	500 mL
1 cup	quinoa, rinsed and drained (see Tips, page 136)	250 mL
3	medium zucchini (each about 12 oz/375 g)	3
1 tbsp	olive oil	15 mL
8 oz	extra lean ground beef	250 g
2	onions, finely chopped	2
4	cloves garlic, minced	4
1 tbsp	dried oregano leaves, crumbled	15 mL
½ tsp	salt	2 mL
½ tsp	ground cinnamon	2 mL
	Freshly ground black pepper	
1	can (28 oz/796 mL) tomatoes with juice, coarsely chopped	1
½ cup	chopped parsley	125 mL
1 cup	crumbled feta	250 mL

1. In a saucepan over medium–high heat, bring stock to a boil. Add quinoa in a steady stream, stirring constantly and return to a boil. Cover and simmer over low heat until tender, about 20 minutes. Remove from heat and let stand for 10 minutes.

2. Cut zucchini in half lengthwise and, using a large spoon, scoop out the centers, leaving a solid frame. Finely chop pulp and set aside. Place halves in baking dish.

3. In a skillet, heat oil over medium heat for 30 seconds. Add ground beef and onions and cook, stirring and breaking up with a spoon, until beef is no longer pink, about 8 minutes. Add garlic, oregano, salt, cinnamon and pepper to taste and cook, stirring, for 1 minute. Add reserved zucchini pulp and cook, stirring, for 2 minutes. Stir in reserved quinoa and tomatoes with juice and bring to a boil. Stir in parsley.

4. Spoon tomato mixture over zucchini, filling the shells. (Don't worry about spillover; it will cook nicely, too.) Bake in preheated oven until mixture is hot and bubbly and zucchini shells are tender but still a bit firm, about 45 minutes. Sprinkle feta over top of shells and bake just until the cheese begins to melt, about 5 minutes.

Variation

Substitute ground lamb for the beef.

Peppery Meat Loaf with Quinoa

I love the range of mouthwatering tastes in this recipe, which combines old-fashioned meat loaf with Mediterranean flavors such as red peppers, paprika, cumin and coriander. Serve this with baked potatoes in their skins and a tossed salad.

Makes 8 servings

Tips

To enhance the pleasantly nutty flavor of the quinoa, toast it in a dry skillet (or the saucepan you are using for cooking) for about 4 minutes over medium heat, stirring constantly until fragrant.

Buy your sausage from a butcher who makes it on-site and can tell you exactly what it contains, or read the label to make sure that no ingredients containing gluten have been added to the meat.

Nutrients per serving

Calories	276
Protein	21 g
Carbohydrates	17.3 g
Fat (Total)	13.5 g
Saturated Fat	4.4 g
Monounsaturated Fat	5.5 g
Polyunsaturated Fat	1.6 g
Dietary Fiber	2.6 g
Sodium	452 mg
Cholesterol	93 mg

EXCELLENT SOURCE OF vitamin C, niacin, iron, zinc and selenium.

GOOD SOURCE OF vitamin A, folate, riboflavin, thiamine, phosphorus, manganese, magnesium and copper.

SOURCE OF vitamin E (alpha-tocopherol), pantothenic acid and calcium.

CONTAINS a moderate amount of dietary fiber.

* Preheat oven to 350°F (180°C)
* 9- by 5-inch (2 L) loaf pan
* Instant-read thermometer

¾ cup	water	175 mL
½ cup	reduced-sodium beef stock or water (see Tips, page 133)	125 mL
¾ cup	quinoa, rinsed and drained (see Tips, left)	175 mL
1 lb	extra lean ground beef	500 g
8 oz	Italian sausage, removed from casings and crumbled (see Tips, left)	250 mL
1	onion, diced	1
1	red bell pepper, seeded and diced	1
½ cup	finely chopped parsley	125 mL
2	eggs, beaten	2
1 cup	reduced-sodium tomato sauce, divided (see Tips, page 133)	250 mL
1 tbsp	sweet paprika	15 mL
1 tbsp	ground cumin (see Tips, page 111)	15 mL
1 tsp	ground coriander	5 mL
½ tsp	salt	2 mL
¼ tsp	cayenne pepper	1 mL

1. In a saucepan, bring water and beef stock to a boil. Gradually stir in quinoa. Return to a boil. Cover and simmer over low heat for 15 minutes. Remove from heat, cover and set aside for 5 minutes. Fluff with a fork before using.

2. In a large bowl, combine ground beef, sausage, onion, bell pepper, parsley, eggs, all but 2 tbsp (30 mL) of the tomato sauce, paprika, cumin, coriander, salt, cayenne and quinoa. Using your hands, mix until well blended. Transfer to loaf pan and spread remaining 2 tbsp (30 mL) of tomato sauce over top. Bake in preheated oven until temperature reaches 165°F (75°C) on a thermometer, about 1 hour.

Variation

Substitute millet for the quinoa. For the best flavor, before using, toast it in a dry skillet, stirring until fragrant, about 5 minutes. Complete Step 1, simmering the millet over low heat for 20 minutes, then remove from the heat and let stand for 10 minutes.

Southwestern-Style Rice-Stuffed Peppers

The addition of corn and chili powder adds a nice Southwestern touch to this classic preparation. It's filling enough to be a meal in itself and it has enough nutrients, including a very high amount of dietary fiber, to justify being a complete meal. It's a great dish for those evenings when everyone is coming and going, as you can keep it warm and people can help themselves.

Makes 4 servings

Tips

I prefer to use chili powder made from ground ancho or New Mexico chiles in this recipe but a good blend works well, too.

If you are using a blended chili powder, check the label to make sure it doesn't contain gluten.

Blanching the peppers in salted water adds a significant amount (387 mg per serving) of sodium to this recipe. If you're watching your sodium intake, blanch them in unsalted water.

Nutrients per serving

Calories	502
Protein	21.5 g
Carbohydrates	72.1 g
Fat (Total)	13.2 g
Saturated Fat	4 g
Monounsaturated Fat	6.5 g
Polyunsaturated Fat	1.4 g
Dietary Fiber	14.7 g
Sodium	817 mg
Cholesterol	34 mg

EXCELLENT SOURCE OF vitamins A and C, niacin, phosphorus, magnesium, manganese, zinc and selenium.

GOOD SOURCE OF folate, thiamine, riboflavin, iron and copper.

SOURCE OF vitamin E (alpha-tocopherol), pantothenic acid and calcium.

CONTAINS a very high amount of dietary fiber.

- **Preheat oven to 350°F (180°C)**
- **Baking dish, lightly greased**

2 cups	cooked brown rice (see cooking instructions, page 28)	500 mL
4	large green bell peppers	4
1 tbsp	olive oil	15 mL
1	onion, finely chopped	1
2	stalks celery, diced	2
8 oz	lean ground beef	250 g
4	cloves garlic, minced	4
1 tbsp	chili powder (see Tips, left)	15 mL
2 tsp	dried oregano leaves	10 mL
1/2 tsp	salt	2 mL
1/2 tsp	cracked black peppercorns	2 mL
1 1/2 cups	cooked corn kernels	375 mL
2 cups	reduced-sodium tomato sauce	500 mL

1. Cut a thin slice off the top of bell peppers and remove the stems, seeds and veins. (A grapefruit spoon makes easy work of scraping out the veins in the pepper.) Place peppers in a large pot of boiling salted water. Return to a boil and blanch for 10 minutes. Set aside to drain upside down on several layers of paper towels.

2. In a skillet, heat oil over medium heat for 30 seconds. Add onion, celery and ground beef and cook, stirring and breaking up beef with a spoon, until beef is no longer pink, about 6 minutes. Add garlic, chili powder, oregano, salt and peppercorns and cook, stirring for 1 minute. Remove from heat. Stir in cooked rice and corn.

3. Fill peppers and place in prepared baking dish. Cover with tomato sauce. Cover loosely with foil and bake in preheated oven until hot and steamy, about 45 minutes.

Tailgaters' Favorite Stew

On a blustery day, a big serving of this ambrosial stew is perfect. It's great for potlucks and outdoor get-togethers because it's easily transportable and there is nothing to add.

Makes 8 servings

Tips

The orange juice and zest add wonderful depth to this stew.

If you like heat, increase the cayenne to as much as ½ tsp (2 mL).

You'll need to simmer the stew for about 1 hour to ensure the Job's tears are tender.

It is always a good idea when using canned products such as tomato paste or beef stock to check the label. Manufacturers are constantly changing their formulae and gluten may suddenly appear in a previously gluten-free product.

Nutrients per serving

Calories	378
Protein	32.8 g
Carbohydrates	30.1 g
Fat (Total)	13.4 g
Saturated Fat	4.6 g
Monounsaturated Fat	5.6 g
Polyunsaturated Fat	0.9 g
Dietary Fiber	2.7 g
Sodium	582 mg
Cholesterol	70 mg

EXCELLENT SOURCE OF
vitamin A, riboflavin, niacin, phosphorus, iron, zinc and selenium.
GOOD SOURCE OF thiamine, pantothenic acid, magnesium and manganese.
SOURCE OF vitamins C and E (alpha-tocopherol), folate, copper and calcium.
CONTAINS a moderate amount of dietary fiber.

6	slices bacon (about 4 oz/125 g)	6
3 tbsp	sorghum flour	45 mL
1 tbsp	potato starch or cornstarch	15 mL
1 tsp	salt	5 mL
½ tsp	cracked black peppercorns	2 mL
¼ tsp	cayenne pepper (see Tips, left)	1 mL
2 lbs	trimmed stewing beef, cut into 1-inch (2.5 cm) chunks	1 kg
2	onions, finely chopped	2
2	stalks celery, diced	2
2	carrots, peeled and diced	2
4	cloves garlic, minced	4
2	bay leaves	2
½ tsp	freshly grated nutmeg	2 mL
	Grated zest and juice of 1 orange	
1 cup	Job's tears, soaked, rinsed and drained	250 mL
1 cup	dry red wine	250 mL
1	can (5½ oz/156 mL) tomato paste (see Tips, left)	1
2 cups	reduced-sodium beef stock	500 mL

1. In a Dutch oven over medium-high heat, sauté bacon until crisp. Transfer to a paper towel–lined plate to drain. When cool, crumble and set aside. Drain off all but 2 tbsp (30 mL) fat from pan, reserving extra.

2. On a plate, combine sorghum flour, potato starch, salt, peppercorns and cayenne. Dredge beef in mixture until coated. Discard any excess. Add beef to pan, in batches, and cook, stirring, until nicely browned on all sides, about 5 minutes per batch. Add more bacon drippings, if required. Remove beef to a plate and reserve. Reduce heat to medium.

3. Add onions, celery and carrots to pan and cook, stirring, until carrots are softened, about 7 minutes. Add garlic, bay leaves, nutmeg and orange zest and cook, stirring, for 1 minute. Add Job's tears, orange juice, red wine, tomato paste, stock and 1½ cups (375 mL) water and bring to a boil. Return beef and bacon to pot and bring to a boil. Reduce heat to low. Cover and simmer until Job's tears are tender.

Slow Cooker Method: Follow Steps 1 through 3, then transfer mixture to slow cooker stoneware, adding just 1 cup (250 mL) of water along with the Job's tears. Cover and cook on Low for 8 hours or on High for 4 hours, until Job's tears are tender.

Cuban-Style Hash with Fried Plantains

This take on picadillo, a classic Cuban dish, is a fabulous weeknight meal — it makes a large serving and you don't need to serve anything else. Make it the night before you intend to serve it because the flavors will improve. (Complete Steps 1 and 2, but don't add the olives.)

Makes 6 servings

Tips

Tomato paste should be gluten-free, but manufacturers often change their formulae so check the label. The same is true of canned tomatoes.

According to my friend Ana Thompson, who is Cuban, plantains should have black skins before they are cooked. In Cuba, they are usually fried in copious amounts of vegetable oil, but I find my method produces a very acceptable result.

Nutrients per serving

Calories	428
Protein	16.6 g
Carbohydrates	65.6 g
Fat (Total)	13.5 g
Saturated Fat	5 g
Monounsaturated Fat	6.2 g
Polyunsaturated Fat	1 g
Dietary Fiber	6.5 g
Sodium	646 mg
Cholesterol	41 mg

EXCELLENT SOURCE OF vitamin C, niacin, iron, magnesium, manganese, zinc and selenium.

GOOD SOURCE OF vitamins A and E (alpha-tocopherol), thiamine, riboflavin, folate, pantothenic acid, phosphorus and copper.

SOURCE OF calcium.

CONTAINS a very high amount of dietary fiber.

2 cups	cooked brown or red rice (see cooking instructions, page 28)	500 mL
1 tbsp	olive oil	15 mL
1	onion, finely chopped	1
1	green bell pepper, seeded and diced	1
1	jalapeño pepper, seeded and diced	1
4	cloves garlic, minced	4
12 oz	extra lean ground beef	375 g
2 tsp	dried oregano leaves	10 mL
½ tsp	salt	2 mL
½ tsp	freshly ground black pepper	2 mL
1	stick cinnamon, about 2 inches (5 cm) long	1
1	bay leaf	1
1	can (28 oz/796 mL) no-salt-added diced tomatoes with juice (see Tips, left)	1
2 tbsp	tomato paste (see Tips, left)	30 mL
2 tbsp	red wine vinegar	30 mL
8	large pimento-stuffed olives, sliced	8

FRIED PLANTAINS

2 tbsp	butter	30 mL
4	very ripe plantains, thinly sliced	4
2 tbsp	freshly squeezed lime or lemon juice	30 mL
4	hot runny fried or poached eggs, optional	4

1. In a large skillet or saucepan, heat oil over medium heat for 30 seconds. Add onion, bell pepper, jalapeño and garlic and stir well. Reduce heat to low. Cover and cook until vegetables are softened, about 10 minutes.

2. Increase heat to medium–high. Add beef, oregano, salt, pepper, cinnamon and bay leaf and cook, stirring and breaking up beef with a spoon, until beef is browned and no longer pink, about 5 minutes. Add tomatoes, tomato paste and vinegar and stir well. Stir in rice and season to taste with salt and pepper. Reduce heat to low. Cover and simmer until flavors meld, about 15 minutes. Stir in olives and remove from heat.

3. *Meanwhile, make Fried Plantains:* In a skillet, melt butter over low heat. Add plantains and cook, stirring occasionally, until caramelized, about 25 minutes. Pour lime juice over top.

4. *To serve:* Spoon picadillo onto a plate and top with a fried egg, if using. Serve fried plantains alongside.

Asian-Spiced Beef with Soba Noodles

Although the flavorings lean toward being Chinese, and the soba noodles are traditionally Japanese, this is a variation on the theme of Vietnamese pho.

Tips

If you are using prepared stock, check the label to make sure it doesn't contain gluten.

Depending upon the size of your baby bok choy, you may have trouble fitting them all in the pan. If so, stir in gradually.

Nutrient Tip

Most of the sodium in this dish comes from beef stock, which contributes 852 mg. So, if you're concerned about your sodium intake, make your own beef stock with no salt added.

Nutrients per serving

Calories	504
Protein	41.4 g
Carbohydrates	50.3 g
Fat (Total)	15.9 g
Saturated Fat	5.1 g
Monounsaturated Fat	7.8 g
Polyunsaturated Fat	1.4 g
Dietary Fiber	5.6 g
Sodium	1327 mg
Cholesterol	51 mg

EXCELLENT SOURCE OF vitamins A and C, thiamine, niacin, folate, phosphorus, iron, manganese, zinc and selenium.
GOOD SOURCE OF riboflavin, pantothenic acid, magnesium and calcium.
SOURCE OF vitamin E (alpha-tocopherol) and copper.
CONTAINS a high amount of dietary fiber.

2 tbsp	olive oil, divided	30 mL
1	flank steak, about 1½ lbs (750 g)	1
1	whole star anise	1
2 tsp	Szechuan peppercorns	10 mL
1 tsp	cracked black peppercorns	5 mL
1 tsp	fennel seeds	5 mL
1	stick cinnamon, about 2 inches (5 cm) long	1
1	piece (2 inches/5 cm) gingerroot, coarsely chopped	1
8 cups	reduced-sodium beef stock (see Tips, left)	2 L
¼ cup	dry sherry or dry white wine	60 mL
2 tbsp	gluten-free reduced-sodium soy sauce	30 mL
12 oz	100% buckwheat soba noodles (see Tips, page 158)	375 g
1 tsp	sesame oil	5 mL
2	cloves garlic, minced	2
8 oz	sliced fresh shiitake mushroom caps	250 g
2 cups	shredded peeled carrots	500 mL
12	baby bok choy, halved lengthwise	12
2 tbsp	thinly sliced green onions	30 mL
	Minced Thai chiles or lime wedges, optional	

1. In a skillet, heat 1 tbsp (15 mL) of the oil over medium heat for 30 seconds. Add steak and brown well on both sides, about 5 minutes. Transfer to a large saucepan set over medium heat. Add star anise, Szechuan and cracked peppercorns, fennel seeds, cinnamon, ginger, stock and sherry. Bring to a boil. Reduce heat to low. Cover and simmer until meat is very tender, about 1 hour. Lift out meat and shred. Strain liquid, discarding solids. Stir in soy sauce and keep stock warm.

2. Meanwhile, cook soba noodles according to package instructions. Drain and rinse under cold running water. Toss with sesame oil and set aside.

3. In a large wok or skillet, heat remaining 1 tbsp (15 mL) of oil over medium–high heat for 30 seconds. Add garlic, shredded meat and mushrooms and cook, stirring, until mushrooms have softened. Add carrots and bok choy and cook, stirring, until bok choy is slightly wilted.

4. *To serve:* Divide steak mixture and cooked noodles evenly among soup bowls. Pour stock over. Sprinkle with green onions and chile pepper, if using. Serve with lime wedges to squeeze over top, if using.

Millet-Crusted Tamale Pie

This is a great weeknight meal — the perfect thing to serve on a night your teenager spontaneously invites a friend or two for dinner. If you have a can of beans in the pantry and cooked rice in the freezer, you can quickly defrost the ingredients, toss a salad and in less than an hour produce a nutritious dinner the kids will rave about.

Makes 6 servings

Tip

Use spicy or not-so-spicy salsa. However, check the label to make sure it is gluten-free. Some brands of prepared salsa contain hydrolyzed wheat gluten.

Nutrient Tip

Much of the fat in this dish comes from the regular-fat cheese (5.7 g) and the Italian sausage, which contributes a total of 9.3 grams. To reduce your consumption of fat, use lower-fat cheese and reduce the quantity of sausage in the dish.

Nutrients per serving	
Calories	437
Protein	20.8 g
Carbohydrates	46.5 g
Fat (Total)	19.1 g
Saturated Fat	7.5 g
Monounsaturated Fat	8 g
Polyunsaturated Fat	2.4 g
Dietary Fiber	6.5 g
Sodium	768 mg
Cholesterol	43 mg

EXCELLENT SOURCE OF thiamine, phosphorus, magnesium, manganese and selenium.

GOOD SOURCE OF niacin, riboflavin, folate, calcium, iron, copper and zinc.

SOURCE OF vitamins A and E (alpha-tocopherol) and pantothenic acid.

CONTAINS a very high amount of dietary fiber.

- Preheat oven to 375°F (190°C)
- 10-inch (25 cm) deep-dish glass pie dish or 8- or 9-inch (2 or 2.5 L) square baking dish

1 cup	cooked brown rice (see cooking instructions, page 28)	250 mL
TOPPING		
1 cup	millet, rinsed and drained	250 mL
3 cups	water or chicken or vegetable stock	750 mL
	Salt and freshly ground black pepper	
1 cup	shredded Monterey Jack cheese	250 mL
FILLING		
1 tbsp	olive oil	15 mL
12 oz	hot or mild Italian sausage (see Tips, page 136), casings removed	375 g
2 tsp	chili powder (see Tips, page 138)	10 mL
¾ cup	tomato salsa (see Tip, left)	175 mL
1 cup	corn kernels	250 mL
1 cup	cooked pinto beans, drained and rinsed (see Variation, below)	250 mL

1. *Topping:* In a saucepan over medium heat, toast millet, stirring constantly, until it crackles and releases its aroma, about 5 minutes. Add water and salt and pepper to taste and bring to a boil. Reduce heat to low. Cover and cook until millet is tender and all of the water is absorbed, about 20 minutes. Stir in cheese.

2. *Filling:* Meanwhile, in a skillet, heat oil over medium heat for 30 seconds. Add sausage and cook, breaking up with a spoon, until no longer pink, about 8 minutes. Drain off all but 1 tbsp (15 mL) fat from pan, if necessary. Add chili powder and cook, stirring, for 1 minute. Add salsa and stir well. Stir in corn, beans and rice and cook, stirring, until heated through. Place in pie dish.

3. Spread topping evenly over filling. Bake in preheated oven until top is nicely browned, about 25 minutes.

Variation

If you don't have pinto beans, substitute an equal quantity of red kidney beans, small red beans or cranberry beans. Be aware that although you can use canned beans, rinse them well because many brands are very high in sodium, or you can cook dried beans yourself with no salt added.

Sausage-Spiked Peas 'n' Rice

What could be easier than this combination of brown and wild rice and split peas, seasoned with sausage and fennel? The flavors are fantastic and I love the way the split peas dissolve into the sauce, creating a luscious texture that I find extremely satisfying. Add a simple green salad or some steamed green beans and enjoy.

Makes 6 servings

Tips

You can cook the split peas yourself, reserving ¼ cup (60 mL) of the cooking liquid or you can use a can (14 to 19 oz/398 to 540 mL) yellow split peas, rinsed and drained, plus ¼ cup (60 mL) water, instead. Be aware that the canned peas will be much higher in sodium than those you cook yourself.

If you have fresh thyme on hand, substitute 2 whole sprigs, stem and all, for the dried. Remove and discard before serving.

2 cups	cooked yellow split peas, with ¼ cup (60 mL) cooking liquid (see Tips, left)	500 mL
1 tbsp	olive oil	15 mL
12 oz	hot or mild Italian sausage, removed from casings (see Tips, page 136)	375 g
1	bulb fennel, cored and chopped	1
1	onion, finely chopped	1
4	cloves garlic, minced	4
1 tsp	dried thyme leaves (see Tips, left)	5 mL
	Freshly ground black pepper	
1 cup	brown and wild rice mixture, rinsed and drained	250 mL
2 cups	reduced-sodium chicken stock (see Tips, page 150)	500 mL

1. In a large saucepan with a tight-fitting lid or Dutch oven, heat oil over medium heat for 30 seconds. Add sausage, fennel and onion and cook, stirring and breaking sausage up with a spoon, until meat is cooked through, about 6 minutes. Add garlic, thyme, pepper to taste and rice and cook, stirring, for 1 minute. Stir in peas with reserved liquid and stock and bring to a boil.

2. Reduce heat to low. Cover tightly and simmer until grains of wild rice begin to split, about 50 minutes. Ladle into soup plates.

Slow Cooker Method: Complete Step 1. Transfer mixture to slow cooker stoneware. Cover and cook on Low for 8 hours or on High for 4 hours, until wild rice is tender and grains begin to split.

Nutrients per serving

Calories	385
Protein	18.7 g
Carbohydrates	41.7 g
Fat (Total)	16.5 g
Saturated Fat	4.6 g
Monounsaturated Fat	7.3 g
Polyunsaturated Fat	2.1 g
Dietary Fiber	5.1 g
Sodium	606 mg
Cholesterol	30 mg

EXCELLENT SOURCE OF thiamine, magnesium and manganese.

GOOD SOURCE OF niacin, folate, zinc, selenium, phosphorus, iron and copper.

SOURCE OF vitamin C, riboflavin, pantothenic acid and calcium.

CONTAINS a high amount of dietary fiber.

Pork Pozole

I love the robust flavors in this traditional Mexican dish, which is perfect for a casual evening with friends. Add the chipotle pepper if you like heat and a bit of smoke. To continue the Mexican theme, serve with a tossed green salad that includes a diced avocado, and warm fresh corn tortillas.

Makes 8 servings

Tips

It is always a good idea when using canned products, such as tomatoes, chicken stock or chipotle peppers in adobo sauce, to check the label. Manufacturers are constantly changing their formulae and gluten may suddenly appear in a previously gluten-free product.

If you prefer, substitute 3 cups (750 mL) cooked dried hominy (see page 18), drained for the canned version.

4	slices bacon	4
2 lbs	trimmed pork shoulder, cut into 1-inch (2.5 cm) cubes	1 kg
2	onions, finely chopped	2
4	cloves garlic, minced	4
1 tbsp	dried oregano leaves	15 mL
½ tsp	cracked black peppercorns	2 mL
2 tsp	finely grated lime zest	10 mL
1	can (14 oz/398 mL) no-salt-added diced tomatoes with juice (see Tips, left)	1
2 cups	reduced-sodium chicken stock	500 mL
1	can (29 oz/824 mL) hominy, drained and rinsed (see Tips, left)	1
2	poblano or green bell peppers, seeded and diced (see Tip, right)	2
2	dried ancho or guajillo chiles	2
2 cups	boiling water	500 mL
2 tbsp	freshly squeezed lime juice	30 mL
2 tbsp	finely chopped cilantro	30 mL
1	chipotle pepper in adobo sauce, optional	1
	Salt	
	Shredded lettuce, optional	
	Chopped radish, optional	
	Chopped red or green onion, optional	
	Fried gluten-free tortilla strips, optional	
	Lime wedges	

Nutrients per serving

Calories	242
Protein	22.9 g
Carbohydrates	19.6 g
Fat (Total)	8.4 g
Saturated Fat	2.9 g
Monounsaturated Fat	3.5 g
Polyunsaturated Fat	1.4 g
Dietary Fiber	4.4 g
Sodium	371 mg
Cholesterol	63 mg

EXCELLENT SOURCE OF
vitamin C, thiamine, niacin, folate and zinc.

GOOD SOURCE OF
pantothenic acid, riboflavin, phosphorus, iron, magnesium, manganese and copper.

SOURCE OF vitamins A and E (alpha-tocopherol), calcium and selenium.

CONTAINS a high amount of dietary fiber.

1. In a Dutch oven, cook bacon over medium–high heat until crisp. Drain on paper towel and crumble. Cover and refrigerate until ready to use. Drain all but 2 tbsp (30 mL) fat from pan. Add pork, in batches, and brown, about 3 minutes per batch. Transfer to a plate. Reduce heat to medium.

2. Add onions to pan and cook, stirring, until softened, about 3 minutes. Add garlic, oregano, peppercorns and lime zest and cook, stirring, for 1 minute. Add tomatoes with juice, stock, hominy and reserved pork and any accumulated juices and return to a boil.

3. Reduce heat to low. Cover and simmer until pork is almost tender, for 1½ hours. Stir in reserved bacon and poblano peppers.

Tip

Poblano peppers, one of the mildest chile peppers, are often available in markets. Triangular in shape, they are a deep shade of green and have a wonderful hot-fruity flavor that is lovely in this dish. However, if you can't find them, green bell peppers make a more than acceptable substitute. In their dried form, poblano peppers are known as ancho peppers.

4. Meanwhile, in a heatproof bowl, soak ancho chiles in boiling water for 30 minutes, weighing down with a cup to keep submerged. Drain and discard soaking liquid and stems. Chop chiles coarsely. Transfer to a blender. Scoop out ½ cup (125 mL) cooking liquid from the pozole and add to blender along with lime juice, cilantro and chipotle pepper, if using. Purée and stir into pozole. Add salt to taste and continue cooking until pork is tender and flavors meld, about 30 minutes.

5. *To serve:* Ladle into soup plates and top with the garnishes of your choice. Season to taste with lime juice.

Slow Cooker Method: Complete Steps 1 and 2, reducing the quantity of chicken stock to 1½ cups (375 mL). Cover and cook on Low for 8 to 10 hours or on High for 4 to 5 hours, until pork is tender. Stir in reserved bacon, poblano pepper and ancho chile mixture and adjust seasoning. Cover and cook on High for 30 minutes, until peppers are tender.

FOLATE

One serving of this dish is an excellent source of folate, a B vitamin that has long been known to prevent neural tube defects in babies. Now information from the Harvard Nurses' Study suggests that an adequate supply of folate has more wide-ranging effects. Consumption of folate may help to prevent high blood pressure and keep homocysteine levels under control, protecting blood vessels from plaque. And Finnish researchers found a link between the consumption of folate and a reduced risk of depression. Although previous information linked folate intake with a decreased risk of colon cancer, a recent study published in *The Journal of the American Medical Association* reported that large daily doses of the nutrient actually seemed to increase the risk of the disease. Once again, it appears that supplementation, not the nutrient itself, may be the problem. Folate is not easily obtained in a typical North American diet. Sources include leafy greens, legumes, nuts and whole grains.

Coconut-Spiked Pork with Quinoa and Peanuts

I love the unusual combination of flavors in this one-dish meal. It's easy enough to make for a weeknight dinner and particularly colorful if made with red quinoa.

Makes 6 servings

Tips

Coconut milk should be suitable for people who are allergic to gluten. However, some brands contain guar gum, which although it does not contain gluten, is not recommended for people with celiac disease. Also it may be processed in a facility where gluten is present. Check the label.

Use the kind of chile pepper you have on hand — jalapeño, long red or green or even half a habanero.

Nutrients per serving

Calories	320
Protein	21.8 g
Carbohydrates	32 g
Fat (Total)	12.9 g
Saturated Fat	5 g
Monounsaturated Fat	4.6 g
Polyunsaturated Fat	2.2 g
Dietary Fiber	5.1 g
Sodium	455 mg
Cholesterol	34 mg

EXCELLENT SOURCE OF thiamine, niacin, phosphorus, iron, magnesium, manganese, copper and selenium.

GOOD SOURCE OF vitamin E (alpha-tocopherol), riboflavin, folate and zinc.

SOURCE OF vitamins A and C, pantothenic acid and calcium.

CONTAINS a high amount of dietary fiber.

1½ cups	reduced-sodium chicken or vegetable stock or water (see Tips, page 150)	375 mL
½ cup	coconut milk (see Tips, left)	125 mL
¼ cup	dry-roasted peanuts	60 mL
1 tbsp	olive oil	15 mL
12 oz	pork tenderloin, thinly sliced	375 g
2	leeks, white part only, cleaned and sliced (see Tips, page 70)	2
4	cloves garlic, minced	4
1	chile pepper, minced (see Tips, left)	1
2 tsp	ground cumin	10 mL
½ tsp	salt	2 mL
	Freshly ground black pepper	
1	can (14 oz/398 mL) no-salt-added diced tomatoes with juice (see Tips, page 146)	1
1 cup	quinoa, rinsed and drained	250 mL
1 cup	sliced green beans	250 mL

1. In a blender, combine stock, coconut milk and peanuts. Process until smooth. Set aside.

2. In a skillet, heat oil over medium-high heat for 30 seconds. Add pork, in batches if necessary, and cook until lightly browned, about 1 minute per side. Transfer to a plate and set aside.

3. Add leeks to pan and cook, stirring, until softened, about 5 minutes. Add garlic, chile pepper, cumin, salt and black pepper to taste and cook, stirring, for 1 minute. Add tomatoes with juice and reserved peanut mixture and bring to a boil. Stir in quinoa and green beans and return to a boil. Reduce heat to low. Stir in pork and any accumulated juices. Cover and simmer until quinoa is tender, about 20 minutes.

Chinese-Style Pork Fried Rice

This zesty rice is a perfect weekday meal, ideal for those days when everyone is coming and going at different times. Just keep it warm and set out the fixins' for salad.

Makes 6 servings

Tips

Shaoxing wine is a Chinese rice wine. It should not contain gluten, but apparently some brands do so consult the label.

When using any canned product, such as chicken stock, check the label to make sure ingredients containing gluten have not been added.

Check the label to make sure your curry paste does not contain gluten.

Nutrients per serving

Calories	325
Protein	25.1 g
Carbohydrates	23 g
Fat (Total)	14.1 g
Saturated Fat	2.4 g
Monounsaturated Fat	6.8 g
Polyunsaturated Fat	3.9 g
Dietary Fiber	3.3 g
Sodium	419 mg
Cholesterol	107 mg

EXCELLENT SOURCE OF vitamin C, thiamine, niacin, phosphorus, magnesium, manganese and selenium.

GOOD SOURCE OF vitamin E (alpha-tocopherol), riboflavin, folate, zinc and iron.

SOURCE OF vitamin A, pantothenic acid, calcium and copper.

CONTAINS a moderate amount of dietary fiber.

2 cups	cooked brown rice (see cooking instructions, page 28)	500 mL
MARINADE		
2 tbsp	gluten-free reduced-sodium soy sauce	30 mL
2 tbsp	Shaoxing wine, dry sherry or vodka	30 mL
1 tbsp	minced gingerroot	15 mL
1 tsp	sesame oil	5 mL
1 lb	pork tenderloin, thinly sliced	500 g
SAUCE		
2 tbsp	reduced-sodium chicken stock	30 mL
2 tbsp	Shaoxing wine (see Tips, left), dry sherry or vodka	30 mL
1 tbsp	gluten-free reduced-sodium soy sauce	15 mL
2 tsp	sesame oil	10 mL
2 tbsp	vegetable oil, divided	30 mL
1 tsp	red curry paste (see Tips, left), optional	5 mL
2	eggs, beaten	2
6	green onions, white part with a bit of green, thinly sliced	6
2	cloves garlic, minced	2
2 cups	sliced green beans, cooked until tender	500 mL
1	red bell pepper, seeded and diced	1
¼ cup	roasted peanuts	60 mL

1. *Marinade:* In a bowl, combine soy sauce, wine, ginger and oil. Stir will. Add pork and toss until well coated. Cover and set aside at room temperature for 20 minutes.

2. *Sauce:* In a small bowl, combine stock, Shaoxing wine, soy sauce and sesame oil. Set aside.

3. In a large skillet or wok, heat 1 tbsp (15 mL) of the oil over medium–high heat for 30 seconds. Add pork with marinade and cook, stirring, until cooked through, about 4 minutes. Transfer to a plate and wipe skillet clean.

4. Add remaining 1 tbsp (15 mL) of oil to skillet. Add curry paste, if using, and cook, stirring and watching carefully to ensure it doesn't burn, until fragrant, about 30 seconds. Add eggs and cook, stirring, until scrambled, about 30 seconds. Add green onions, garlic, green beans and bell pepper and cook, stirring, until fragrant and pepper begins to soften, about 3 minutes. Add rice, breaking it up with your fingers while dropping it into the pan, and cook, stirring, until well combined and heated through, for 3 minutes. Add cooked pork and any accumulated juices and stir well. Add sauce and toss well. Garnish with peanuts and serve.

Home-Style Skillet Rice with Tomato Crust

Here's a great dish to serve if your kids call to say they are bringing friends home after soccer practice. It has great robust flavor and is very quick to make so long as you have some precooked rice on hand. Add the cheese for a creamy mellow finish. Serve a tossed green salad and warm gluten-free bread to complete the meal.

Makes 6 servings

Tips

Lundberg sells a variety of brown rice mixes, all of which would work well in this recipe. Their Jubilee blend, which includes Wehani and Black Japonica, is particularly nice in this dish.

Check the label to make sure your tomato sauce is gluten-free.

Nutrients per serving

Calories	318
Protein	11.6 g
Carbohydrates	37.7 g
Fat (Total)	14 g
Saturated Fat	3.7 g
Monounsaturated Fat	6.1 g
Polyunsaturated Fat	1.7 g
Dietary Fiber	4.8 g
Sodium	509 mg
Cholesterol	82 mg

EXCELLENT SOURCE OF vitamin C and folate.

GOOD SOURCE OF vitamin E (alpha-tocopherol), thiamine, niacin, iron and selenium.

SOURCE OF vitamin A, riboflavin, pantothenic acid, phosphorus, magnesium, manganese, copper, calcium and zinc.

CONTAINS a high amount of dietary fiber.

- Preheat oven to 350°F (180°C)

3 cups	cooked red, brown, or brown and wild rice mixture (see cooking instructions, page 28, and Tips, left)	750 mL
1 tbsp	olive oil	15 mL
8 oz	hot or mild Italian sausage, removed from casings (see Tips, page 136)	250 g
1	onion, finely chopped	1
4	stalks celery, diced	4
2	green bell peppers, seeded and diced	2
4	cloves garlic, minced	4
1 tbsp	chili powder (see Tips, page 138)	15 mL
2 tsp	caraway seeds	10 mL
1 tsp	dried oregano leaves	5 mL
1/2 tsp	salt or to taste	2 mL
	Freshly ground black pepper	
1 1/2 cups	reduced-sodium tomato sauce (see Tips, left)	375 mL
2	eggs, beaten	2
8 oz	sliced mozzarella, optional	250 g

1. In a cast-iron or other ovenproof skillet, heat oil over medium heat for 30 seconds. Add sausage, onion, celery and bell peppers and cook, stirring and breaking up sausage with a spoon, until vegetables are very tender and sausage is no longer pink, about 7 minutes. Add garlic, chili powder, caraway seeds, oregano, salt and black pepper to taste and cook, stirring, for 1 minute. Add cooked rice and cook, stirring, until heated through. Remove from heat.

2. In a bowl, beat tomato sauce and eggs until blended. Spread evenly over rice in skillet. Lay sliced mozzarella, if using, evenly over top. Place skillet in preheated oven and bake until top is crusty and cheese, if using, is melted, about 15 minutes.

Peppery Polenta Bake with Mushrooms and Sausages

I have a real weakness for this combination of ingredients and flavors: the zesty sausage, sweet peppers and mushrooms surrounded by creamy polenta and cheese is a marriage made in heaven. I love having leftovers so I can heat some up for an afternoon snack.

Makes 8 servings

Tips

Creamy Polenta contains a bit of milk and Parmesan, which works nicely with this recipe.

For convenience, cool both the polenta and the sausage mixture separately, assemble the dish without the cheese and refrigerate for up to 2 days, until ready to cook. Bake until hot, about 40 minutes, adding cheese for the last 10 minutes.

- 10-cup (2.5 L) baking dish, greased

1	batch Creamy Polenta (see Variations, page 183)	1
1 tbsp	extra virgin olive oil	15 mL
12 oz	hot or mild Italian sausage, removed from casings (see Tips, page 136)	375 g
1	onion, finely chopped	1
1	red bell pepper, seeded and diced	1
1	green bell pepper, seeded and diced	1
2	cloves garlic, minced	2
2 tbsp	crumbled dried mushrooms, such as porcini or portobello	30 mL
2 tsp	dried Italian seasoning	10 mL
1	can (14 oz/398 mL) no-salt-added diced tomatoes with juice (see Tips, page 146)	1
	Salt and freshly ground black pepper	
2 cups	shredded mozzarella cheese (see Tips, page 160)	500 mL

1. Spread warm polenta evenly over the bottom of baking dish and set aside to firm up.

2. Meanwhile, in a skillet, heat oil over medium heat for 30 seconds. Add sausage, onion and bell peppers and cook, breaking sausage up with a spoon, until vegetables are quite soft and sausage is no longer pink, about 7 minutes. Drain off all fat from pan. Add garlic, mushrooms and Italian seasoning and cook, stirring, for 1 minute. Add tomatoes with juice and bring to a boil. Season to taste with salt and black pepper. Reduce heat to low. Cover and simmer until flavors meld, about 10 minutes.

3. Meanwhile, preheat oven to 350°F (180°C). Spread sausage mixture evenly over polenta. Sprinkle cheese evenly over top. Bake in preheated oven until cheese is melted and mixture is bubbly, about 15 minutes.

Nutrients per serving

Calories	278
Protein	14.8 g
Carbohydrates	21.8 g
Fat (Total)	15.4 g
Saturated Fat	6.8 g
Monounsaturated Fat	6.2 g
Polyunsaturated Fat	1.5 g
Dietary Fiber	4 g
Sodium	474 mg
Cholesterol	43 mg

EXCELLENT SOURCE OF vitamin C and selenium.

GOOD SOURCE OF vitamin A, thiamine, calcium, phosphorus, magnesium, zinc and copper.

SOURCE OF vitamin E (alpha-tocopherol), riboflavin, folate, pantothenic acid, manganese and iron.

CONTAINS a high amount of dietary fiber.

Fragrant Lamb Curry with Chinese "Barley"

Make this delicious curry any time you have a craving for something lusciously different. It's a great Sunday night dinner and is perfect for a potluck or on a buffet.

Makes 6 servings

Tips

If you are using prepared stock, check the label to make sure it doesn't contain gluten.

Plain yogurt should be gluten-free but you should check the label before purchasing. Manufacturers often add gluten to flavored varieties and formulae frequently change.

Nutrients per serving

Calories	353
Protein	25.4 g
Carbohydrates	30.9 g
Fat (Total)	12.6 g
Saturated Fat	3.7 g
Monounsaturated Fat	5.5 g
Polyunsaturated Fat	1.9 g
Dietary Fiber	1.3 g
Sodium	676 mg
Cholesterol	65 mg

EXCELLENT SOURCE OF riboflavin, niacin, phosphorus, zinc and selenium.
GOOD SOURCE OF vitamin C, iron and magnesium.
SOURCE OF vitamins A and E (alpha-tocopherol), folate, thiamine, pantothenic acid, manganese, copper and calcium.

- Preheat oven to 325°F (160°C)
- 13- by 9-inch (3 L) baking dish

2 tbsp	olive oil, divided	30 mL
1 lb	trimmed stewing lamb	500 g
2	onions, finely chopped	2
4	cloves garlic, minced	4
1 tbsp	minced gingerroot	15 mL
1 to 2	long red or green chile peppers, seeded and diced	1 to 2
1 tsp	sweet paprika	5 mL
1 tsp	turmeric	5 mL
1 tsp	salt	5 mL
1/2 tsp	cracked black peppercorns	2 mL
1/4 tsp	cayenne pepper	1 mL
2	black cardamom pods, crushed	2
4	whole cloves	4
1	stick cinnamon, about 3 inches (7.5 cm) long	1
2	bay leaves	2
1 cup	Job's tears, soaked, rinsed and drained	250 mL
2 cups	reduced-sodium chicken stock or water	500 mL
1 1/2 cups	plain yogurt (minimum 4% M.F.)	375 mL
1/4 cup	finely chopped cilantro	60 mL

1. In a skillet, heat 1 tbsp (15 mL) of the oil over medium heat for 30 seconds. Add lamb, in batches, and cook, stirring, until browned, about 4 minutes per batch. Transfer to a plate and set aside.

2. Add remaining 1 tbsp (15 mL) of oil to pan. Add onions and cook, stirring, until softened, about 3 minutes. Add garlic, ginger, chile peppers, paprika, turmeric, salt, peppercorns, cayenne, cardamom, cloves, cinnamon stick and bay leaves and cook, stirring, for 2 minutes. Add Job's tears and toss until coated with mixture. Stir in stock and bring to a boil.

3. Return lamb and any accumulated juices to pan and stir well. Transfer to baking dish and stir in yogurt. Cover with foil and bake in preheated oven until Job's tears and lamb are tender, about 1 hour. Garnish with cilantro.

Variation

Spicy Beef Curry with Chinese "Barley": Substitute an equal quantity of stewing beef for the lamb.

Quinoa

Meatless Mains

Zuni Stew

Zuni stew, which is often made with meat, has its roots firmly in New Mexico, where the key ingredients, corn and chile peppers, thrive. It also happens to be home to the Zuni people, who make it from whatever they have on hand. Serve this with warm corn tortillas.

Makes 8 servings

Tips

Use canned hominy, drained and rinsed or cook dried hominy yourself (see page 18).

If you've cooked your own beans, save the cooking liquid and use it to moisten the stew instead of water or stock (Step 3).

I like to use a single-source chili powder (ancho or New Mexico) that differs from the dried chile used but a blend will work well, too. If using a blend, check the label to make sure no gluten has been added.

Nutrients per serving

Calories	268
Protein	14.3 g
Carbohydrates	34.4 g
Fat (Total)	9.5 g
Saturated Fat	4.4 g
Monounsaturated Fat	3.2 g
Polyunsaturated Fat	1.1 g
Dietary Fiber	8.1 g
Sodium	447 mg
Cholesterol	18 mg

EXCELLENT SOURCE OF vitamin A, folate, calcium, phosphorus, iron and manganese.

GOOD SOURCE OF vitamin C, riboflavin, magnesium, zinc and selenium.

SOURCE OF vitamin E (alpha-tocopherol), niacin, thiamine, pantothenic acid and copper.

CONTAINS a very high amount of dietary fiber.

3 cups	cooked drained hominy (see Tips, left)	750 mL
1 cup	drained, rinsed, cooked or canned pinto beans (see Tips, left)	250 mL
2	dried ancho, New Mexico or guajillo chiles	2
2 cups	boiling water	500 mL
1 tbsp	olive oil	15 mL
2	onions, finely chopped	2
4	stalks celery, diced	4
1	green bell pepper, seeded and diced	1
2	cloves garlic, minced	2
2 tbsp	chili powder (see Tips, left)	30 mL
2 tsp	ground cumin (see Tips, page 111)	10 mL
1 tsp	dried oregano leaves	5 mL
1/2 tsp	salt	2 mL
	Freshly ground black pepper	
1	chipotle pepper in adobo sauce, minced (see Tips, page 163)	1
1	can (28 oz/796 mL) no-salt-added diced tomatoes with juice	1
2 cups	corn kernels	500 mL
2	small zucchini (each about 8 oz/250 g), cut into 1/2-inch (1 cm) cubes	2
1 cup	sliced green beans	250 mL
	Water or reduced-sodium vegetable stock	
2 cups	shredded reduced-fat Monterey Jack cheese (see Tips, page 160)	500 mL

1. In a heatproof bowl, soak dried chiles in boiling water, weighing down with a cup to keep submerged, for 30 minutes. Drain, discarding soaking liquid and stems. Pat chiles dry, chop finely and set aside.

2. In a Dutch oven, heat oil over medium heat for 30 seconds. Add onions, celery, bell pepper and garlic and stir well. Reduce heat to low. Cover and cook until vegetables are softened, for 10 minutes. Add chili powder, cumin, oregano, salt, black pepper to taste, reserved chiles and chipotle pepper. Cook, stirring, for 1 minute. Add hominy and pinto beans and stir well.

3. Add tomatoes with juice and bring to a boil. Stir in corn, zucchini and green beans. Add water or stock barely to cover. Cover and simmer until vegetables are tender and flavors meld, about 30 minutes. Ladle into soup plates and pass the cheese at the table for sprinkling.

Roasted Mushrooms with Millet and Goat Cheese

Accompanied by a salad, this makes a nice light dinner. In season, I like to serve this with a sliced tomato salad, but tossed greens work well, too.

Makes 4 servings

Tips

Depending upon the size of your mushrooms, you may need a bit more olive oil to complete the brushing.

Try to time this so the preliminary baking of the mushrooms is completed at about the same time as the filling.

The mushrooms will be rather flat after roasting, so be aware that you will be piling on the filling rather than filling the tops.

Nutrients per serving

Calories	310
Protein	13.4 g
Carbohydrates	28.8 g
Fat (Total)	17.2 g
Saturated Fat	5.8 g
Monounsaturated Fat	7.4 g
Polyunsaturated Fat	2.7 g
Dietary Fiber	5.3 g
Sodium	156 mg
Cholesterol	14 mg

EXCELLENT SOURCE OF
vitamin A, riboflavin, niacin, folate, pantothenic acid, phosphorus, iron, magnesium, manganese, copper and selenium.

GOOD SOURCE OF vitamin E (alpha-tocopherol), thiamine and zinc.

SOURCE OF vitamin C and calcium.

CONTAINS a high amount of dietary fiber.

- **Preheat oven to 400°F (200°C)**
- **Rimmed baking sheet, lightly greased**

1½ cups	cooked toasted millet (see cooking instructions, page 22)	375 mL
4	large portobello mushrooms, stems and gills removed (each about 6 oz/175 g, after stemming)	4
2 tbsp	olive oil, divided	30 mL
	Salt and freshly ground black pepper	
2 tbsp	freshly squeezed lemon juice	30 mL
½ cup	finely chopped shallots	125 mL
2	cloves garlic, minced	2
6 cups	loosely packed chopped spinach leaves	1.5 L
½ cup	soft goat cheese	125 mL
2 tbsp	pine nuts	30 mL
2 tsp	balsamic vinegar	10 mL

1. Brush mushrooms all over with 1 tbsp (15 mL) of the oil and place on prepared baking sheet, gill side down. Roast in preheated oven until the edges are browning, about 15 minutes. Remove from oven and turn over. Season to taste with salt and pepper and drizzle with lemon juice. Set aside. Preheat broiler.

2. Meanwhile, in a skillet, heat remaining 1 tbsp (15 mL) of oil over medium heat for 30 seconds. Add shallots and cook, stirring, until softened, about 3 minutes. Add garlic and cook, stirring, for 1 minute. Add spinach and toss until wilted, about 2 minutes. Add millet and cook, stirring, until heated through, about 1 minute. Spoon mixture evenly into warm mushroom caps (see Tips, left).

3. Spoon 2 tbsp (30 mL) of goat cheese over each filled mushroom, evening out as best you can. Sprinkle with pine nuts. Heat under broiler until pine nuts brown, about 4 minutes. Drizzle balsamic vinegar evenly over mushrooms.

Variation

Roasted Mushrooms with Quinoa and Goat Cheese: Substitute an equal quantity of cooked quinoa (see cooking instructions, page 26) for the millet.

Soba Noodles with Broccoli Sauce

VEGAN FRIENDLY

This flavorful combination makes a great light weekday dinner. You can also serve smaller portions as a side dish. It is particularly enjoyable alongside miso-glazed tofu or fish.

Makes 4 servings

Tips

Most soba noodles contain some wheat flour. Those made only with buckwheat are available in Japanese markets or some natural foods stores.

If you are a heat seeker, increase the quantity of chili sauce to suit your taste.

I make this using sambal oelek, which is widely available, but other hot Asian chili sauces, such as chili-garlic and Sriracha, will also work.

8 oz	dried 100% buckwheat soba noodles (see Tips, left)	250 g
1 tsp	sesame oil	5 mL
BROCCOLI SAUCE		
3 tbsp	gluten-free reduced-sodium soy sauce	45 mL
1 tbsp	sake or vodka	15 mL
1 tbsp	cornstarch	15 mL
½ tsp	granulated sugar	2 mL
½ tsp	hot Asian chili sauce (see Tips, left)	2 mL
	Freshly ground black pepper	
1 tbsp	vegetable oil	15 mL
2	cloves garlic, minced	2
1 tbsp	minced gingerroot	15 mL
4 cups	broccoli florets	1 L
2 tbsp	reduced-sodium vegetable or chicken stock or water	30 mL
2	green onions, white part with a bit of green, thinly sliced	2
	Sesame oil	

1. In a large pot of boiling salted water, cook noodles until tender to the bite, about 7 minutes. Drain, rinse well in cold running water and drain again. Toss with sesame oil. Transfer to a serving bowl or deep platter and set aside.

2. *Broccoli Sauce:* In a small bowl, combine soy sauce, sake, cornstarch, sugar, chili sauce and pepper to taste. Mix well and set aside.

3. In a skillet or wok, heat oil over medium heat for 30 seconds. Add garlic and ginger and cook, stirring, for 1 minute. Add broccoli and toss to coat. Sprinkle with stock. Reduce heat to low. Cover and cook until broccoli is tender, about 5 minutes. Add soy sauce mixture and cook, stirring, until thickened, about 30 seconds.

4. Arrange broccoli mixture over noodles, sprinkle with green onions and drizzle with sesame oil. Serve immediately or let cool to room temperature.

Nutrients per serving

Calories	375
Protein	12.9 g
Carbohydrates	75 g
Fat (Total)	5 g
Saturated Fat	0.5 g
Monounsaturated Fat	2.5 g
Polyunsaturated Fat	1.7 g
Dietary Fiber	2.5 g
Sodium	804 mg
Cholesterol	0 mg

EXCELLENT SOURCE OF vitamin C and manganese.
GOOD SOURCE OF vitamin A, thiamine, niacin, folate and magnesium.
SOURCE OF vitamin E (alpha-tocopherol), calcium, phosphorus, riboflavin, pantothenic acid, iron, zinc and selenium.
CONTAINS a moderate amount of dietary fiber.

158 MEATLESS MAINS

Wild Rice Cakes

These make a nice light dinner accompanied by a salad or you can serve them as a substantial side dish. I top them with homemade ketchup or the red pepper coulis, both of which are delicious, but chili sauce, tomato sauce, or even a dab of pesto, also work quite well.

Makes 4 main servings or 8 side servings

Tips

Be careful when turning the cakes, as they have a tendency to fall apart until they are thoroughly cooked.

The basil adds a nice note to the coulis, but if you can't get fresh leaves, omit it — the coulis will be quite tasty, anyway.

If you are using pre-shredded cheese, check the label to make sure the manufacturer has not added a product containing gluten to prevent sticking.

Nutrients per serving

Calories	386
Protein	21.4 g
Carbohydrates	41.9 g
Fat (Total)	14.7 g
Saturated Fat	4.4 g
Monounsaturated Fat	7.8 g
Polyunsaturated Fat	1.7 g
Dietary Fiber	3.5 g
Sodium	547 mg
Cholesterol	113 mg

EXCELLENT SOURCE OF vitamin C, calcium, phosphorus, magnesium, manganese, riboflavin, zinc and selenium.
GOOD SOURCE OF vitamins A and E (alpha-tocopherol), folate and niacin.
SOURCE OF thiamine, pantothenic acid, iron and copper.
CONTAINS a moderate amount of dietary fiber.

- Preheat oven to 400°F (200°C)
- Large rimmed baking sheet, lightly greased

2½ cups	water	625 mL
1 cup	wild and brown rice mixture, rinsed and drained	250 mL
½ tsp	salt	2 mL
1½ cups	shredded reduced-fat Swiss cheese (see Tips, left)	375 mL
½ cup	plain yogurt, preferably full fat (see Tips, page 153)	125 mL
¼ cup	chopped red or green onion	60 mL
¼ cup	finely chopped parsley	60 mL
2	eggs, beaten	2
	Freshly ground black pepper	

RED PEPPER COULIS

2	roasted red peppers	2
3	drained oil-packed sun-dried tomatoes, chopped	3
2 tbsp	extra virgin olive oil	30 mL
1 tbsp	balsamic vinegar	15 mL
10	fresh basil leaves, optional	10

1. In a large saucepan, bring water to a rolling boil. Add rice and salt. Return to a boil. Reduce heat, cover and simmer until rice is tender and about half of the wild rice grains have split, about 1 hour. Set aside until cool enough to handle, about 20 minutes.

2. In a bowl, combine rice, Swiss cheese, yogurt, red onion, parsley, eggs and pepper to taste. Mix well. Using a large spoon, drop mixture in 8 batches, onto prepared baking sheet. Flatten lightly with a spatula or large spoon.

3. Bake in preheated oven for 15 minutes, then flip and cook until lightly browned and heated through, for 5 minutes. Let cool on pan for 5 minutes before serving. Top with Red Pepper Coulis, if using.

4. *Red Pepper Coulis:* In a food processor, combine roasted peppers, sun–dried tomatoes, oil, balsamic vinegar and basil, if using, and process until smooth.

Rice-Stuffed Eggplant

This one-dish meal is very tasty and particularly handy for those nights when everyone is coming and going at different times. Cover the cooked eggplants and leave them out so people can help themselves, and leave the fixins' for salad alongside. If you roast the eggplant in the oven while you're chopping the vegetables, it's actually quite time-efficient.

Makes 6 servings

Tips

Herbes de Provence is a traditional French combination of dried herbs such as thyme, marjoram, tarragon and parsley. It is available premixed or you can make your own simplified version by combining 2 tsp (10 mL) dried thyme leaves with 1 tsp (5 mL) each marjoram and dried parsley.

When using any canned product, such as tomatoes, check the label to make sure ingredients containing gluten have not been added.

Nutrients per serving

Calories	281
Protein	8.9 g
Carbohydrates	42.4 g
Fat (Total)	10.6 g
Saturated Fat	2.6 g
Monounsaturated Fat	6 g
Polyunsaturated Fat	1.3 g
Dietary Fiber	8 g
Sodium	556 mg
Cholesterol	7 mg

EXCELLENT SOURCE OF vitamin C, magnesium and manganese.

GOOD SOURCE OF vitamins A and E (alpha-tocopherol), thiamine, niacin, folate, calcium, phosphorus, iron, copper and selenium.

SOURCE OF riboflavin, pantothenic acid and zinc.

CONTAINS a very high amount of dietary fiber.

- Preheat oven to 350°F (180°C)
- Rimmed baking sheet

2 cups	cooked brown or red rice, cooled	500 mL
3	eggplants (each about 10 oz/300 g)	3
3 tbsp	olive oil (approx.), divided	45 mL
1	onion, finely chopped	1
1	green bell pepper, seeded and diced	1
1	red bell pepper, seeded and diced	1
4	cloves garlic, minced	4
1 tbsp	herbes de Provence (see Tips, left)	15 mL
1 tsp	salt	5 mL
	Freshly ground black pepper	
1	can (28 oz/796 mL) no-salt-added diced tomatoes, drained (see Tips, left)	1
½ cup	freshly grated Parmesan cheese (see Tips, page 174)	125 mL

1. Halve eggplants lengthwise and brush cut sides liberally with about 2 tbsp (30 mL) of the olive oil. Place cut side down on baking sheet and roast in preheated oven until softened, about 35 minutes. Let cool. Scoop out flesh, leaving about ½ inch (1 cm) of the shell, and return to baking sheet, hollow side up. Chop flesh finely. Set both parts aside.

2. In a large skillet, heat remaining 1 tbsp (15 mL) of olive oil over medium heat for 30 seconds. Add onion, bell peppers and garlic and stir well. Reduce heat to low. Cover and cook until vegetables are softened, about 10 minutes. Increase heat to medium. Add herbes de Provence, salt and black pepper to taste and cook, stirring, for 1 minute. Add reserved eggplant flesh, cooked rice and diced tomatoes and cook, stirring, until heated through.

3. Spoon filling into eggplant shells to form a generous mound. Bake in preheated oven for 20 minutes. Sprinkle Parmesan evenly over tops and bake until cheese is melted and slightly crusty, about 10 minutes.

Mushroom Varnishkes

This traditional dish of buckwheat groats with bowtie pasta and mushrooms can be categorized as Jewish comfort food. I've embellished it a bit with celery and spice, and specified farfalle to bump up the whole-grain content, but haven't strayed far from its roots. This is a substantial but simple dish deeply rooted in Eastern European cuisine. Serve it with steamed green beans or a tossed green salad.

Makes 6 servings

Tip

Buckwheat groats that are already toasted are known as kasha. If you prefer a milder buckwheat flavor, use groats rather than kasha in this dish. Cooking them with the egg serves the same purpose as toasting — to bring out the flavor.

1	egg	1
½ tsp	salt	2 mL
¼ tsp	cayenne pepper	1 mL
	Freshly ground black pepper	
1 cup	buckwheat groats or kasha (see Tip, left)	250 mL
2 tbsp	olive oil, divided	30 mL
2 tbsp	butter, divided	30 mL
8 oz	cremini mushrooms, stems removed and thinly sliced	250 g
2 tbsp	freshly squeezed lemon juice	30 mL
1	onion, finely chopped	1
2	stalks celery, diced	2
2	cloves garlic, minced	2
1 tsp	sweet paprika	5 mL
2 cups	reduced-sodium vegetable stock or water	500 mL
1 cup	gluten-free corn bowtie pasta (farfalle)	250 mL
½ cup	finely chopped parsley or dill	125 mL

1. In a bowl, beat egg, salt, cayenne and black pepper to taste until eggs are frothy. Add groats and stir to coat. Heat a skillet over medium heat for 30 seconds. Add groat mixture, stirring, until egg sets and grains separate, about 3 minutes. Transfer to a bowl and wipe skillet clean.

2. In same skillet, heat 1 tbsp (15 mL) each of the oil and butter over medium–high heat. Add mushrooms and cook, stirring, until their liquid evaporates, about 8 minutes. Sprinkle with lemon juice and, using a slotted spoon, transfer to a bowl and set aside.

3. Add remaining 1 tbsp (15 mL) of oil to pan. Add onion, celery, garlic and paprika and cook, stirring, until celery is softened, about 5 minutes. Add cooled groats and egg mixture and reserved mushrooms and toss well. Add stock and bring to a boil. Reduce heat to low. Cover and simmer for 5 minutes. Remove from heat and set aside until groats are tender and liquid is absorbed, about 10 minutes.

4. Meanwhile, in a large pot of boiling salted water, cook bowtie pasta until tender to the bite, about 12 minutes. Toss with remaining 1 tbsp (15 mL) of butter. Add to cooked groats and mix well. Garnish with parsley.

Nutrients per serving

Calories	266
Protein	7.3 g
Carbohydrates	39.4 g
Fat (Total)	10.3 g
Saturated Fat	3.5 g
Monounsaturated Fat	5 g
Polyunsaturated Fat	1.2 g
Dietary Fiber	6.8 g
Sodium	250 mg
Cholesterol	41 mg

EXCELLENT SOURCE OF magnesium, manganese and selenium.

GOOD SOURCE OF riboflavin, niacin, folate, pantothenic acid, phosphorus, zinc and copper.

SOURCE OF vitamins A, C and E (alpha-tocopherol), thiamine and iron.

CONTAINS a very high amount of dietary fiber.

Quinoa-Stuffed Tomatoes

Here's a delightfully different main course. Make this in late summer or early fall when field tomatoes are in season and use the largest reddest tomatoes you can find for a spectacular presentation.

Makes 6 servings

Tips

A grapefruit spoon makes easy work of scooping out the tomato pulp.

If you are using pre-shredded cheese, check the label to make sure the manufacturer has not added a product containing gluten to prevent sticking.

If you're shredding your own cheese, you'll need about a 6-oz (175 g) block.

Chipotle peppers are dried smoked jalapeño peppers. Not all brands of chipotle peppers in abodo sauce are gluten-free so be sure to check the label.

Nutrients per serving

Calories	257
Protein	13.5 g
Carbohydrates	21.1 g
Fat (Total)	14 g
Saturated Fat	8.1 g
Monounsaturated Fat	3.9 g
Polyunsaturated Fat	1.1 g
Dietary Fiber	3.6 g
Sodium	453 mg
Cholesterol	40 mg

EXCELLENT SOURCE OF vitamin A, calcium, phosphorus and manganese.

GOOD SOURCE OF vitamin C, riboflavin, iron, magnesium and zinc.

SOURCE OF vitamin E (alpha-tocopherol), niacin, folate, thiamine, pantothenic acid, copper and selenium.

CONTAINS a moderate amount of dietary fiber.

- **Preheat oven to 350°F (180°C)**

6	large firm tomatoes	6
FILLING		
2 cups	cooked quinoa (see cooking instructions, page 26)	500 mL
2 cups	shredded Cheddar cheese, divided (see Tips, left)	500 mL
¼ cup	finely chopped red onion	60 mL
1	finely chopped chipotle pepper in adobo sauce (see Tips, left)	1
1 tsp	sweet paprika	5 mL
½ tsp	salt	2 mL
	Freshly ground black pepper	

1. Cut ½ inch (1 cm) off tops of tomatoes. Remove the core and discard. Carefully scoop out remaining pulp, leaving a thin wall and being careful not to puncture the shell. Place tomatoes in a baking dish. Finely chop pulp and set aside.

2. *Filling:* In a bowl, combine quinoa, 1½ cups (375 mL) of the cheese, onion, chipotle pepper with sauce, paprika, salt, pepper to taste and reserved tomato pulp. Mix well. Spoon into tomato shells. Sprinkle remaining cheese over top. Bake in preheated oven until cheese is melted and browned and tomatoes are tender, about 30 minutes. Serve hot.

Variation

Millet-Stuffed Tomatoes: Substitute an equal quantity of toasted cooked millet (see cooking instructions, page 22) for the quinoa.

VITAMIN A

One serving of this dish is an excellent source of vitamin A. Although this vitamin is famous for keeping your eyes healthy, it has other important functions, such as contributing to your ability to see at night, supporting bone growth and keeping cells functioning well. Dietary intake studies suggest that diets rich in beta-carotene (which the body makes into vitamin A) and vitamin A may lower the risk of many types of cancer. However, studies testing beta-carotene supplements found no such correlation.

Korean-Style Rice Bowl

This version of a Korean dish known as bibimbap, which is served in a hot stone bowl called a tukbaege. Vegans can omit the egg.

Makes 4 servings

Tips

If you're not concerned about using butter, brush the rice with about 2 tsp (10 mL) melted butter instead of the vegetable oil prior to baking to ensure a nicely crusted top.

This quantity of chili paste and sesame oil likely makes more hot sauce than you will need to satisfy most palates, but if you have heat seekers among your diners, you may require this amount. For subsequent meals, just combine an equal quantity of Asian chili paste and sesame oil to suit your needs.

Nutrients per serving

Calories	315
Protein	6.3 g
Carbohydrates	47.7 g
Fat (Total)	11.8 g
Saturated Fat	1.3 g
Monounsaturated Fat	5.8 g
Polyunsaturated Fat	4 g
Dietary Fiber	6.2 g
Sodium	63 mg
Cholesterol	0 mg

EXCELLENT SOURCE OF vitamins A and C, magnesium and manganese.
GOOD SOURCE OF vitamin E (alpha-tocopherol), thiamine, niacin, folate, pantothenic acid, phosphorus, iron, zinc and copper.
SOURCE OF riboflavin and calcium.
CONTAINS a very high amount of dietary fiber.

- **Preheat oven to 400°F (200°C)**
- **12-inch (30 cm) ovenproof skillet**

3 cups	hot cooked short-grain brown rice	750 mL
3 tbsp	vegetable oil, divided (approx.)	45 mL
8 oz	shiitake mushrooms, stemmed and sliced	250 g
2	cloves garlic, minced	2
	Salt and freshly ground black pepper	
1 tbsp	freshly squeezed lemon juice	15 mL
1 cup	sliced green beans, blanched	250 mL
1 cup	diced carrots, blanched	250 mL
1	red bell pepper, seeded and diced	1
6	green onions, thinly sliced	6
1 cup	diced English cucumber	250 mL
1 tsp	rice vinegar	5 mL
1 tbsp	hot Asian chili paste, such as sambal oelek	15 mL
1 tbsp	sesame oil	15 mL
4	eggs, optional	4
	Kimchi, optional	

1. In skillet, heat 2 tsp (10 mL) of the oil over medium heat. Add rice and spread evenly. Cook until bottom begins to brown, about 4 minutes. Brush top with 2 tsp (10 mL) vegetable oil. Transfer to preheated oven and bake until crusty, about 15 minutes. Set aside.

2. Meanwhile, in a wok, heat 1 tbsp (15 mL) of the oil over medium–high heat for 30 seconds. Add mushrooms and garlic and cook, stirring, until mushrooms lose their liquid, about 8 minutes. Season to taste with salt and pepper. Sprinkle with lemon juice. Transfer to a bowl and set aside.

3. Add 1 tbsp (15 mL) of oil to wok. Add green beans, carrots and bell pepper and cook, stirring, until vegetables are softened, about 5 minutes. Remove from heat and set aside.

4. In a bowl, combine green onions and cucumber. Toss with rice vinegar. Season to taste with salt and pepper and set aside.

5. In a small bowl, combine chili paste and sesame oil. Set aside.

6. Divide baked rice into 4 bowls. Arrange mushroom, green bean and cucumber mixtures over top. Drizzle with a small amount of chili–sesame oil and place remainder in a small dish to pass at the table.

7. If using eggs, heat 1 tbsp (15 mL) of oil in wok. Add eggs, 2 at a time, and fry until crispy brown around the edges. Top each rice bowl with a fried egg and serve immediately. Serve with kimchi, if using.

Mushroom Ragoût

You can't go wrong with this combination of ingredients. The addition of Chinese seasonings and lentils to mushrooms and Job's tears adds interesting flavors and expands the range of nutrients in the dish. Just add a sliced tomato or green salad to complete the meal.

Makes 8 servings

Tips

Be careful not to use more Chinese 5-spice powder than the quantity called for. It has a very pronounced flavor and will overpower the dish. Also, check the label to make sure your brand is gluten-free.

Tamari is a type of soy sauce that shouldn't contain wheat. However, check the label.

3 cups	cooked Job's tears (see cooking instructions, page 20)	750 mL
4	dried shiitake mushrooms	4
2 cups	hot water	500 mL
1 tbsp	butter or oil	15 mL
8 oz	cremini mushrooms, stemmed and sliced	250 g
1 tbsp	olive oil	15 mL
2	onions, finely chopped	2
4	stalks celery, diced	4
2	carrots, diced	2
4	cloves garlic, minced	4
2 tbsp	minced gingerroot	30 mL
1 tsp	cracked black peppercorns	5 mL
½ tsp	Chinese 5-spice powder (see Tips, left)	2 mL
1 cup	dried brown lentils, rinsed and drained	250 mL
4 cups	reduced-sodium vegetable stock (see Tips, page 78)	1 L
¼ cup	gluten-free reduced-sodium soy sauce (see Tips, left)	60 mL
	Finely chopped green onions	

1. In a bowl, combine dried shiitake mushrooms with hot water. Stir well. Let stand for 30 minutes. Strain through a fine sieve, reserving mushrooms and liquid separately. Pat mushrooms dry, remove stems and chop finely.

2. Meanwhile, in a deep skillet, melt butter over medium heat. Add cremini mushrooms and cook, stirring, until they begin to release liquid, about 5 minutes. Transfer to a bowl.

3. Add oil to pan and heat for 30 seconds. Add onions, celery and carrots and cook, stirring, until vegetables are softened, about 7 minutes. Add garlic, ginger, peppercorns and 5-spice powder and cook, stirring, for 1 minute. Stir in reconstituted and fresh mushrooms. Add Job's tears and lentils and stir well. Stir in stock and reserved mushroom soaking liquid. Bring to a boil. Reduce heat to low. Cover and simmer until lentils are tender, about 40 minutes. Stir in soy sauce. Garnish with green onions.

Variation

Mushroom and Rice Ragoût: Substitute an equal quantity of cooked brown or red rice for the Job's tears.

Nutrients per serving

Calories	276
Protein	13 g
Carbohydrates	47 g
Fat (Total)	5.4 g
Saturated Fat	1.2 g
Monounsaturated Fat	1.7 g
Polyunsaturated Fat	0.4 g
Dietary Fiber	6.1 g
Sodium	312 mg
Cholesterol	4 mg

EXCELLENT SOURCE OF vitamin A, folate, pantothenic acid, phosphorus, iron, manganese, copper and selenium.
GOOD SOURCE OF thiamine, niacin, riboflavin, zinc and magnesium.
SOURCE OF vitamins C and E (alpha-tocopherol) and calcium.
CONTAINS a very high amount of dietary fiber.

Quinoa Chili

This chili is easy to make, very tasty and different enough to perk up your taste buds if they have grown tired of the same old thing. Like most whole-grain dishes, it soaks up liquid if left to sit, so keep some extra vegetable stock on hand to add if you're reheating leftovers. I like to serve this with a tossed green salad.

Makes 6 servings

Tip

In all the recipes calling for beans (as in legumes, not green beans), you can cook dried beans from scratch, in which case soak and cook 1 cup (250 mL) of dried beans. Or use canned beans, which are already cooked, and thoroughly rinse and drain. Beans do not contain gluten, but canned beans may be processed in a facility where gluten is present. It is always a good idea to check the label and, if necessary, contact the manufacturer.

Nutrients per serving

Calories	293
Protein	11.5 g
Carbohydrates	55.1 g
Fat (Total)	5.3 g
Saturated Fat	0.7 g
Monounsaturated Fat	2.4 g
Polyunsaturated Fat	1.5 g
Dietary Fiber	10.6 g
Sodium	303 mg
Cholesterol	0 mg

EXCELLENT SOURCE OF vitamins A and C, folate, iron, magnesium, manganese and copper.
GOOD SOURCE OF vitamin E (alpha-tocopherol), thiamine, riboflavin, niacin, phosphorus and zinc.
SOURCE OF pantothenic acid, calcium and selenium.
CONTAINS a very high amount of dietary fiber.

1 tbsp	olive oil	15 mL
2	onions, finely chopped	2
2	stalks celery, diced	2
1	carrot, peeled and diced	1
1	green bell pepper, seeded and diced	1
4	cloves garlic, minced	4
2 tbsp	chili powder	30 mL
1	chipotle pepper in adobo sauce, minced	1
1	can (28 oz/796 mL) no-salt-added diced tomatoes with juice	1
2 cups	reduced-sodium vegetable stock (see Tips, page 153)	500 mL
	Salt and freshly ground black pepper	
1 cup	quinoa, rinsed and drained	250 mL
2 cups	drained, rinsed cooked or canned pinto beans (see Tip, left)	500 mL
1 cup	corn kernels	250 mL

1. In a large deep skillet with a tight-fitting lid, heat oil over medium heat for 30 seconds. Add onions, celery, carrot, bell pepper and garlic and stir well. Reduce heat to low. Cover and cook until vegetables are softened, about 10 minutes.

2. Increase heat to medium. Add chili powder and chipotle pepper and cook, stirring, for 1 minute. Add tomatoes with juice and stock and bring to a boil. Season to taste with salt and black pepper. Add quinoa, beans and corn and cook, stirring, until mixture returns to a boil. Reduce heat to low. Cover and simmer until quinoa is tender, about 25 minutes.

Variations

Millet Chili: Substitute an equal quantity of toasted millet for the quinoa. Increase the quantity of vegetable stock to $2\frac{1}{2}$ cups (625 mL) and increase cooking time to about 25 minutes.

Substitute red kidney, cranberry or small red beans for the pinto beans.

Khitchuri with Tomatoes and Green Peppers

This traditional Indian dish of rice and lentils makes a delicious main course when topped off with a mélange of peppers and tomatoes, so expect requests for seconds. I like to use red lentils because they dissolve in the liquid, adding creaminess to the sauce. The pilaf will be liquidy when the rice is cooked, so serve this in soup plates. You don't need to add much — a simple green salad and perhaps some gluten-free bread to soak up the sauce.

Makes 6 servings

Tips

Substitute 2 cups (500 mL) halved cherry tomatoes for the chopped tomatoes, if you prefer.

Heinz ketchup is gluten-free but if you're using another brand, check the label to make sure ingredients containing gluten have not been added.

2 tbsp	olive oil, divided	30 mL
1	onion, finely chopped	1
2	cloves garlic, minced	2
2 tsp	curry powder	10 mL
1	bay leaf	1
1 cup	brown basmati or brown long-grain rice, rinsed and drained	250 mL
1 cup	dried red lentils	250 mL
4 cups	reduced-sodium vegetable stock (see Tips, page 150)	1 L
2	green bell peppers, seeded and diced	2
½ tsp	ground cumin (see Tips, page 111)	2 mL
½ tsp	salt	2 mL
½ tsp	freshly ground black pepper	2 mL
1	hot pepper, long red or green or Thai chile pepper, optional	1
4	small tomatoes, peeled and chopped (see Tips, left)	4
⅓ cup	ketchup (see Tips, left)	75 mL
3	hard-cooked eggs, sliced, optional	3

1. In a saucepan, heat 1 tbsp (15 mL) of the oil over medium heat. Add onion and garlic and cook, stirring, until onion softens, about 3 minutes. Stir in curry powder and bay leaf. Add rice and lentils and stir until coated. Add stock and bring to a boil. Reduce heat to low. Cover and simmer until rice is tender, about 50 minutes.

2. Meanwhile, in a skillet, heat remaining 1 tbsp (15 mL) of oil over medium heat. Add bell peppers, cumin, salt, black pepper and chile pepper, if using, and cook, stirring, until peppers are softened, about 5 minutes. Add tomatoes and cook, stirring, for 1 minute. Stir in ketchup. Reduce heat to low and simmer, stirring occasionally, until flavors meld, about 10 minutes.

3. *To serve:* Spread rice mixture evenly over a large deep platter. Arrange pepper mixture over top and garnish with eggs, if using.

Nutrients per serving

Calories	310
Protein	12.2 g
Carbohydrates	54 g
Fat (Total)	6.1 g
Saturated Fat	0.9 g
Monounsaturated Fat	3.8 g
Polyunsaturated Fat	1.1 g
Dietary Fiber	7.9 g
Sodium	347 mg
Cholesterol	0 mg

EXCELLENT SOURCE OF vitamins A and C, thiamine, folate, riboflavin, phosphorus, iron, magnesium and manganese.

GOOD SOURCE OF niacin, pantothenic acid, zinc and copper.

SOURCE OF vitamin E (alpha-tocopherol), calcium and selenium.

CONTAINS a very high amount of dietary fiber.

Chile-Spiked Quinoa Pudding with Corn

This is a tasty and versatile dish. I like to serve it on weekdays as a main course, accompanied by a salad of bibb lettuce, green onions and diced avocado in a white wine vinaigrette. If you're having a large number of guests for dinner and looking to stretch the meal, it also works as an unusual side, serving eight to ten.

Makes 6 servings

Tip
Chipotle peppers are dried smoked jalapeño peppers. Not all brands of chipotle peppers in abodo sauce are gluten-free so be sure to check the label. If you are a heat seeker, add an extra half chipotle pepper in adobo sauce.

Nutrients per serving

Calories	212
Protein	8.5 g
Carbohydrates	31.4 g
Fat (Total)	6.8 g
Saturated Fat	1.3 g
Monounsaturated Fat	3.2 g
Polyunsaturated Fat	1.4 g
Dietary Fiber	3.8 g
Sodium	331 mg
Cholesterol	93 mg

EXCELLENT SOURCE OF vitamin C, iron, magnesium and manganese.

GOOD SOURCE OF riboflavin, niacin, thiamine, folate, phosphorus, zinc, copper and selenium.

SOURCE OF vitamins A and E (alpha-tocopherol), pantothenic acid and calcium.

CONTAINS a moderate amount of dietary fiber.

- Preheat oven to 375°F (190°C)
- Shallow 8-cup (2 L) baking dish, lightly greased

3 cups	cooked quinoa (see cooking instructions, page 26)	750 mL
1 tbsp	olive oil	15 mL
1	onion, finely chopped	1
1	red bell pepper, seeded and diced	1
1	clove garlic, minced	1
2 tsp	dried oregano leaves	10 mL
1/2 tsp	salt	2 mL
1/2 tsp	freshly ground black pepper	2 mL
1	chipotle pepper in adobo sauce, minced (see Tip, left)	1
1	can (14 oz/398 mL) diced tomatoes with juice (see Tips, page 161)	1
1 cup	corn kernels	250 mL
3	eggs, beaten	3

1. In a large saucepan, heat oil over medium heat for 30 seconds. Add onion and bell pepper. Reduce heat to low. Cover and cook until vegetables are softened, about 10 minutes.

2. Add garlic, oregano, salt and black pepper and cook, stirring, for 1 minute. Stir in chipotle pepper. Add quinoa and mix well. Stir in tomatoes with juice and corn. Remove from heat.

3. In a small bowl, combine beaten eggs with about 1/2 cup (125 mL) of the hot mixture, beating until combined. Gradually return to pot, mixing well. Transfer to prepared baking dish. Bake in preheated oven until pudding sets and top is crispy and browned, about 45 minutes.

Variation
Chile-Spiked Millet Pudding with Corn: Substitute an equal quantity of cooked toasted millet (see cooking instructions, page 22) for the quinoa.

Wild Rice

Sides, Sundries and Basics

Italian-Style Green Rice

Here's a deliciously different rice that makes a perfect companion for grilled meats and fish. Your guests will be very impressed, as the short-grain rice is quite glutinous and the results mimic risotto. You can fib and say you spent endless time stirring to produce such a stunning effect.

Makes 6 servings

Tips

If you are using prepared stock, check the label to make sure it doesn't contain gluten.

If your spinach has not been prewashed, be sure to rinse it thoroughly in a basin of lukewarm water. Swish it around to remove all traces of grit, then rinse it again in a colander under cold running water.

1 cup	short-grain brown rice	250 mL
1¼ cups	water, divided	300 mL
2 cups	reduced-sodium chicken or vegetable stock (see Tips, left)	500 mL
1 lb	fresh spinach leaves, stems removed (see Tips, left)	500 g
	Salt and freshly ground black pepper	
2	green onions, white part only, finely chopped	2
2 tbsp	extra virgin olive oil	30 mL
¼ cup	freshly grated Parmesan cheese (see Tips, page 174)	60 mL

1. In a bowl, combine rice and 1 cup (250 mL) of the water. Stir well. Cover and set aside for at least 3 hours or overnight. Drain, reserving liquid.

2. In a heavy saucepan with a tight-fitting lid, combine stock and reserved soaking water. Bring to a boil. Stir in rice and return to a boil. Reduce heat to low. Cover and simmer for 35 minutes. Remove lid, stir well and simmer, uncovered, stirring occasionally, until liquid is absorbed and rice is tender, about 15 minutes.

3. When rice is almost cooked, in another saucepan over low heat, combine spinach and ¼ cup (60 mL) of water. Cover and cook until wilted, about 5 minutes. Using a slotted spoon, transfer to a cutting board and chop finely. Transfer to a bowl. Season to taste with salt and pepper. Stir in green onions. Set aside.

4. *To serve:* Spread cooked rice evenly over a deep platter. Arrange spinach evenly over the center, leaving some rice exposed around the edge. Drizzle olive oil over the spinach and sprinkle with Parmesan. Serve immediately.

Nutrients per serving

Calories	195
Protein	7 g
Carbohydrates	27.5 g
Fat (Total)	6.8 g
Saturated Fat	1.5 g
Monounsaturated Fat	4 g
Polyunsaturated Fat	0.9 g
Dietary Fiber	3.6 g
Sodium	314 mg
Cholesterol	4 mg

EXCELLENT SOURCE OF vitamin A, folate, magnesium and manganese.

GOOD SOURCE OF vitamin E (alpha-tocopherol) and iron.

SOURCE OF vitamin C, thiamine, riboflavin, niacin, pantothenic acid, zinc, calcium, phosphorus and copper.

CONTAINS a moderate amount of dietary fiber.

Brown Rice Risotto

Short-grain brown rice is glutinous, which means you can use it to make a terrific risotto without the stirring. This dish is so easy to make that I often serve it as a side for weekday dinners. It's a great accompaniment to roasted or grilled meat, fish or a meatless main and is much more nutritious than versions made with white rice.

Makes 6 servings

Tips

I have found that when making this recipe, soaking the rice speeds up the cooking and produces a creamier result. But if you don't have time, add about 10 minutes to the cooking time with the lid on.

The addition of white wine adds a pleasantly acidic note to risotto, but if you prefer, use an additional 1/2 cup (125 mL) of stock.

Nutrient Tip

I used homemade vegetable stock to make this risotto because it is so low in sodium.

Nutrients per serving	
Calories	147
Protein	2.6 g
Carbohydrates	26.3 g
Fat (Total)	3.1 g
Saturated Fat	0.5 g
Monounsaturated Fat	2 g
Polyunsaturated Fat	0.5 g
Dietary Fiber	2.1 g
Sodium	3 mg
Cholesterol	0 mg

EXCELLENT SOURCE OF
manganese.

GOOD SOURCE OF
magnesium.

SOURCE OF thiamin,
niacin, pantothenic acid,
phosphorus, iron, zinc and
copper.

CONTAINS a moderate
amount of dietary fiber.

1 cup	short-grain brown rice (see Tips, left)	250 mL
1 cup	warm water	250 mL
1 tbsp	olive oil	15 mL
1	onion, finely chopped	1
2 cups	Homemade Vegetable Stock (see recipe, page 78) or reduced-sodium chicken stock	500 mL
1/2 cup	dry white wine (see Tips, left)	125 mL
	Freshly ground black pepper	
1 tbsp	butter, optional	15 mL
2 tbsp	finely chopped parsley, optional	30 mL
2 tbsp	freshly grated Parmesan cheese, optional	30 mL

1. In a bowl, combine rice and water. Stir well and set aside for at least 3 hours or overnight. When ready to cook, drain, reserving soaking liquid.

2. In a heavy saucepan with a tight-fitting lid, heat oil over medium heat for 30 seconds. Add onion and cook, stirring, until softened, about 3 minutes. Add stock, wine and reserved soaking liquid and bring to a boil. Add rice and pepper to taste. Stir well and bring to a boil. Reduce heat to low. Cover and simmer for 35 minutes, placing a heat diffuser on the element, if necessary, to keep the mixture at a true simmer. Remove lid, stir well and simmer, uncovered, stirring occasionally, until liquid is absorbed and rice is tender, about 15 minutes.

3. Stir in butter, parsley and cheese, if using.

Variation

Substitute up to 2 tbsp (30 mL) of the short-grain brown rice with a more colorful robust rice, such as Colusari red rice or Wehani, to add texture and visual detail.

Roasted Red Pepper Risotto

This is a great way to dress up a simple dinner or to handle unexpected guests. Pick up a rotisserie chicken or two or a vegetable stir-fry, and a precooked vegetable, such as asparagus vinaigrette. Make this risotto, open a bottle of wine and everyone will think you're amazing.

Makes 6 servings

Tips

You can make this recipe without presoaking the rice, but you'll need to cook it for an extra 15 minutes. If you're not presoaking the rice, don't forget to add 1 cup (250 mL) water along with the stock.

Authentic Parmigiano-Reggiano cheese, which has Protected Designation of Origin status in Italy, is made with calf rennet. If you are a vegetarian, look for generic Parmesan cheese that is suitable for your diet.

Nutrients per serving	
Calories	167
Protein	4.3 g
Carbohydrates	28.2 g
Fat (Total)	3.8 g
Saturated Fat	0.8 g
Monounsaturated Fat	2.2 g
Polyunsaturated Fat	0.6 g
Dietary Fiber	2.6 g
Sodium	241 mg
Cholesterol	2 mg

EXCELLENT SOURCE OF vitamin C and manganese.
GOOD SOURCE OF magnesium.
SOURCE OF vitamins A and E (alpha-tocopherol), thiamine, niacin, folate, pantothenic acid, phosphorus, iron, zinc and copper.
CONTAINS a moderate amount of dietary fiber.

1 cup	short-grain brown rice	250 mL
1 cup	water	250 mL
1 tbsp	olive oil	15 mL
1	onion, finely chopped	1
2 tbsp	diced pancetta, optional	30 mL
½ tsp	sweet or hot paprika	2 mL
¼ tsp	freshly ground black pepper	1 mL
½ cup	dry white wine or additional stock	125 mL
1½ cups	reduced-sodium chicken or vegetable stock (see Tips, page 172)	375 mL
¾ cup	diced roasted red peppers (about 2)	175 mL
2 tbsp	freshly grated Parmesan cheese (see Tips, left)	30 mL

1. In a bowl, combine rice and water. Stir well. Cover and set aside for at least 3 hours or overnight. Drain, reserving liquid (see Tips, left).

2. In a heavy saucepan with a tight-fitting lid, heat oil over medium heat for 30 seconds. Add onion and pancetta, if using, and cook, stirring, until onion softens, about 3 minutes. Add paprika and black pepper and cook, stirring, for 1 minute. Add wine and cook, stirring, until liquid evaporates, about 5 minutes. Add stock and reserved soaking liquid and bring to a boil. Stir in rice and return to a boil. Reduce heat to low. Cover and simmer for 35 minutes.

3. Stir in red peppers. Simmer, uncovered, stirring occasionally, until liquid is absorbed and rice is tender, about 15 minutes. Remove from heat and stir in Parmesan. Serve immediately.

Variations

Risotto with Cabbage: Substitute 2 cups (500 mL) thinly shredded cabbage (preferably Savoy) for the roasted red peppers and ½ tsp (2 mL) dried thyme leaves for the paprika.

Smoked Cheese Risotto: Omit pancetta, paprika and roasted red peppers. Add 2 cloves minced garlic, along with the onion. After the rice is tender (Step 3), stir in 1 cup (250 mL) shredded smoked Gouda or mozzarella until melted, then add Parmesan.

Chile Rice

This robust rice makes a great accompaniment to grilled fish or meat or a platter of roasted vegetables and is superb with Saffron-Scented Shrimp (see recipe, page 122). Use two chiles if you're a heat seeker and one if you prefer a tamer result. Either way, this is a winner.

Makes 6 servings

Tips

Unless you have a stove with a true simmer, after reducing the heat to low I recommend placing a heat diffuser under the pot to prevent the mixture from boiling. This device also helps to ensure the rice will cook evenly and prevents hot spots, which might cause scorching, from forming.

Heat diffusers are available at kitchen supply and hardware stores and are made to work on gas or electric stoves.

1 tbsp	olive oil	15 mL
1	onion, thinly sliced on the vertical	1
2	cloves garlic, minced	2
1 tbsp	minced gingerroot	15 mL
1 to 2	long red or green chile peppers, seeded and minced	1 to 2
2	bay leaves	2
1 tsp	ground cumin	5 mL
	Salt and freshly ground black pepper	
1 cup	brown basmati or brown long-grain rice, rinsed and drained	250 mL
1	can (28 oz/796 mL) no-salt-added diced tomatoes with juice (see Tips, page 161)	1
1 cup	water	250 mL
½ cup	finely chopped parsley	125 mL

1. In a large saucepan with a tight-fitting lid, heat oil over medium-high heat for 30 seconds. Add onion and cook, stirring, until well browned, about 10 minutes. Add garlic, ginger, chile pepper, bay leaves, cumin and salt and black pepper to taste and cook, stirring, for 1 minute.

2. Add rice and toss until coated. Stir in tomatoes with juice and water. Bring to a boil. Reduce heat to low. Cover and simmer until rice is tender, about 1 hour. Remove from heat and let stand for 5 minutes. Fluff with a fork and garnish with parsley.

Variation

For variety, try adding some red rice to the brown rice when cooking it. Two tablespoons (30 mL) of Colusari or Camargue red rice or Wehani per cup (250 mL) adds a visual and textural spark to the dish.

Nutrients per serving

Calories	194
Protein	5.1 g
Carbohydrates	37.3 g
Fat (Total)	3.7 g
Saturated Fat	0.4 g
Monounsaturated Fat	1.8 g
Polyunsaturated Fat	1.2 g
Dietary Fiber	5 g
Sodium	46 mg
Cholesterol	0 mg

EXCELLENT SOURCE OF magnesium and manganese.
GOOD SOURCE OF vitamins A and C, thiamine, niacin, iron and copper.
SOURCE OF vitamin E (alpha-tocopherol), riboflavin, folate, pantothenic acid, calcium, phosphorus and zinc.
CONTAINS a high amount of dietary fiber.

Baked Rice with Rosemary-Roasted Tomatoes

This is a great dish for entertaining — it's delicious, impressive and different enough to inspire your guests. It's a wonderful accompaniment to grilled fish and meat, a perfect way to finish simple roast chicken and is delicious alongside grilled or roasted eggplant. If you're cooking for a crowd, double the quantity. You may even want to serve this as a light main course accompanied by a tossed green salad.

Makes 6 servings

Nutrient Tip

This recipe contains a very high amount of dietary fiber, which comes from three basic sources. The whole wheat bread crumbs and the brown rice each provide 2.3 grams, while the tomatoes provide 1.8 grams.

Nutrients per serving

Calories	326
Protein	6.9 g
Carbohydrates	51.2 g
Fat (Total)	10.7 g
Saturated Fat	3.6 g
Monounsaturated Fat	5 g
Polyunsaturated Fat	1.6 g
Dietary Fiber	6.6 g
Sodium	577 mg
Cholesterol	10 mg

EXCELLENT SOURCE OF thiamine, magnesium and manganese.
GOOD SOURCE OF vitamins A and C, niacin, folate, phosphorus and iron.
SOURCE OF vitamin E (alpha-tocopherol), riboflavin, pantothenic acid, zinc, calcium, copper and selenium.
CONTAINS a very high amount of dietary fiber.

- Preheat oven to 425°F (220°C)
- Shallow 8-cup (2 L) baking dish, lightly greased
- 6-cup (1.5 L) baking dish

2½ cups	reduced-sodium vegetable or chicken stock or water (see Tips, page 172)	625 mL
1¼ cups	short-grain brown rice, rinsed and drained	300 mL
2 tbsp	melted butter, divided	30 mL
5	large tomatoes, cored and thinly sliced	5
2 tbsp	extra virgin olive oil, divided	30 mL
4	cloves garlic, minced	4
1 tbsp	finely chopped fresh rosemary leaves	15 mL
	Salt and freshly ground black pepper	
1 cup	dry gluten-free whole-grain bread crumbs (see Tips, page 187)	250 mL
2 tbsp	finely chopped parsley or chives	30 mL

1. In a large saucepan with a tight-fitting lid over medium-high heat, bring stock to a boil. Add rice and return to a boil. Reduce heat to low. Cover and simmer until rice is tender, about 50 minutes. Spread in prepared 8-cup (2 L) baking dish and brush with 1 tbsp (15 mL) of the melted butter.

2. Meanwhile, place tomatoes in 6-cup (1.5 L) baking dish, overlapping as necessary, and sprinkle with garlic and rosemary. Drizzle with 1 tbsp (15 mL) of the olive oil and season with salt and pepper to taste. Roast in preheated oven for 15 minutes. Turn tomatoes over and drizzle with a bit more oil (about 1½ tsp/7 mL). Roast for 10 minutes more. Remove from oven.

3. In a bowl, combine bread crumbs with remaining 1 tbsp (15 mL) of melted butter and parsley. Set aside.

4. *To assemble:* Preheat broiler. Broil rice until lightly browned and crusty, about 2 minutes. Spread roasted tomatoes evenly over rice. Sprinkle bread crumb mixture evenly over tomatoes. Drizzle with remaining olive oil. Broil until crumbs are lightly browned, about 2 minutes.

Variation

If you prefer, substitute 4 cups (1 L) halved cherry tomatoes for the regular ones.

Red Beans and Red Rice

Here's a fresh twist on the classic Southern dish of red beans and rice. Bulked up with muscular red rice, this is very hearty — with the addition of salad, it's a meal in itself. The green peas add a burst of color, making this a visually attractive dish that looks good on a buffet. It is particularly tasty as an accompaniment to roast chicken or pork, or pork chops or a platter of roasted vegetables.

Makes 8 servings

Tips

If you're using chicken stock to cook the rice, you may not need the added salt.

When using any canned product, such as chicken stock or beans, check the label to make sure ingredients containing gluten have not been added.

You can cook your own beans or use 1 can (14 to 19 oz/398 to 540 mL) no-salt-added red kidney or small red beans, drained and rinsed.

1 tbsp	olive oil	15 mL
1	onion, finely chopped	1
1	green bell pepper, seeded and diced	1
4	stalks celery, diced	4
4	cloves garlic, minced	4
1 tsp	dried thyme leaves	5 mL
½ tsp	salt (see Tips, left)	2 mL
½ tsp	cracked black peppercorns	2 mL
¼ tsp	cayenne pepper	1 mL
1 cup	Wehani or Camargue red rice, rinsed and drained (see Tips, page 110)	250 mL
2 cups	water or reduced-sodium chicken stock (see Tips, left)	500 mL
2 cups	drained, rinsed cooked or canned red beans (see Tips, left)	500 mL
2 cups	cooked green peas	500 mL

1. In a Dutch oven, heat oil over medium heat for 30 seconds. Add onion, bell pepper, celery and garlic and cook, stirring, until pepper is softened, about 5 minutes. Add thyme, salt, peppercorns and cayenne and cook, stirring, for 1 minute.

2. Add rice and toss to coat. Add water and bring to a boil. Reduce heat to low. Cover and simmer until rice is tender and most of the water is absorbed, about 1 hour. Stir in beans and peas and cook, covered, until heated through, about 10 minutes.

Variations

Red Rice, Sausage and Beans: To turn this into a heartier dish, perfect for a pot luck or buffet, add 4 oz (125 g) diced gluten-free kielbasa along with the peas.

Substitute brown rice or mixture of brown rice and wild rice for the red rice.

Nutrients per serving

Calories	203
Protein	7.9 g
Carbohydrates	38.6 g
Fat (Total)	2.6 g
Saturated Fat	0.3 g
Monounsaturated Fat	1.3 g
Polyunsaturated Fat	0.4 g
Dietary Fiber	6.9 g
Sodium	191 mg
Cholesterol	0 mg

EXCELLENT SOURCE OF folate.
GOOD SOURCE OF thiamine, iron and manganese.
SOURCE OF vitamins A and C, riboflavin, niacin, phosphorus, magnesium, zinc and copper.
CONTAINS a very high amount of dietary fiber.

Fragrant Coconut Rice

This is a deliciously rich rice — perhaps a bit too much for every day, but a wonderful treat now and again. I like to serve it as an accompaniment to a spicy curry because its robustness nicely complements the creamy sweetness of the rice.

Makes 4 servings

Tip

Coconut milk should be suitable for people who are allergic to gluten. However, some brands contain guar gum, which although it does not contain gluten, is not recommended for people with celiac disease. Also it may be processed in a facility where gluten is present. Check the label.

1½ cups	coconut milk (see Tip, left)	375 mL
1 cup	water	250 mL
1	stick cinnamon, about 2 inches (5 cm) long	1
1 cup	brown basmati or brown long-grain rice, rinsed and drained	250 mL

1. In a saucepan over medium–high heat, bring coconut milk, water and cinnamon stick to a rapid boil. Stir in rice and return to a boil. Reduce heat to low. Cover and simmer until rice is tender and liquid is absorbed, about 50 minutes. Discard cinnamon stick.

COCONUT MILK

This dish is high in saturated fat, but the source is coconut, which appears to have many healthy properties. Although the research into coconut oil is in the preliminary stages, it contains a number of fatty acids that have anti-inflammatory properties and may help your body fight infections. Coconut oil (and milk) contain lauric acid, which is found in breast milk and may have cardiovascular benefits. A significant portion of the saturated fats in coconut oil are medium-chain triglycerides, which may boost our immune system and help you to keep your weight under control.

Nutrients per serving

Calories	339
Protein	5.3 g
Carbohydrates	38.6 g
Fat (Total)	19.3 g
Saturated Fat	16.2 g
Monounsaturated Fat	1.2 g
Polyunsaturated Fat	0.7 g
Dietary Fiber	3.6 g
Sodium	13 mg
Cholesterol	0 mg

EXCELLENT SOURCE OF iron, magnesium and manganese.

GOOD SOURCE OF niacin, phosphorus, zinc and copper.

SOURCE OF thiamine, folate, pantothenic acid and selenium.

CONTAINS a moderate amount of dietary fiber.

Currant-Studded Quinoa

This version of quinoa, enhanced with currants and toasted almonds, is very easy to make. If you're serving a plain main course, such as grilled fish or vegetables, and feel it needs a boost, this will do the trick.

Makes 6 servings

Tips

The saffron adds a pleasantly bitter note to the quinoa, which is particularly nice with poultry or fish.

Add the chile pepper if you like a bit of heat.

To toast almonds, preheat oven to 350°F (180°C). Place sliced nuts on a rimmed baking sheet and bake, stirring occasionally, until golden, about 8 minutes.

Nutrients per serving

Calories	176
Protein	5 g
Carbohydrates	29.5 g
Fat (Total)	5.1 g
Saturated Fat	0.5 g
Monounsaturated Fat	2.8 g
Polyunsaturated Fat	1.3 g
Dietary Fiber	3.3 g
Sodium	7 mg
Cholesterol	0 mg

EXCELLENT SOURCE OF manganese.

GOOD SOURCE OF magnesium, iron and copper.

SOURCE OF vitamin E (alpha-tocopherol), thiamine, riboflavin, niacin, folate, pantothenic acid, phosphorus and zinc.

CONTAINS a moderate amount of dietary fiber.

2 cups	Homemade Vegetable Stock with no-salt-added (see recipe, page 78) or reduced-sodium chicken stock	500 mL
¼ tsp	crumbled saffron threads, optional (see Tips, left)	1 mL
1	stick cinnamon, about 2 inches (5 cm) long	1
1	dried red chile pepper, optional (see Tips, left)	1
½ tsp	freshly ground black pepper	2 mL
1 cup	quinoa, rinsed and drained	250 mL
2 tsp	extra virgin olive oil	10 mL
1 tsp	freshly squeezed lemon juice	5 mL
½ cup	currants	125 mL
¼ cup	toasted sliced almonds (see Tips, left)	60 mL

1. In a saucepan over medium heat, bring vegetable stock to a boil. Add saffron, if using, and stir until infused. Add cinnamon stick, chile pepper, if using, and black pepper and return to a boil. Add quinoa in a steady stream, stirring to prevent lumps, and return to a boil. Reduce heat to low and simmer until tender, about 15 minutes. Remove from heat and let stand, covered for 5 minutes. Fluff with a fork.

2. In a small bowl, mix together olive oil and lemon juice. Add to quinoa along with currants and almonds. Stir well and serve.

Variation

Currant-Studded Millet: Substitute an equal quantity of toasted millet for the quinoa. Increase the liquid to 2½ cups (625 mL) and the cooking time to 25 minutes.

SAFFRON

Saffron is the dried stigma of a particular kind of crocus. It has an intensely bitter but extremely appealing taste and a little goes a long way, which is fortunate since it is one of the costliest spices. In this recipe, it adds unmistakable flavor so I recommend using it, if possible.

Basic Polenta and Grits

Polenta, the Italian version of cornmeal mush, is a magnificent way to add whole grains to your diet. When properly cooked, it is a soothing comfort food that functions like a bowl of steaming mashed potatoes, the yummy basis upon which more elaborate dishes can strut their stuff. Many people — and for a long time, I was one of them — aren't keen to make polenta because they think it takes hours of stirring over a hot stove. In fact, even on the stove, you can make great polenta in less than 40 minutes and if, like me, you're inclined to be lazy, you can produce excellent results in a slow cooker or the oven, with virtually no stirring at all. Grits, which are more coarsely ground than cornmeal, are even more delicious if you can find artisanal versions being produced in the southern U.S. They are prepared just like stone-ground cornmeal, but take longer to cook.

Makes about 5 cups (1.25 L) or 6 servings

Tips

If you prefer, substitute gluten-free vegetable or chicken stock for the water.

If you're using the oven method, use an ovenproof saucepan to ease cleanup.

Grits Tip

Grits are very sticky. Greasing the saucepan or using one with a nonstick finish helps with cleanup.

Nutrients per serving	
Calories	73
Protein	1.4 g
Carbohydrates	15.6 g
Fat (Total)	0.8 g
Saturated Fat	0.1 g
Monounsaturated Fat	0.2 g
Polyunsaturated Fat	0.4 g
Dietary Fiber	2.7 g
Sodium	100 mg
Cholesterol	0 mg

SOURCE OF phosphorus, magnesium and manganese.

CONTAINS a moderate amount of dietary fiber.

4½ cups	water (see Tips, left)	1.125 L
¼ tsp	salt	1 mL
1 cup	coarse stone-ground cornmeal or coarse stone-ground grits	250 mL

1. In a saucepan over medium heat, bring water and salt to a boil. Gradually stir in cornmeal in a steady stream. Cook, stirring constantly, until smooth and blended and mixture bubbles like lava, about 5 minutes.

Stovetop Method

Complete Step 1, above.

2. Reduce heat to low (placing a heat diffuser under the pot if your stove doesn't have a true simmer). Continue cooking, stirring frequently, while the mixture bubbles and thickens, until the grains are tender and creamy, about 30 minutes for polenta and about 1 hour for grits. Serve immediately.

Oven Method

- Preheat oven to 350°F (180°C)
- 8-cup (2 L) ovenproof saucepan or baking dish, lightly greased

Complete Step 1, above.

2. Transfer pot to preheated oven or if you don't have an ovenproof saucepan, transfer mixture to lightly greased baking dish. Bake, covered, until cornmeal is tender and creamy, about 40 minutes for cornmeal and 1 hour for grits.

Slow Cooker Methods

There are two ways to make polenta or grits in the slow cooker. You can cook it directly in the slow cooker stoneware, in which case I recommend using a small (maximum 3½ quart) slow cooker, lightly greased. This method produces a soft creamy polenta, which is how my husband likes it. It takes a bit longer to firm up than polenta cooked on the stove or in the oven. If you have a large oval slow cooker, I recommend using a baking dish (see right).

182   SIDES, SUNDRIES AND BASICS

Tip

If you have trouble digesting cornmeal, look for an artisanal source to ensure it has not been genetically modified. Stone-ground grits will most likely be made from heirloom corn and are not likely to be genetically modified. Also, try soaking your cornmeal for at least 8 hours or overnight in warm non-chlorinated water (about 2 parts water to 1 part grain) with a spoonful or so of cider vinegar (preferably with the mother). Drain and rinse before cooking. Your polenta will be particularly creamy.

Direct Method

Complete Step 1, left.

2. Transfer mixture to prepared slow cooker stoneware. Cover and cook polenta on Low for $1\frac{1}{2}$ hours. Cover and cook grits on Low for 3 hours, until set.

Baking Dish Method

Complete Step 1, left.

2. Transfer mixture to a lightly greased 6-cup (1.5 L) baking dish. Cover with foil and secure with a string. Place dish in slow cooker stoneware and pour in enough boiling water to come 1 inch (2.5 cm) up the sides of the dish. Cover and cook polenta on Low for $1\frac{1}{2}$ hours. Cover and cook grits on Low for 3 hours.

Variations

Creamy Polenta: Substitute $2\frac{1}{2}$ cups (625 mL) milk or cream and 2 cups (500 mL) water or stock for the liquid. If you prefer, stir in 2 tbsp (30 mL) freshly grated Parmesan cheese after the cornmeal has been added to the liquid.

Polenta Squares: To make polenta squares, transfer the hot cooked polenta into a greased baking pan or dish (depending upon the thickness you want), using the back of a spoon to even the top. Set aside to cool (it will solidify during the process) and cut into squares.

Cheesy Baked Grits: Complete Step 1. Remove from heat and stir in 2 cups (500 mL) shredded Cheddar or Jack cheese and 2 beaten eggs.

You can also add a finely chopped roasted red pepper or half of a chipotle pepper in adobo sauce, if you prefer. Stir well and transfer to a greased 6-cup (1.5 L) baking dish. Bake at 350°F (180°C) until grits are tender and pudding is set, about 1 hour.

Gluten-Free Pizza Crust

I like this gluten-free crust at least as much as one made with wheat flour.

Makes one 10-inch (25 cm) pizza or four small pizzas

Tips

The amount called for here is 1 package of active dry yeast.

Xanthan gum is available in natural food stores.

- Instant-read thermometer

¾ cup	milk	175 mL
2¼ tsp	active dry yeast (see Tips, left)	11 mL
2 tsp	granulated sugar	10 mL
¾ cup	finely ground brown rice flour	175 mL
⅔ cup	sorghum flour	150 mL
¼ cup	tapioca flour	60 mL
1 tsp	xanthan gum (see Tips, left)	5 mL
1 tsp	salt	5 mL
1 tbsp	olive oil	15 mL
1 tsp	cider vinegar	5 mL
	Fine cornmeal for dusting	

1. In a small saucepan, heat milk over medium heat until temperature reaches 115°F (46°C). Sprinkle yeast and sugar over top. Set aside.

2. In a food processor fitted with metal blade, process brown rice flour, sorghum flour, tapioca flour, xanthan gum and salt until combined. Add olive oil, vinegar and reserved yeast mixture and process until a ball forms. (The dough will be soft.) Use immediately or cover and refrigerate for up to 3 days.

3. When you are ready to bake, ensure oven rack is in lowest position and place pizza stone or an inverted baking sheet on rack. Preheat oven to 425°F (220°C).

4. Meanwhile, sprinkle cornmeal over a sheet of parchment large enough to accommodate the rolled dough. Place dough on top, flatten with your hand and sprinkle lightly with cornmeal. Place a large piece of plastic wrap over the dough and roll into a 12-inch (30 cm) circle. Discard plastic and lift crust with parchment onto preheated stone. Bake on bottom rack until bottom is lightly browned, about 10 minutes. Add toppings of your choice and continue baking until crust is nicely browned, about 15 minutes longer.

Nutrients per serving

Calories	186
Protein	4.5 g
Carbohydrates	34.9 g
Fat (Total)	3.9 g
Saturated Fat	0.8 g
Monounsaturated Fat	2.2 g
Polyunsaturated Fat	0.6 g
Dietary Fiber	1.7 g
Sodium	410 mg
Cholesterol	2 mg

EXCELLENT SOURCE OF manganese.

GOOD SOURCE OF folate.

SOURCE OF vitamin E (alpha-tocopherol), thiamine, riboflavin, niacin, pantothenic acid, phosphorus, iron, magnesium, zinc and copper.

Old English Celery Bake

This dish, which I've adapted from a traditional English recipe, is a great accompaniment to just about anything — from roast poultry and meat to a rich luscious vegetable stew. I make it often because it's a great way to use up the less tender outer stalks of celery, which often linger in the crisper long after the tender heart has been used.

Makes 6 servings

Tips

Large stalks of celery can be fibrous. For best results, I recommend using a vegetable peeler to remove the outer layer.

If you are using prepared stock, check the label to make sure it doesn't contain gluten.

- **Preheat oven to 325°F (160°C)**
- **Shallow 6-cup (1.5 L) baking dish, lightly greased**

1 cup	Job's tears, soaked, rinsed and drained	250 mL
1	bay leaf	1
4	large stalks celery, diced (see Tips, left)	4
2½ cups	reduced-sodium vegetable or chicken stock or water (see Tips, left)	625 mL

1. Spread Job's tears evenly over bottom of prepared baking dish. Place bay leaf in the center and arrange celery evenly over top. Add stock and bake in preheated oven until liquid is absorbed and the grain is tender, about 1½ hours.

CELERY

While not an excellent source of any nutrient, celery does provide a smattering of valuable nutrients such as vitamin K, folate, vitamin A and potassium. However, celery contains apparently valuable phytonutrients, which scientists are now studying. The phenolic acids in celery, such as coumarins, may help to protect against cancer and also appear to have anti-inflammatory properties, as do some of the vegetable's other phytonutrients. In addition, celery appears to provide support to your digestive system and contains phthalides, which may help to keep your blood pressure under control.

Nutrients per serving

Calories	124
Protein	5.1 g
Carbohydrates	21.7 g
Fat (Total)	2 g
Saturated Fat	0 g
Monounsaturated Fat	0 g
Polyunsaturated Fat	0 g
Dietary Fiber	0.8
Sodium	35 mg
Cholesterol	0 mg

SOURCE OF thiamine, niacin, folate, phosphorus and iron.

Wild Rice Stuffing with Cranberries

This stuffing is different enough to satisfy any needs for something exotic, yet traditionally North American in terms of its ingredients. There's enough here to stuff six game hens or an 8- to 10-lb (4 to 5 kg) turkey. Vegans can use it to stuff baked squash or bell peppers.

Makes about 6 cups (1.5 L)

Tips

Look for gluten-free bread crumbs in well-stocked supermarkets. Natural foods stores will stock whole-grain versions.

To toast pecans, preheat oven to 350°F (180°C). Place chopped nuts on a baking sheet and bake, stirring occasionally, until fragrant, about 10 minutes.

If you prefer, rather than using this to stuff poultry, bake it in a greased covered baking dish at 350°F (180°C) for 1 hour.

2 cups	cooked wild rice (see cooking instructions, page 32), cooled	500 mL
1 cup	dry gluten-free bread crumbs (see Tips, left)	250 mL
6	green onions, white part only, finely chopped	6
2	stalks celery, diced	2
½ cup	dried cranberries	125 mL
½ cup	toasted chopped pecans (see Tips, left)	125 mL
1	jalapeño pepper, seeded and minced, optional	1
1 tbsp	fresh thyme leaves or 1 tsp (5 mL) dried thyme	15 mL
1 tbsp	freshly grated orange zest	15 mL
½ cup	freshly squeezed orange juice	125 mL
2 tbsp	melted butter or extra virgin olive oil	30 mL
	Salt and freshly ground black pepper	

1. In a bowl, combine wild rice, bread crumbs, green onions, celery, cranberries, pecans, jalapeño pepper, if using, thyme and orange zest. Mix well. Add orange juice and melted butter or olive oil and stir well. Season to taste with salt and black pepper.

Nutrients per serving

Calories	122
Protein	2.6 g
Carbohydrates	16.8 g
Fat (Total)	5.5 g
Saturated Fat	1.5 g
Monounsaturated Fat	2.4 g
Polyunsaturated Fat	1.2 g
Dietary Fiber	1.6 g
Sodium	76 mg
Cholesterol	5 mg

GOOD SOURCE OF manganese.

SOURCE OF vitamin C, thiamine, folate, magnesium, zinc and copper.

Moroccan-Style Millet Stuffing

This deliciously different stuffing is wonderful with roast chicken or even whole boned fish. I like to use it to stuff a large capon, which I roast and serve as a splendid Sunday dinner. Vegans can use it as a stuffing for roasted bell peppers, squash or eggplant.

Makes about 4 cups (1 L)

Tips

If you don't have saffron, substitute 1 tsp (5 mL) turmeric. Add along with the cinnamon.

To toast millet, place in a dry skillet over medium heat and cook, stirring constantly, until fragrant, about 5 minutes.

If you prefer, rather than using the stuffing to stuff a bird, bake at 350°F (180°C) in a greased covered baking dish for 1 hour.

2 cups	reduced-sodium vegetable or chicken stock	500 mL
Pinch	saffron threads, crumbled (see Tips, left)	Pinch
¾ cup	toasted millet (see Tips, left)	175 mL
⅔ cup	toasted coarsely chopped blanched almonds (see Tip, 189)	150 mL
⅔ cup	chopped pitted dates	150 mL
½ cup	dried cherries	125 mL
1 tbsp	freshly grated orange zest, optional	15 mL
1 tsp	ground cinnamon	5 mL
½ tsp	salt	2 mL
½ tsp	freshly ground black pepper	2 mL

1. In a saucepan over medium–high heat, bring stock to a boil. Add saffron and stir until infused. Add toasted millet in a steady stream, stirring constantly. Return to a rapid boil. Reduce heat to low. Cover tightly and simmer until liquid is absorbed, about 25 minutes. Remove from heat and let stand for 15 minutes. Fluff with a fork.

2. In a food processor fitted with metal blade, combine almonds, dates, cherries, orange zest, if using, cinnamon, salt and pepper. Pulse until chopped and integrated. Add to millet and stir well.

Variations

If you're serving a holiday turkey, double the quantity. If you don't want to entirely break with tradition, substitute dried cranberries for the cherries.

Moroccan-Style Quinoa Stuffing: Substitute an equal quantity of quinoa for the millet. Reduce the quantity of stock to 1½ cups (375 mL) and decrease the cooking time to 15 minutes.

Moroccan-Style Teff Stuffing: Substitute an equal quantity of teff for the millet. Like millet, teff benefits from being toasted before cooking.

Nutrients per serving

Calories	197
Protein	4.8 g
Carbohydrates	34.7 g
Fat (Total)	5.4 g
Saturated Fat	0.5 g
Monounsaturated Fat	3.1 g
Polyunsaturated Fat	1.4 g
Dietary Fiber	4.7 g
Sodium	150 mg
Cholesterol	0 mg

GOOD SOURCE OF vitamin E (alpha-tocopherol), magnesium and manganese.
SOURCE OF niacin, thiamine, riboflavin, folate, calcium, phosphorus, iron, zinc and copper.
CONTAINS a high amount of dietary fiber.

188   SIDES, SUNDRIES AND BASICS

Saffron-Scented Millet Pilaf with Toasted Almonds

This tasty pilaf is very easy to make so long as you have saffron in the house. Its mildly exotic flavors will give your taste buds a lift. It makes a delicious accompaniment to roast chicken or a platter of roasted vegetables.

Makes 6 servings

Tip

To toast almonds, place on a rimmed baking sheet in the center of 350°F (180°C) preheated oven and toast, stirring occasionally, until lightly browned, 5 to 10 minutes.

Nutrient Tip

I like to make this with homemade vegetable stock because it adds flavor to the pilaf and is so low in sodium.

1 cup	millet	250 mL
1 tbsp	olive oil	15 mL
1	onion, finely chopped	1
2½ cups	Homemade Vegetable Stock (see recipe, page 78) or reduced-sodium vegetable or chicken stock, or water	625 mL
¼ tsp	crumbled saffron threads, dissolved in 2 tbsp (30 mL) boiling water	1 mL
	Freshly ground black pepper	
2 tbsp	toasted sliced almonds (see Tip, left)	30 mL
2 tbsp	finely chopped parsley	30 mL

1. In a saucepan over medium heat, toast millet, stirring, until it crackles and releases its aroma, about 5 minutes. Transfer to a bowl.

2. In same saucepan, heat oil over medium heat for 30 seconds. Add onion and cook, stirring, until softened, about 3 minutes. Add stock and saffron liquid and bring to a boil. Gradually stir in reserved millet and return to a boil. Season to taste with pepper.

3. Reduce heat to low. Cover, placing a heat diffuser under the pot if necessary, and simmer until liquid is absorbed, about 25 minutes. Remove from heat and let stand for 5 minutes. Fluff with a fork. Stir in toasted almonds and parsley.

Variation

Saffron-Scented Millet Pilaf with Toasted Pine Nuts: Substitute an equal quantity of toasted pine nuts for the almonds.

Nutrients per serving

Calories	166
Protein	4.4 g
Carbohydrates	27.5 g
Fat (Total)	4.3 g
Saturated Fat	0.6 g
Monounsaturated Fat	2.5 g
Polyunsaturated Fat	1 g
Dietary Fiber	3.6 g
Sodium	4 mg
Cholesterol	0 mg

GOOD SOURCE OF magnesium and manganese.

SOURCE OF vitamin E (alpha-tocopherol), thiamine, riboflavin, niacin, folate, phosphorus, iron, zinc and copper.

CONTAINS a moderate amount of dietary fiber.

Rolled Oats

Desserts

Pretty Traditional Rice Pudding

This is a classic rice pudding, made with more-nutritious brown rice instead of white. If you want to deviate a bit more from tradition, try soaking the raisins in a bit of rum, or substituting them with dried cherries or cranberries (see Variations, below). Whenever I make this, I'm usually in the mood for indulging and finish the dish with a dollop of whipped cream.

Makes 6 servings

Tip

If you don't have a shallow dish, you can make this in a deep baking dish or a soufflé dish of the same volume. It will take longer to cook, about 1 hour and 10 minutes, depending upon the dimensions of your dish.

- Preheat oven to 325°F (160°C)
- Shallow 6-cup (1.5 L) baking dish, greased (see Tip, left)

2 cups	cooked brown rice, cooled (see cooking instructions, page 28)	500 mL
3 cups	2% milk or rice milk	750 mL
½ cup	granulated sugar	125 mL
3	eggs	3
2 tsp	finely grated lemon zest	10 mL
2 tsp	vanilla extract	10 mL
½ cup	raisins	125 mL

CINNAMON-SUGAR TOPPING

1 tbsp + 2 tsp	granulated sugar	25 mL
1 tsp	ground cinnamon	5 mL
	Table (18%) cream, optional	

1. In a large bowl, whisk together milk, sugar, eggs, lemon zest and vanilla. Add rice and raisins and mix well. Transfer to prepared baking dish.

2. *Cinnamon-Sugar Topping:* In a small bowl, combine sugar and cinnamon and mix well. Sprinkle evenly over rice mixture.

3. Bake, uncovered, in preheated oven just until set, about 35 minutes. Serve warm or chill thoroughly. Accompany with whipped cream, if desired.

Variations

Soak raisins in 2 tbsp (30 mL) dark rum for 10 minutes.

Substitute an equal quantity of dried cherries or cranberries for the raisins. If using cranberries, substitute an equal quantity of orange zest for the lemon.

For a different flavor profile, substitute almond milk for the 2%, almond extract for the vanilla and dried cherries for the raisins.

Nutrients per serving

Calories	286
Protein	9.2 g
Carbohydrates	51.1 g
Fat (Total)	5.5 g
Saturated Fat	2.3 g
Monounsaturated Fat	1.9 g
Polyunsaturated Fat	0.7 g
Dietary Fiber	1.7 g
Sodium	85 mg
Cholesterol	103 mg

EXCELLENT SOURCE OF manganese and selenium.

GOOD SOURCE OF phosphorus, calcium, magnesium and riboflavin.

SOURCE OF vitamins A and E (alpha-tocopherol), thiamine, niacin, folate, pantothenic acid, iron, zinc and copper.

Blueberry and Wild Rice Pudding

This delicious pudding exemplifies the theory that foods that grow together taste good in combination. Although blueberries grow on land and wild rice is the seed of an aquatic grass, they are found in the same geographic regions. Remarkably light, slightly sweet and a little bit crunchy, this pudding is comfort food for the new millennia.

Makes 8 servings

Nutrient Tip

Dried blueberries are available in natural food stores. They add concentrated blueberry flavor to dishes and offer the same nutritious profile as their fresh counterparts. Blueberries are particularly high in antioxidants, signaled by their deep dark color. In one laboratory test, USDA researchers found that blueberry consumption improved the learning ability of mice and slowed age-related memory loss.

Nutrients per serving

Calories	186
Protein	7.1 g
Carbohydrates	31.9 g
Fat (Total)	3.9 g
Saturated Fat	1.7 g
Monounsaturated Fat	1.3 g
Polyunsaturated Fat	0.5 g
Dietary Fiber	1.7 g
Sodium	68 mg
Cholesterol	77 mg

GOOD SOURCE OF riboflavin and selenium.

SOURCE OF vitamin A, niacin, folate, pantothenic acid, calcium, phosphorus, iron, magnesium, manganese, zinc and copper.

- Preheat oven to 325°F (160°C)
- Shallow 6-cup (1.5 L) baking dish, greased

2 cups	cooked wild rice, cooled (see cooking instructions, page 32)	500 mL
1/2 cup	dried blueberries	125 mL
3 cups	2% milk or non-dairy alternative	750 mL
1/2 cup	packed Demerara or other raw cane sugar	125 mL
3	eggs	3
1 tbsp	finely grated lemon zest	15 mL
1 tsp	vanilla extract	5 mL
1/2 tsp	freshly grated nutmeg	2 mL
	Maple syrup, optional	

1. In prepared baking dish, combine wild rice and blueberries.

2. In a saucepan over medium heat, heat milk and sugar, just until bubbles appear around the edges, stirring occasionally to dissolve the sugar. Remove from heat.

3. In a bowl, beat together eggs, lemon zest, vanilla and nutmeg. Add a bit of the milk mixture and stir well. Add to saucepan and mix well. Pour over rice mixture and carefully stir to blend. Bake in preheated oven until top is set and edges just begin to brown, about 1 hour. Serve warm with a drizzle of maple syrup, if using.

Variation

Cranberry and Wild Rice Pudding: Substitute an equal quantity of dried cranberries for the dried blueberries and 1 tbsp (15 mL) grated orange zest for the lemon.

Black Sticky Rice Pudding

Years ago, when my husband, daughter and I traveled in Thailand, we became addicted to mangos and sticky rice, a truly delicious sweet. After our return, we tried but could never duplicate the superb taste and texture of the authentic version. Although this black sticky rice pudding is a different dish, it reminds me of that delightful concoction. In fact, it's so good you don't even need the fruit. Although it's high in saturated fat, it comes from the coconut milk, which may have healthful benefits.

Makes 6 servings

Tips

Thai black sticky rice is available in Asian markets.

I like to make this pudding using piloncillo, unrefined Mexican sugar, which is sold in cones in Latin markets. Use a 4-oz (125 g) cone in this recipe.

If you prefer, cook the rice in your rice cooker on the brown rice setting.

1½ cups	water	375 mL
¾ cup	cooked Thai black sticky rice (see Tips, left)	175 mL
1	can (14 oz/400 mL) coconut milk	1
½ cup	packed Demerara or other raw cane sugar (see Tips, left)	125 mL
½ tsp	salt	2 mL
1 cup	sliced strawberries or kiwifruit or chopped peaches or mango	250 mL
¼ cup	toasted shredded sweetened coconut Finely chopped mint, optional	60 mL

1. In a bowl, combine water and rice. Set aside to soak for at least 4 hours or overnight. When you're ready to cook, transfer rice and soaking water to a heavy pot with a tight-fitting lid. Bring to a rapid boil over medium heat. Reduce heat to low and simmer until rice is tender, 30 to 45 minutes. (Don't lift the lid; see Tips, left).

2. In a saucepan, combine coconut milk, brown sugar and salt. Bring to a boil over medium heat and cook, stirring, until sugar dissolves. Stir in cooked rice and cook, stirring, until thickened, about 10 minutes. Transfer to a serving bowl and chill, if desired.

3. When you're ready to serve, top with fruit and garnish with coconut and mint, if using.

Nutrients per serving

Calories	305
Protein	3.3 g
Carbohydrates	41.4 g
Fat (Total)	15.4 g
Saturated Fat	13.2 g
Monounsaturated Fat	0.6 g
Polyunsaturated Fat	0.2 g
Dietary Fiber	1 g
Sodium	221 mg
Cholesterol	0 mg

EXCELLENT SOURCE OF manganese.

GOOD SOURCE OF iron and magnesium.

SOURCE OF vitamin C, thiamine, niacin, folate, phosphorus, zinc, copper and selenium.

Amaretto-Spiked Quinoa Pudding with Cherries

This pudding is so deliciously decadent it's almost impossible to believe it is loaded with whole-grain goodness. Enjoy every succulent mouthful.

Makes 8 servings

Tips

To highlight the pleasantly nutty flavor of quinoa, toast it before using in this recipe. Place rinsed, drained quinoa in a dry skillet over medium heat, and stir constantly until it darkens, about 4 minutes.

If you prefer, substitute an equal quantity of plain almond milk for the regular milk.

If you don't have almond liqueur, substitute an additional ½ tsp (2 mL) almond extract plus 2 tbsp (30 mL) water.

Nutrients per serving

Calories	327
Protein	9.9 g
Carbohydrates	55.7 g
Fat (Total)	7.7 g
Saturated Fat	3.4 g
Monounsaturated Fat	2.5 g
Polyunsaturated Fat	1 g
Dietary Fiber	2.5 g
Sodium	97 mg
Cholesterol	87 mg

EXCELLENT SOURCE OF manganese.
GOOD SOURCE OF riboflavin, magnesium, selenium, calcium, phosphorus and iron.
SOURCE OF vitamins A and C, thiamine, niacin, folate, pantothenic acid, copper and zinc.
CONTAINS a moderate amount of dietary fiber.

- **Preheat oven to 350°F (180°C)**
- **6-cup (1.5 L) baking dish, greased**

1½ cups	water	375 mL
1 tbsp	finely grated orange zest	15 mL
½ cup	freshly squeezed orange juice	125 mL
1 cup	quinoa, rinsed and drained (see Tips, left)	250 mL
1	can (14 oz/396 g or 300 mL) sweetened condensed milk	1
¾ cup	dried cherries	175 mL
½ cup	milk or half-and-half (10%) cream (see Tips, left)	125 mL
2 tbsp	almond-flavored liqueur, such as Amaretto (see Tips, left)	30 mL
1 tsp	almond extract	5 mL
½ tsp	ground cinnamon	2 mL
3	eggs, beaten	3

1. In a saucepan over medium–high heat, bring water, orange zest and juice to a boil. Add quinoa in a steady stream, stirring to prevent lumps from forming, and return to a boil. Reduce heat to low. Cover and simmer until tender and liquid is absorbed, about 15 minutes. Remove from heat and let stand for 5 minutes. Fluff with a fork and let cool slightly.

2. Add condensed milk, cherries, milk, almond liqueur, almond extract, cinnamon and eggs and mix well. Transfer to prepared dish. Bake in preheated oven until set, about 45 minutes. Serve warm.

Middle Eastern Millet Pudding with Almonds and Dates

A version of this pudding is traditionally made with bulgur and, depending upon the source, its origins are Jewish, Egyptian or Syrian. In any case, it's Mediterranean and is a light and delicious dessert. It is also surprisingly easy to make.

Makes 8 servings

Tip

When buying nuts be sure to source them from a purveyor with high turnover. Because nuts are very high in unsaturated fats, they tend to become rancid very quickly. This is especially true of walnuts. In my experience, the vast percentage of walnuts sold in supermarkets have already passed their peak. Taste before you buy.

1 cup	millet	250 mL
2½ cups	boiling water	625 mL
½ cup	heavy or whipping (35%) cream or soy creamer	125 mL
½ cup	liquid honey or ¼ cup (60 mL) agave nectar	125 mL
2 tsp	finely grated lemon zest	10 mL
1 tsp	ground cinnamon	5 mL
Pinch	salt	Pinch
1 cup	toasted chopped almonds or walnuts (see Tip, left and page 189)	250 mL
1 cup	chopped pitted Medjool dates Pomegranate seeds, optional	250 mL

1. In a dry saucepan over medium heat, toast millet, stirring constantly, until fragrant, about 5 minutes. Remove from heat, stand well back (it will spatter) and add boiling water. Stir well. Return to heat and bring to a boil. Reduce heat to low. Cover tightly and simmer until liquid is absorbed and millet is tender, 20 minutes. Remove from heat and let stand, covered, for 5 minutes.

2. Meanwhile, in a saucepan, combine cream, honey, lemon zest, cinnamon and salt. Heat over medium heat until honey is dissolved and bubbles form around the edge of the mixture. Add to cooked millet and stir well. Stir in almonds and dates. Serve warm or chilled sprinkled with pomegranate seeds, if using.

Variation

Middle Eastern Teff Pudding with Almonds and Dates: Substitute an equal quantity of teff for the millet.

Nutrients per serving

Calories	339
Protein	6.2 g
Carbohydrates	56 g
Fat (Total)	12 g
Saturated Fat	3.8 g
Monounsaturated Fat	5.5 g
Polyunsaturated Fat	2 g
Dietary Fiber	5.3 g
Sodium	13 mg
Cholesterol	19 mg

EXCELLENT SOURCE OF magnesium and manganese.
GOOD SOURCE OF vitamin E (alpha-tocopherol), phosphorus and copper.
SOURCE OF vitamin A, thiamine, riboflavin, niacin, folate, pantothenic acid, calcium, iron and zinc.
CONTAINS a high amount of dietary fiber.

Oatmeal Shortbread Squares

These crisp cookies make a great accompaniment to fresh berries or, with a glass of cold milk, a refreshing snack. They are rich and delicious. One will certainly be enough.

Makes 25 cookies

Tips

Make sure your shortbread has cooked completely before you remove it from the pan. Otherwise, it will crumble.

Store shortbread at room temperature in an airtight container, between layers of waxed or parchment paper, for up to 1 week.

- **Preheat oven to 350°F (180°C)**
- **9-inch (2.5 L) square cake pan, ungreased**

2 cups	gluten-free old-fashioned (large flake) rolled oats	500 mL
½ cup	brown rice flour	125 mL
¼ cup	cornstarch	60 mL
¾ cup	packed Demerara or other raw cane sugar	175 mL
½ tsp	baking soda	2 mL
½ tsp	salt	2 mL
½ tsp	xanthan gum	2 mL
1 cup	cold butter, cubed	250 mL
1 tsp	vanilla extract	5 mL

1. In a food processor fitted with metal blade, combine oats, rice flour, cornstarch, sugar, baking soda, salt and xanthan gum. Process for 30 seconds to blend and grind sugar. Add butter and process until mixture resembles coarse crumbs. Sprinkle vanilla over top and pulse until blended. Using your hands, knead to form a smooth dough.

2. Press dough evenly into pan and bake in preheated oven until edges begin to brown, about 25 minutes. Place pan on a wire rack. Using a serrated knife, score the top to form 25 squares. Let cool completely in pan on rack. Recut and remove squares from pan.

Nutrients per serving

(1 cookie)

Calories	135
Protein	1.5 g
Carbohydrates	15.1 g
Fat (Total)	7.9 g
Saturated Fat	4.8 g
Monounsaturated Fat	2.1 g
Polyunsaturated Fat	0.5 g
Dietary Fiber	0.9 g
Sodium	129 mg
Cholesterol	20 mg

GOOD SOURCE OF manganese.
SOURCE OF vitamin A, phosphorus and magnesium.

Gingery Shortbread

I love the gingery flavor and crumbly texture of this shortbread. It's delicious with a cup of tea, as a complement to fresh berries, or anytime a cookie will do.

Makes about 30 cookies

Tip

Store shortbread at room temperature in an airtight container, between layers of waxed or parchment paper, for up to 1 week.

- **Preheat oven to 350°F (180°C)**
- **Baking sheets, ungreased**

1 cup	finely ground brown rice flour	250 mL
¾ cup	sorghum flour	175 mL
2 tbsp	tapioca flour	30 mL
½ cup	packed Demerara or other raw cane sugar	125 mL
1 tsp	ground ginger	5 mL
½ tsp	xanthan gum	2 mL
¼ tsp	gluten-free baking powder	1 mL
¼ tsp	salt	1 mL
1 cup	cold butter, cubed	250 mL
⅓ cup	chopped crystallized ginger	75 mL
1 tsp	vanilla extract	5 mL

1. In food processor fitted with the metal blade, combine brown rice flour, sorghum flour, tapioca flour, sugar, ground ginger, xanthan gum, baking powder and salt. Process for 30 seconds to blend and grind sugar.

2. Add butter and process until integrated. Add crystallized ginger and vanilla and process until mixture begins to form a ball. Roll into 2 logs, each about 6 inches (15 cm) long. Wrap in plastic wrap and refrigerate until firm enough to slice, about 30 minutes.

3. Slice into cookies about ½ inch (1 cm) thick and place on baking sheets. Bake in preheated oven until edges are golden, about 20 minutes. Let cool completely on sheet on a wire rack.

Nutrients per serving

(1 cookie)

Calories	108
Protein	0.8 g
Carbohydrates	12.6 g
Fat (Total)	6.4 g
Saturated Fat	3.9 g
Monounsaturated Fat	1.7 g
Polyunsaturated Fat	0.3 g
Dietary Fiber	0.3 g
Sodium	70 mg
Cholesterol	16 mg

GOOD SOURCE OF manganese.
SOURCE OF vitamin A and iron.

Chewy Oatmeal Coconut Cookies with Cranberries and Pecans

The luscious cookies are appealingly chewy with just a hint of honey flavor. Once you've had one, it's hard to resist another.

Makes about 48 cookies

Tip

These cookies are a bit soft when they come out of the oven, but they firm up while cooling. Make sure they are just golden while baking — they continue to cook on the sheet after removal from the oven.

- Preheat oven to 350°F (180°C)
- Baking sheets, lightly greased or lined with parchment

1 cup	sorghum flour	250 mL
1/3 cup	coconut flour	75 mL
2 tbsp	cornstarch	30 mL
1 tsp	gluten-free baking powder	5 mL
1 tsp	xanthan gum	5 mL
1/2 tsp	salt	2 mL
1 cup	butter, softened	250 mL
1 cup	packed Demerara or other raw cane sugar	250 mL
2	eggs	2
1 tsp	vanilla extract	5 mL
1/2 cup	liquid honey	125 mL
2 cups	gluten-free old-fashioned (large flake) rolled oats	500 mL
1 cup	sweetened flaked coconut	250 mL
1/2 cup	dried cranberries	125 mL
1/2 cup	chopped pecans	125 mL

1. In a bowl, combine sorghum and coconut flours, cornstarch, baking powder, xanthan gum and salt.

2. In a separate bowl, beat butter and sugar until light and creamy. Add eggs, vanilla and honey, beating and scraping down the sides of the bowl until blended. Gradually add flour mixture, beating until smooth. Stir in oats, coconut, cranberries and pecans.

3. Drop dough by tablespoonfuls (15 mL), about 2 inches (5 cm) apart, on prepared baking sheet. Bake in preheated oven until tops begin to brown, about 12 minutes. Let cool for 5 minutes on sheets, then transfer to a wire rack and let cool completely.

Variations

If you don't like nuts, eliminate the pecans and double the quantity of cranberries. Similarly, if you don't like cranberries, leave them out and double the amount of pecans.

Nutrients per serving

(1 cookie)

Calories	107
Protein	1.2 g
Carbohydrates	14.1 g
Fat (Total)	5.6 g
Saturated Fat	3 g
Monounsaturated Fat	1.6 g
Polyunsaturated Fat	0.6 g
Dietary Fiber	0.7 g
Sodium	67 mg
Cholesterol	14 mg

GOOD SOURCE OF manganese.

Wine-Soaked Cornmeal Cake with Balsamic Berries

The best sweet cornmeal cakes are usually Italian, but the addition of white wine is a French touch. This makes a great dessert when fresh berries are in season — in my opinion as delicious as shortcake and more nutritious, containing a wide range of nutrients and a very high amount of dietary fiber, almost half of which comes from the whole grains. Although I've called for raspberries here, I have also made this with strawberries or blueberries and a "bumbleberry" mix.

Makes 10 servings

Tip

If you have leftover cake, use it to make trifle.

Nutrients per serving

Calories	272
Protein	4.1 g
Carbohydrates	36.8 g
Fat (Total)	12.7 g
Saturated Fat	6.7 g
Monounsaturated Fat	3.8 g
Polyunsaturated Fat	1.2 g
Dietary Fiber	6.2 g
Sodium	270 mg
Cholesterol	62 mg

EXCELLENT SOURCE OF manganese.

GOOD SOURCE OF magnesium.

SOURCE OF vitamins A, C and E (alpha-tocopherol), thiamine, riboflavin, niacin, folate, pantothenic acid, calcium, phosphorus, iron, zinc, selenium and copper.

CONTAINS a very high amount of dietary fiber.

- **Preheat oven to 350°F (180°C)**
- **8-inch (2 L) square cake pan, lined with parchment**

1 cup	stone-ground yellow cornmeal	250 mL
¾ cup	packed Demerara or other raw cane sugar	175 mL
¼ cup	sorghum flour	60 mL
¼ cup	coconut flour	60 mL
¼ cup	ground almonds	60 mL
2 tsp	gluten-free baking powder	10 mL
½ tsp	salt	2 mL
¼ tsp	xanthan gum	1 mL
½ cup	cold butter, cut into 1-inch (2.5 cm) cubes	125 mL
2	eggs	2
2 tsp	finely grated lemon zest	10 mL
1 cup	dry white wine	250 mL
2 tbsp	freshly squeezed lemon juice	30 mL

FRUIT TOPPING

4 cups	fresh raspberries (see Variations, below)	1 L
1 tbsp	balsamic vinegar	15 mL
	Granulated sugar	
	Whipped cream, optional	

1. In a food processor fitted with metal blade, combine cornmeal, sugar, sorghum and coconut flours, almonds, baking powder, salt and xanthan gum. Pulse until cornmeal is quite fine. Add butter and pulse until mixture is crumbly. Add eggs, lemon zest, wine and lemon juice and pulse until blended. Pour into prepared pan, smoothing top. Bake in preheated oven until center springs back when lightly pressed, about 45 minutes. Let cool completely in pan on rack.

2. *Fruit Topping:* In a bowl, combine raspberries, balsamic vinegar and sugar to taste. Cut cake into serving size pieces and top with berry mixture, and a dollop of whipped cream, if using.

Variations

Substitute an equal quantity of sliced hulled strawberries for the raspberries, or use blueberries and substitute freshly squeezed lemon juice for the balsamic vinegar.

Tunisian Fruit and Grain Cake

This "cake," which I adapted from a recipe for a couscous cake in Claudia Roden's The Book of Jewish Food, is a pleasing combination of texture and flavors that is oddly addictive. Once I start eating it, I have trouble putting down my spoon. For dessert, I serve it with pouring cream. I thoroughly enjoy leftovers for breakfast, chilled, and with milk.

Makes 8 servings

Tip

If you use a large saucepan, it will be cool enough after standing to act as a mixing bowl. Add the remaining ingredients to the pot and, using your hands, mix them into the teff, being sure to scrape up the bits that will be stuck to the bottom.

Nutrients per serving	
Calories	361
Protein	7.5 g
Carbohydrates	65.5 g
Fat (Total)	9.2 g
Saturated Fat	0.9 g
Monounsaturated Fat	2.9 g
Polyunsaturated Fat	4.8 g
Dietary Fiber	6.7 g
Sodium	13 mg
Cholesterol	0 mg

EXCELLENT SOURCE OF magnesium, manganese and copper.
GOOD SOURCE OF niacin, phosphorus and zinc.
SOURCE OF vitamins A, C and E (alpha-tocopherol), thiamine, riboflavin, pantothenic acid, folate, calcium and iron
CONTAINS a very high amount of dietary fiber.

- Preheat oven to 350°F (180°C)
- 8-inch (2 L) square cake pan, lightly greased

1½ cups	millet or teff	375 mL
2¼ cups	boiling water	550 mL
½ cup	packed Demerara or other raw cane sugar	125 mL
2 tsp	finely grated orange zest	10 mL
¼ cup	freshly squeezed orange juice	60 mL
½ tsp	ground cinnamon	2 mL
½ cup	chopped pitted Medjool dates	125 mL
½ cup	chopped pitted dried apricots	125 mL
½ cup	dried cherries	125 mL
½ cup	toasted chopped walnuts	125 mL
½ cup	toasted sliced almonds (see Tips, page 189)	125 mL
	Confectioner's (icing) sugar, optional	
	Table (18%) cream or non-dairy alternative	

1. In a dry saucepan over medium heat, toast millet, stirring constantly, until fragrant, about 5 minutes. Remove from heat, stand well back (it may spatter) and add boiling water. Stir well. Add sugar, orange zest and juice and cinnamon and stir well. Return to heat and bring to a boil. Reduce heat to low. Cover tightly and simmer until liquid is absorbed and millet is tender, 20 minutes. Remove from heat and let stand, covered, for 5 minutes. Fluff up with a fork, and break up, using your fingers.

2. Add dates, apricots, cherries, walnuts and almonds and, using your hands, mix well. Transfer to prepared cake pan and press down with your fingers. Cover tightly with foil and bake in preheated oven until heated through, about 20 minutes. Turn out onto a serving plate and dust with confectioner's sugar, if using. Serve warm or chilled. Pass the cream at the table.

Rhubarb-Strawberry Cobbler

There are few things that symbolize the arrival of summer more vividly than the luscious combination of strawberries and rhubarb. You can enjoy these fruits in a traditional fruit cobbler that is deliciously gluten-free. Finish with a scoop of homemade vanilla ice cream.

Makes 8 servings

Tips

You'll need a long shallow baking dish rather than a deep square one to accommodate the topping in a single layer.

If you prefer a more intense orange flavor, add up to 2 tbsp (30 mL) orange liqueur, such as Triple Sec or Cointreau to the fruit mixture, along with the orange zest.

Nutrients per serving

Calories	389
Protein	5.3 g
Carbohydrates	63.4 g
Fat (Total)	14.3 g
Saturated Fat	9.2 g
Monounsaturated Fat	3.3 g
Polyunsaturated Fat	0.7 g
Dietary Fiber	6.8 g
Sodium	330 mg
Cholesterol	34 mg

EXCELLENT SOURCE OF vitamin C, riboflavin and manganese.
SOURCE OF vitamins A and E (alpha-tocopherol), thiamine, niacin, folate, pantothenic acid, calcium, phosphorus, iron, magnesium, zinc and copper.
CONTAINS a very high amount of dietary fiber.

- Preheat oven to 375°F (190°C)
- 8 cup (2 L) baking dish, greased (see Tips, left)

FRUIT

1¼ cups	granulated sugar	300 mL
1 tbsp	tapioca flour	15 mL
1 tsp	ground cinnamon	5 mL
4 cups	halved hulled strawberries	1 L
4 cups	chopped (½-inch/1 cm) rhubarb	1 L
1 tbsp	finely grated orange zest (see Tips, left)	15 mL

TOPPING

⅔ cup	each sorghum flour and coconut flour	150 mL
3 tbsp	tapioca flour	45 mL
2 tbsp	granulated sugar (approx.)	30 mL
1 tsp	gluten-free baking powder	5 mL
1 tsp	xanthan gum	5 mL
1 tsp	finely grated orange zest	5 mL
½ tsp	salt	2 mL
½ cup	cold butter, cut into 1-inch (2.5 mL) cubes	125 mL
1¼ cups	buttermilk + 1 tbsp (15 mL) for brushing	300 mL

1. *Fruit:* In a large bowl, combine sugar, tapioca flour and cinnamon. Mix well. Add strawberries, rhubarb and orange zest and toss well. Transfer to prepared baking dish.

2. *Topping:* In a bowl, combine sorghum, coconut and tapioca flours, sugar, baking powder, xanthan gum, orange zest and salt. Using your fingers or a pastry blender, cut in butter until mixture resembles coarse crumbs. Drizzle with buttermilk and stir with a fork until a batter forms. Divide dough into 8 equal parts and flatten each into a rough circle. Place on top of fruit mixture. Brush tops with remaining buttermilk and sprinkle with sugar. Place dish on a baking sheet and bake in preheated oven until fruit is hot and bubbly and top is golden, about 45 minutes. Remove from oven and let cool for at least 10 minutes before serving. Serve warm.

Variations

You can make cobblers with an endless variety of fruits. You'll need about 8 cups (2 L) of cubed fruit that is roughly ½-inch (1 cm). Orange flavoring is good with rhubarb, but lemon zest and lemon juice work well with most other combinations.

Diabetes Food Values

The diabetes food values for all the recipes were prepared by Info Access (1988) Inc.

Info Access is a Canadian firm of registered dietitians and computer experts specializing in computer-assisted nutrient analysis, assessing more than 4,000 recipes annually for a broad range of international clients. The Nutritional Accounting System component of the CBORD Menu Management System is used, as well as the Canadian Nutrient File, augmented as necessary with data from other reliable sources.

Info Access has also been involved with the assignment of food choice values in Canada, acting as the consulting firm assigning values for the Canadian Diabetes Association. The U.S. determinations were based on Exchange List Guidelines for Recipe/Food Label Calculations, Page 174, Diabetes Medical Nutrition Therapy, The American Dietetic Association/American Diabetes Association, 1997.

Recipes	Page No.	Canadian Diabetes Association Values	American Diabetes Association Values
Amaranth (1/2 cup/125 mL)	14	1/2 Carbohydrate	1 Starch
Buckwheat Groats (1/2 cup/125 mL)	15	1 1/2 Carbohydrates	1 1/2 Starch
Job's Tears (1/2 cup/125 mL)	20	1 1/2 Carbohydrates, 1/2 Fat	1 1/2 Starch
Long-Grain Brown Rice (1/2 cup/125 mL)	26	1 1/2 Carbohydrates	1 1/2 Starch
Millet Seeds (1/2 cup/125 mL)	21	1 Carbohydrate	1 1/2 Starch
Quinoa (1/2 cup/125 mL)	25	1 Carbohydrate	1 Starch
Rolled Oats (1/2 cup/125 mL)	23	1/2 Carbohydrate	1/2 Starch
Sorghum (1/2 cup/125 mL)	30	2 Carbohydrates	2 Starch
Stone-Ground Yellow Cornmeal (1/2 cup/125 mL)	18	1 Carbohydrate	1 Starch
Wild Rice (1/2 cup/125 mL)	31	1 Carbohydrate	1 Starch

Note: Based on instructions for cooking grains provided in *The Complete Gluten-Free Whole Grains Cookbook,* pages 14 through 33.

Recipes	Page No.	Canadian Diabetes Association Values	American Diabetes Association Values
Almond-Flavored Millet with Cherries (1/6 of recipe)	46	2 1/2 Carbohydrates, 1/2 Fat	2 Starch, 1 Fruit
Amaretto-Spiked Quinoa Pudding with Cherries (1/8 of recipe)	196	3 1/2 Carbohydrates, 1 Fat	1 Starch, 1 Fruit, 1 1/2 Other, 1 Low-Fat Meat, 1 Fat
Arroz con Pollo (1/6 of recipe)	100	1 1/2 Carbohydrates, 4 Meat, 1 Fat	1 1/2 Starch, 2 Vegetables, 4 Medium-Fat Meat
Asian-Spiced Beef with Soba Noodles (1/6 of recipe)	142	2 1/2 Carbohydrates, 3 Meat, 1 Fat	3 Starch, 1 Vegetable, 4 Low-Fat Meat
Asian-Style Beef and Chinese "Barley" Salad with Arugula (1/4 of recipe)	86	1 1/2 Carbohydrates, 3 Meat	1 1/2 Starch, 1 Vegetable, 3 Medium-Fat Meat
Asian-Style Quinoa Salad with Chili-Orange Dressing (1/6 of recipe)	84	1 1/2 Carbohydrates, 1/2 Fat	1 1/2 Starch, 1 Vegetable
Baked Rice with Rosemary-Roasted Tomatoes (1/6 of recipe)	177	2 1/2 Carbohydrates, 2 Fat	3 Starch, 1 Vegetable, 1 1/2 Fat
Basic Grits (1/6 of recipe)	182	1 Carbohydrate	1 1/2 Starch
Basic Polenta (1/6 of recipe)	182	1 Carbohydrate	1 Starch
Beef Biriyani (1/10 of recipe)	132	2 Carbohydrates, 2 1/2 Meat	2 Starch, 1 Vegetable, 3 Low-Fat Meat
Black Sticky Rice Pudding (1/6 of recipe)	194	2 1/2 Carbohydrates, 3 Fat	1 Starch, 1 1/2 Other, 3 Fat
Blueberry and Wild Rice Pudding (1/8 of recipe)	193	2 Carbohydrates, 1/2 Fat	1 Starch, 1 Other, 1 Low-Fat Meat
Blueberry Wild Rice Pancakes (1/4 of recipe)	39	3 Carbohydrates, 1/2 Fat	2 1/2 Starch, 1 Other
Brown Rice Risotto (1/6 of recipe)	173	1 1/2 Carbohydrates, 1/2 Fat	1 1/2 Starch, 1/2 Fat
Buckwheat Blini (1/36 of recipe)	54	1/2 Carbohydrate	1/2 Starch
Buttermilk Buckwheat Pancakes (1/14 of recipe)	38	1 Carbohydrate, 1/2 Fat	1 Starch
Cheesy Jalapeño Cornbread (1/8 of recipe)	42	2 Carbohydrates, 1/2 Meat, 2 Fat	2 Starch, 1/2 High-Fat Meat, 1 1/2 Fat
Chewy Oatmeal Coconut Cookies with Cranberries and Pecans (1/48 of recipe)	200	1 Carbohydrate, 1 Fat	1/2 Starch, 1/2 Other, 1 Fat

Recipes	Page No.	Canadian Diabetes Association Values	American Diabetes Association Values
Chili Rice ($\frac{1}{6}$ of recipe)	176	2 Carbohydrates, $\frac{1}{2}$ Fat	2 Starch, 1 Vegetable, $\frac{1}{2}$ Fat
Chile-Spiked Quinoa Pudding with Corn ($\frac{1}{6}$ of recipe)	169	$1\frac{1}{2}$ Carbohydrates, $\frac{1}{2}$ Meat, 1 Fat	2 Starch, 1 Vegetable, 1 Fat
Chinese-Style Chicken Fried Rice ($\frac{1}{4}$ of recipe)	103	2 Carbohydrates, 2 Meat, 1 Fat	$2\frac{1}{2}$ Starch, 1 Vegetable, 2 Medium-Fat Meat
Chinese-Style Pork Fried Rice ($\frac{1}{6}$ of recipe)	150	1 Carbohydrate, 3 Meat	1 Starch, 1 Vegetable, 3 Medium-Fat Meat
Cockaleekie ($\frac{1}{8}$ of recipe)	70	$1\frac{1}{2}$ Carbohydrates, 3 Meat	1 Starch, $\frac{1}{2}$ Fruit, 2 Vegetables, 3 Low-Fat Meat
Coconut Chicken With Quinoa ($\frac{1}{4}$ of recipe)	102	$1\frac{1}{2}$ Carbohydrates, 4 Meat, 1 Fat	$1\frac{1}{2}$ Starch, 2 Vegetables, 4 Low-Fat Meat, 2 Fat
Coconut-Spiked Pork with Quinoa and Peanuts ($\frac{1}{6}$ of recipe)	148	$1\frac{1}{2}$ Carbohydrates, 2 Meat, 1 Fat	$1\frac{1}{2}$ Starch, 2 Vegetables, 2 Medium-Fat Meat
Cold Soba Noodles ($\frac{1}{6}$ of recipe)	88	2 Carbohydrates, 2 Fat	2 Starch, $1\frac{1}{2}$ Fat
Congee with Chinese Greens and Barbecued Pork ($\frac{1}{6}$ of recipe)	80	1 Carbohydrate, 1 Meat	$1\frac{1}{2}$ Starch, 1 Low-Fat Meat
Corn and Sausage Salad with Shredded Hearts of Romaine ($\frac{1}{8}$ of recipe)	94	$\frac{1}{2}$ Carbohydrate, 1 Meat, 2 Fat	$\frac{1}{2}$ Starch, 1 Vegetable, 1 High-Fat Meat, 1 Fat
Corn Cakes ($\frac{1}{24}$ of recipe)	52	$\frac{1}{2}$ Carbohydrate, $\frac{1}{2}$ Fat	$\frac{1}{2}$ Starch, $\frac{1}{2}$ Fat
Cranberry-Orange Pecan Muffins ($\frac{1}{12}$ of recipe)	36	2 Carbohydrates, $2\frac{1}{2}$ Fat	1 Starch, 1 Other, 2 Fat
Cranberry Pecan Millet Salad ($\frac{1}{8}$ of recipe)	95	$1\frac{1}{2}$ Carbohydrates, $2\frac{1}{2}$ Fat	$1\frac{1}{2}$ Starch, $\frac{1}{2}$ Fruit, 2 Fat
Cranberry Quinoa Porridge ($\frac{1}{6}$ of recipe)	47	$1\frac{1}{2}$ Carbohydrates, $\frac{1}{2}$ Fat	1 Starch, 1 Fruit
Creole Chicken with Red Rice ($\frac{1}{6}$ of recipe)	108	2 Carbohydrates, 3 Meat, 1 Fat	2 Starch, 2 Vegetables, 3 Medium-Fat Meat, $\frac{1}{2}$ Fat
Crêpes Parmentier ($\frac{1}{24}$ of recipe)	56	1 Fat	$\frac{1}{2}$ Starch, $\frac{1}{2}$ Fat
Cuban-Style Hash with Fried Plantains ($\frac{1}{6}$ of recipe)	140	$3\frac{1}{2}$ Carbohydrates, $1\frac{1}{2}$ Meat, 1 Fat	1 Starch, $2\frac{1}{2}$ Fruit, 2 Vegetables, 1 Medium-Fat Meat, $1\frac{1}{2}$ Fat
Currant-Studded Quinoa ($\frac{1}{6}$ of recipe)	181	2 Carbohydrates, 1 Fat	1 Starch, 1 Fruit, 1 Fat

Recipes	Page No.	Canadian Diabetes Association Values	American Diabetes Association Values
Curried Sweet Potato and Millet Soup (1/6 of recipe)	72	2½ Carbohydrates, ½ Fat	2 Starch, 1 Vegetable, 1 Other, ½ Fat
Everyday Tuna and Warm Red Rice Salad (1/4 of recipe)	97	1½ Carbohydrates, 1 Meat, 2 Fat	2 Starch, 1 Low-Fat Meat, 2 Fat
Fennel-Scented Tomato and Wild Rice Soup (1/8 of recipe)	74	1 Carbohydrate, ½ Fat	1 Starch, 2 Vegetables, ½ Fat
Fragrant Beef and Chinese "Barley" Soup with Shiitake Mushrooms (1/6 of recipe)	66	1 Carbohydrate, 1½ Meat	1 Starch, 2 Vegetables, 1 High-Fat Meat
Fragrant Coconut Rice (1/4 of recipe)	180	2 Carbohydrates, 4 Fat	2½ Starch, 3½ Fat
Fragrant Lamb Curry with Chinese "Barley" (1/6 of recipe)	153	1½ Carbohydrates, 2½ Meat	½ Whole Milk, 1½ Starch, ½ Vegetable, 2½ Low-Fat Meat, ½ Fat
Fusion Corn Soup (1/16 of recipe)	67	1 Carbohydrate, 1 Fat	1 Starch, ½ Vegetable, 1 Fat
Gingery Chicken and Wild Rice Soup (1/6 of recipe)	76	1½ Carbohydrates, 2½ Meat	1½ Starch, 1 Vegetable, 2 Low-Fat Meat
Gingery Shortbread (1/30 of recipe)	199	1 Carbohydrate, 1 Fat	1 Starch, 1 Fat
Gluten-Free Pizza Crust (1/6 of recipe)	184	2 Carbohydrates, 1 Fat	2 Starch, ½ Fat
Hearty Miso-Spiked Vegetable Soup (1/6 of recipe)	78	2 Carbohydrates, 1 Fat	1½ Starch, 3 Vegetables, ½ Fat
Home-Style Skillet Rice with Tomato Crust (1/6 of recipe)	151	2 Carbohydrates, 1 Meat, 2 Fat	2 Starch, 2 Vegetables, 2½ Fat
Hot Millet Amaranth Cereal (1/6 of recipe)	44	1 Carbohydrate ½ Fat	1½ Starch
Indonesian-Style Shrimp Fried Rice (1/4 of recipe)	121	2½ Carbohydrates, 3½ Meat, 1 Fat	2½ Starch, 3 Medium-Fat Meat
Italian-Style Chicken and Rice (1/6 of recipe)	106	2 Carbohydrates, 3½ Meat, 1 Fat	2½ Starch, 2 Vegetables, 3 Medium-Fat Meat, 1 Fat
Italian-Style Chicken in White Wine with Olives and Polenta (1/8 of recipe)	112	1 Carbohydrate, 3½ Meat	1 Starch, 1 Vegetable, 3½ Meat
Italian-Style Green Rice (1/6 of recipe)	172	1½ Carbohydrates, 1½ Fat	1½ Starch, 1 Vegetable, 1 Fat

Recipes	Page No.	Canadian Diabetes Association Values	American Diabetes Association Values
Jambalaya (1/6 of recipe)	107	1 Carbohydrate, 3 Meat	1 Starch, 3 Vegetables, 2 1/2 Medium-Fat Meat
Kasha and Beet Salad with Celery and Feta (1/8 of recipe)	92	1 Carbohydrate, 1 1/2 Fat	1 Starch, 1 Vegetable, 1 1/2 Fat
Khitchuri with Tomatoes and Green Peppers (1/6 of recipe)	168	2 1/2 Carbohydrates, 1/2 Meat 1 Fat	3 Starch, 2 Vegetables, 1/2 Fat
Korean-Style Rice Bowl (1/4 of recipe)	164	2 1/2 Carbohydrates, 2 1/2 Fat	2 1/2 Starch, 2 Vegetables, 2 Fat
Mexican-Style Millet and Shrimp (1/6 of recipe)	129	1 1/2 Carbohydrates, 2 Meat, 1 Fat	2 Starch, 1 Vegetable, 2 Medium-Fat Meat
Mexican-Style Seafood Stew with Hominy (1/6 of recipe)	128	1/2 Carbohydrates, 3 Meat	1/2 Starch, 2 Vegetables, 3 Low-Fat Meat
Middle Eastern Millet Pudding with Almonds and Dates (1/8 of recipe)	197	3 1/2 Carbohydrates, 2 1/2 Fat	1 1/2 Starch, 1 Fruit, 1 Other, 2 Fat
Millet-Crusted Tamale Pie (1/6 of recipe)	143	2 1/2 Carbohydrates, 2 Meat, 2 Fat	3 Starch, 2 Medium-Fat Meat, 1 Fat
Millet Salad with Lemony Chickpeas and Tomatoes (1/10 of recipe)	96	1 1/2 Carbohydrates, 2 Fat	1 1/2 Starch, 1 Vegetable, 1 1/2 Fat
Minestrone with Leafy Greens (1/6 of recipe)	68	3 Carbohydrates, 1/2 Meat, 1/2 Fat	2 Starch, 5 Vegetables, 1/2 Fat
Moroccan-Style Chicken Stew with Chickpeas and Rice (1/4 of recipe)	114	2 Carbohydrates, 3 Meat	2 Starch, 2 Vegetables, 3 Low-Fat Meat
Moroccan-Style Millet Stuffing (1/8 of recipe)	188	2 Carbohydrates, 1 Fat	1 Starch, 1 Fruit, 1 Fat
Multigrain Cereal with Fruit (1/8 of recipe)	43	2 Carbohydrates	1 1/2 Starch, 1 Fruit
Mushroom Ragoût (1/8 of recipe)	166	2 Carbohydrates, 1 Meat	2 Starch, 3 Vegetables, 1/2 Fat
Mushroom-Scented Quinoa Congee With Zucchini (1/6 of recipe)	81	1 Carbohydrate, 1/2 Fat	1 Starch, 2 Vegetables, 1/2 Fat
Mushroom Varnishkes (1/6 of recipe)	162	2 Carbohydrates, 2 Fat	2 1/2 Starch, 1 Vegetable, 1 1/2 Fat
Mussels in Spicy Lemongrass Broth with Chinese Black Rice (1/4 of recipe)	123	2 Carbohydrates, 1 Meat	2 Starch, 1 Vegetable, 1 Low-Fat Meat

Recipes	Page No.	Canadian Diabetes Association Values	American Diabetes Association Values
Oatmeal Shortbread Squares (1/25 of recipe)	198	1 Carbohydrate, 1½ Fat	½ Starch, ½ Other, 1½ Fat
Old English Celery Bake (1/6 of recipe)	186	1½ Carbohydrates	1½ Starch
Old-Fashioned Cornbread (1/8 of recipe)	42	2 Carbohydrates, 1 Fat	2 Starch, 1 Fat
Peppery Chicken Quinoa (1/4 of recipe)	104	2 Carbohydrates, 3 Meat, 1 Fat	2 Starch, 1 Vegetable, 4 Low-Fat Meat
Peppery Meat Loaf with Quinoa (1/8 of recipe)	136	1 Carbohydrate, 2½ Meat	1 Starch, 1 Vegetable, 2½ Medium-Fat Meat
Peppery Polenta Bake with Mushrooms and Sausages (1/8 of recipe)	152	1 Carbohydrate, 2 Meat, 1 Fat	1 Starch, 1 Vegetable, 1 Medium-Fat Meat, 2 Fat
Peppery Quinoa Stew with Corn and Crispy Snapper (1/6 of recipe)	127	2 Carbohydrates, 3 Meat	2 Starch, 2 Vegetables, 3 Low-Fat Meat, ½ Fat
Peppery Shrimp with Quinoa (1/4 of recipe)	126	1½ Carbohydrates, 2 Meat, 1 Fat	2 Starch, 1½ Vegetables, 2½ Low-Fat Meat, 1½ Fat
Polenta Crostini (1/36 of recipe)	58	1 Extra	1 Free
Pork Pozole (1/8 of recipe)	146	½ Carbohydrate, 3 Meat	½ Starch, 2 Vegetables, 3 Low-Fat Meat
Pretty Traditional Rice Pudding (1/6 of recipe)	192	3 Carbohydrates, ½ Fat	2½ Starch, 1 Other, ½ Fat
Quinoa and Radish Salad with Avocado Dressing (1/6 of recipe)	90	1 Carbohydrate, 2½ Fat	1½ Starch, 1 Vegetable, 2½ Fat
Quinoa Chili (1/6 of recipe)	167	2½ Carbohydrates, 1 Fat	3 Starch, 2 Vegetables, ½ Fat
Quinoa-Stuffed Tomatoes (1/6 of serving)	163	1 Carbohydrate, 1 Meat 2 Fat	1 Starch, 1 Vegetable, 1 Medium-Fat Meat, 2 Fat
Red Beans and Red Rice (1/8 of recipe)	178	2 Carbohydrates, ½ Fat	2 Starch, 2 Vegetables
Rhubarb Strawberry Cobbler (1/8 of recipe)	204	4 Carbohydrates, 3 Fat	1 Starch, 1 Fruit, 2½ Other, 2½ Fat
Rice Salad Niçoise (1/4 of recipe)	91	1 Carbohydrate, 1 Meat, 3½ Fat	1½ Starch, 1 Vegetable, 1 Medium-Fat Meat, 3 Fat
Rice-Stuffed Eggplant (1/6 of recipe)	161	2 Carbohydrates, ½ Meat, 1½ Fat	2 Starch, 2 Vegetables, 1½ Fat

Recipes	Page No.	Canadian Diabetes Association Values	American Diabetes Association Values
Roasted Mushrooms with Millet and Goat Cheese (1/4 of recipe)	157	1 Carbohydrate, 1 Meat, 3 Fat	1 Starch, 2 Vegetables, 1 Medium-Fat Meat, 2 Fat
Roasted Red Pepper Risotto (1/6 of recipe)	174	1½ Carbohydrates, 1 Fat	1½ Starch, 1 Vegetable, ½ Fat
Saffron-Scented Millet Pilaf with Toasted Almonds (1/6 of recipe)	189	1½ Carbohydrates, 1 Fat	2 Starch, ½ Fat
Saffron-Scented Shrimp With Chile Rice (1/6 of recipe)	122	2 Carbohydrates, 2 Meat, 2 Fat	2 Starch, 2 Vegetables, 2 Low-Fat Meat, 1½ Fat
Salmon and Wild Rice Cakes with Avocado-Chili Topping (1/4 of recipe)	120	1 Carbohydrate, 2 Meat, 2 Fat	1½ Starch, 2 Medium-Fat Meat, 1 Fat
Salmon Stew with Corn and Quinoa (1/8 of recipe)	124	1½ Carbohydrates, 2½ Meat, 2 Fat	1½ Starch, 1 Vegetable, 2 Medium-Fat Meat, 1½ Fat
Sausage-Spiked Peas 'n' Rice (1/6 of recipe)	144	2 Carbohydrates, 2 Meat, 2 Fat	2½ Starch, 1 Vegetable, 1 Medium-Fat Meat
Savory Lamb Shanks with Eggplant (1/8 of recipe)	134	1 Carbohydrate, 3 Meat	1 Starch, 3 Vegetables, 3 Medium-Fat Meat
Scotch Broth (1/8 of recipe)	71	2 Carbohydrates, 1½ Meat	1½ Starch, 3 Vegetables, 1½ Low-Fat Meat
Shrimp Tempura (1/12 of recipe)	62	½ Carbohydrate, ½ Meat	½ Starch, ½ Low-Fat Meat
Sloppy Joes Zucchini (1/6 of recipe)	135	1 Carbohydrate, 2 Meat	1½ Starch, 3 Vegetables, 1 High-Fat Meat
Smoked Salmon and Grits Cakes (1/64 of recipe)	60	½ Fat	½ Fat
Soba Noodles with Broccoli Sauce (1/4 of serving)	158	4½ Carbohydrates, 1 Fat	3 Starch, 1 Vegetable, 1½ Other, ½ Fat
Southwestern Bean and Chinese "Barley" Salad with Roasted Peppers (1/8 of recipe)	85	2 Carbohydrates, ½ Meat, 2½ Fat	2½ Starch, ½ Vegetable, 2½ Fat
Southwestern-Style Chile Chicken with Wehani Rice (1/8 of recipe)	110	1½ Carbohydrates, 3½ Meat	1½ Starch, 1 Vegetable, 4 Low-Fat Meat, 1 Fat
Southwestern-Style Rice-Stuffed Peppers (1/4 of recipe)	138	3½ Carbohydrates, 1 Meat, 2 Fat	4 Starch, 2 Vegetables, 1 Medium-Fat Meat, 1 Fat
Southwestern Turkey Chowder (1/8 of recipe)	75	2 Carbohydrates, 2 Meat	2½ Starch, 2 Vegetables, 1 Low-Fat Meat

Recipes	Page No.	Canadian Diabetes Association Values	American Diabetes Association Values
Southwestern Turkey Stew with Cornmeal Dumplings (1/6 of recipe)	115	1 1/2 Carbohydrates, 2 Meat	1 1/2 Starch, 2 Vegetables, 2 Low-Fat Meat
Tailgaters' Favorite Stew (1/8 of recipe)	139	1 1/2 Carbohydrates, 3 Meat	1 1/2 Starch, 1 Vegetable, 4 Low-Fat Meat
Thai-Inspired Peanut and Wild Rice Soup (1/6 of recipe)	79	1 1/2 Carbohydrates, 1 1/2 Meat, 3 Fat	1 1/2 Starch, 1 Vegetable, 1 Medium-Fat Meat, 3 Fat
Tunisian Fruit and Grain Cake (1/8 of recipe)	203	4 Carbohydrates, 2 Fat	2 Starch, 1 1/2 Fruit, 1 Other, 1 1/2 Fat
Turkey Cutlets in Gingery Lemon Gravy with Cranberry Rice (1/4 of recipe)	116	2 1/2 Carbohydrates, 2 1/2 Meat	2 Starch, 1/2 Fruit, 1/2 Other, 2 1/2 Low-Fat Meat, 1 1/2 Fat
Vegetable Tempura (1/8 of recipe)	63	1 Carbohydrate, 1/2 Fat	1 Starch, 1/2 Fat
Wild Rice and Smoked Turkey Salad with Dried Cherries (1/6 of recipe)	89	1 1/2 Carbohydrates, 1/2 Meat, 2 Fat	1 Starch, 1 Fruit, 1 Medium-Fat Meat, 1 Fat
Wild Rice Cakes (1/4 of recipe)	160	2 Carbohydrates, 2 Meat, 1 Fat	2 1/2 Starch, 1 Vegetable, 2 Low-Fat Meat, 1 Fat
Wild Rice Stuffing with Cranberries (1/12 of recipe)	187	1 Carbohydrate, 1 Fat	1/2 Starch, 1/2 Fruit, 1 Fat
Wine-Soaked Cornmeal Cake with Balsamic Berries (1/10 of recipe)	202	2 Carbohydrates, 3 Fat	1 Starch, 1/2 Fruit, 1 Other, 2 1/2 Fat
Yogurt Flatbread (1/30 of recipe)	57	1/2 Carbohydrate, 1/2 Fat	1/2 Starch
Zesty Cheddar Crisps (1/36 of recipe)	53	1 Fat	1/2 Starch, 1 Fat
Zucchini Fritters (1/24 of recipe)	50	1/2 Fat	1/2 Starch, 1/2 Fat
Zuni Stew (1/8 of recipe)	156	1 Carbohydrates, 1 Meat, 1 Fat	1 1/2 Starch, 2 Vegetables, 1 High-Fat Meat

Library and Archives Canada Cataloguing in Publication

Finlayson, Judith
  The complete gluten-free whole grains cookbook : 125 delicious recipes from amaranth to quinoa to wild rice / Judith Finlayson.

Includes index.
ISBN 978-0-7788-0438-3

1. Gluten-free diet—Recipes. 2. Cooking (Cereals). 3. Grain. 4. Cookbooks. I. Title.

RM237.86.F56 2013   641.5'638   C2012-907473-X

Index